BALL HAWKS

BALL HAWKS

THE ARRIVAL
AND DEPARTURE
OF THE NBA
IN IOWA

·

TIM HARWOOD

UNIVERSITY OF IOWA PRESS   IOWA CITY

University of Iowa Press, Iowa City 52242
Copyright © 2018 by the University of Iowa Press
www.uipress.uiowa.edu
Printed in the United States of America

Design by Rich Hendel

The University of Iowa Press is a member of Green Press Initiative
and is committed to preserving natural resources.

Printed on acid-free paper

Library of Congress Cataloging-in-Publication Data
Names: Harwood, Tim, 1981– author.
Title: Ball Hawks : the arrival and departure of the NBA in Iowa /
by Tim Harwood.
Description: Iowa City : University of Iowa Press, 2018. |
Includes bibliographical references and index.
Identifiers: LCCN 2018005478 (print) | LCCN 2018021158 (ebook) |
ISBN 978-1-60938-589-7 | ISBN 978-1-60938-588-0 (paperback : alk. paper)
Subjects: LCSH: Waterloo Hawks (Basketball team)—History. |
Basketball—Iowa—Waterloo—History. | BISAC: SPORTS & RECREATION /
Basketball. | HISTORY / United States / State & Local / Midwest
(IA, IL, IN, KS, MI, MN, MO, ND, NE, OH, SD, WI).
Classification: LCC GV885.52.W395 (ebook) |
LCC GV885.52.W395 H37 2018 (print) | DDC 796.323/640977737—dc23
LC record available at https://lccn.loc.gov/2018005478

For those
who dream of reaching
the big leagues,
and for those
who get there
but can't stay as long
as they planned

CONTENTS

Photos follow page 98

PREFACE

Imagine the New York Knicks and the Boston Celtics coming to Waterloo, Iowa, during the same week. It sounds like something Ray Kinsella and Terence Mann might have discussed in a basketball sequel to *Field of Dreams*. When I found out that it had actually happened in 1949, I felt compelled to explore the details. I will not take so much artistic license as to suggest that I could hear the voice of James Earl Jones saying, "People will read, Tim; people will most definitely read." But nevertheless I expected to find a story worth sharing.

I came to Waterloo in 2005 to cover the local amateur baseball team on radio. The opportunity materialized for me to stay year-round and broadcast hockey games just across the Cedar River. In many ways, it was an ideal situation, but holding two seasonal part-time jobs—and a third job outside sports or radio—was taxing. Starting in 2008, I stepped away from baseball into a full-time hockey position and toward my first long-form writing project.

The Waterloo Black Hawks hockey team originally took to the ice in 1962. Many local fans remembered the successes of the Hawks' early seasons. Still, much of the team's history was obscure, especially history from the 1980s, when popularity waned after the transition from the semiprofessional senior level to amateur junior hockey. Even the United States Hockey League's records were sparse for long stretches of time.

Two summers of reading through newspaper articles on microfilm and scanning old box scores gave me more information than I could cram into the media guide I had first intended to produce. Instead, in 2011, I pieced together the book *Black Hawks Chronicle: Five Decades of Teams, Games, and Players* in time for the fiftieth season of local hockey. A few years later, using the same methods, I was able to produce *The Legion Team: Forgotten Hockey in Waterloo, 1927–1930*, a book about Waterloo's American Legion hockey club of the late 1920s.

Professional basketball in the Cedar Valley had come and gone between these two hockey eras. I knew that the stories of those teams, including the faintly remembered 1949–50 National Basketball Association squad, could be found in the same archives I was already familiar with. As a result, this current project is based on similar research tactics. Statistics from the era are limited: rebounds, steals, and turnovers were not tracked, and a formal conception of the assist was only just coming into existence. Since the quantitative measures of games and players are incomplete by modern standards, the qualitative judgments of the writers on hand from jump ball to final horn play a special role in this retelling. The story is also enriched by the firsthand accounts of Waterloo Hawks players Leo Kubiak and Wayne See; reminiscences of Wayne See's daughter, Vicki Sidey, and player-coach Jack Smiley's son, Mark Smiley; and memories of Waterloo resident Danny Steiber, who helped with the team's radio broadcasts while still in high school.

Major league basketball did not survive long in northeast Iowa. From a purely statistical standpoint, the Waterloo Hawks' record is not impressive. The team never stepped onto the court for a postseason game. Yet the Hawks did play, and to date, Waterloo's postwar basketball club is the only team to represent the state in a contemporary major league.

For that reason alone, I hope you will go the distance for the unique story that follows.

INTRODUCTION

I n the winter of 1891, as he typed the first thirteen rules that brought basketball to life, James Naismith could never have imagined that the game he created for his students in Springfield, Massachusetts, would be played around the world in his lifetime. Yet Naismith witnessed the sport take root in colleges and high schools. He was on hand to see it debut in the Olympics and bring thousands of fans to huge arenas in just the few decades that followed. Within a century of its invention, the game had transformed into one of the four major team sports avidly followed by fans in the United States, and ultimately it became a multibillion-dollar worldwide phenomenon.

Professional basketball leagues are now everywhere, from Europe to Asia to Australia, with the National Basketball Association (NBA) remaining the world's premier league. During the 2013–14 season, more than 21 million fans attended NBA games played by one of the thirty league clubs in cities across North America.[1] Perhaps more impressively, the NBA Finals are televised in nearly every country, and league officials eagerly anticipate attracting even more international fans through aggressive marketing in China, India, and elsewhere.[2] Professional basketball is big global business.

Of course, the NBA didn't start out that way. The league's beginnings after World War II were themselves as modest as Naismith's gym activity for his students nearly sixty years earlier. Forerunners of today's clubs operated in towns like Syracuse, New York, and Moline, Illinois. Their opponents came from places like Anderson, Indiana, and Sheboygan, Wisconsin. This is the story of one of those unlikely major league towns and teams: Waterloo, Iowa, and its Waterloo Hawks.

Waterloo was already calling itself Iowa's City of Factories by the early twentieth century. John Deere tractors and Black Hawk–brand bacon cut by the Rath Packing Company were the town's two most significant exports, and the majority of local factory workers were employed by those two companies. Waterloo's location in northeast Iowa, at the convergence of three rail lines, provided an inherent advantage for manufacturers. Illinois Central trains could roll from Waterloo through the Mississippi Valley as far south as the Gulf of Mexico. The Chicago Great Western line stretched to Minneapolis and St. Paul in the north, Des Moines and Kansas City to the south, and toward the route's namesake city in the east. Chicago was also accessible by way of Cedar Rapids and Davenport on the Rock Island Railroad, with other tracks on that network stretching south and west.

Notable growth in Waterloo at the turn of the twentieth century came from immigration, and the town quickly stood out for being more ethnically diverse than most parts of the state. Wage-earning men—some anticipating a return to their homelands, others planning to stay permanently—often arrived individually, establishing themselves before being joined later by their families. Significant numbers of Greeks and Croatians as well as Italian and Bulgarian populations moved to the city in search of opportunities. Waterloo also attracted a strong Jewish community; its synagogue, established in 1905, was a rarity in the region.

Although federal restrictions severely curbed international immigration in the 1920s, increased domestic migration from an influx of African American workers helped sustain the city's growth. The new arrivals began coming to Waterloo in the early 1910s in the midst of an Illinois Central strike. Unbeknownst to the relocating black workers, most of whom were already employed by the railroad in Mississippi, they were brought in to replace the strikers, attracting immediate prejudice and animosity from the mostly white workforce in town. Segregation—in fact if not in law—was established; black families rarely found homes outside a small neighborhood on the city's east side near the Illinois Central railyard. Yet Waterloo's black community persisted and grew, especially as African American coal miners from other parts of the state moved to the city when Iowa coal production diminished.

Waterloo's racial situation, like race relations in the rest of America by the mid-twentieth century, might best be described as complex. Even by the postwar period, Waterloo's black and white communities still interacted in only limited contexts. Black workers found jobs at John Deere and Rath Packing, typically in the most challenging and least desirable aspects of production. As such, they were important to the growth of both industries and to the community in general. And although black entertainers like Cab Calloway or Marian Anderson could draw a large white audience in the community, an everyday homemaker like Millie Saffold, who moved to Waterloo in the late 1940s, experienced a far different reception. "There weren't a lot of places for black folks to go around here. We kept to ourselves mostly," she remembered. "You just didn't go some places. . . . They didn't want you in there and you knew it."[3]

Those were different times for basketball as well. In 1946–47, the National Basketball League (NBL), a forerunner of the National Basketball Association, was briefly integrated. A small number of black players, including William "Pop" Gates, were signed by league clubs. Gates had excelled with the all-black New York Renaissance (often shortened to the "Rens") touring club and would eventually be inducted into the Naismith Basketball Hall of Fame in Springfield. He joined the Buffalo Bison and, early in the 1946–47 season, moved with the club when it relocated to become the Tri-Cities Blackhawks in western Illinois. According to an account in an NBL magazine a few years later, "The Tri-City fans speak of him as being the greatest ball handler they have ever seen."[4]

But Gates and the other black athletes left the NBL by season's end. It was often difficult for them to find accommodations. "As far as the team was concerned, I had no problems," Gates recounted years later. "But our home base was Moline, and they were used to keeping blacks out of hotels. . . . I wound up being shunted to a YMCA there."[5]

Occasionally, hostile opposing crowds were a concern in places not accustomed to seeing blacks and whites together. In an era when punches were thrown in professional basketball games with some regularity, Gates was involved in an on-court fight during a February game in Syracuse. The altercation became a melee, and Gates needed an escort to the locker room as the home crowd surged onto the floor. Integration ebbed temporarily, and the NBL was again all white in 1947–48.

Aside from segregation, professional squads of the late 1940s would have looked different from NBA teams of later generations for other reasons. With limited exceptions, most players had attended college for a full four years. Many were even older than typical graduates after deferring their education to serve during World War II. Some were decorated war heroes who had earned a maturity unattainable from any sports experience or college course.

On the court, a shift in emphasis toward height and high-scoring offense was slowly moving the focus away from the systematic ball control and unrelenting defense prized in earlier decades. The traditional style of play was athletically challenging in its emphasis on endurance, but the low-scoring games were not particularly crowd-pleasing. Indeed, many of the innovations from 1950 onward, including the shot clock and, later, the three-point line, were intentionally designed to make the game more entertaining for crowds, encouraging higher scores and lifting final point totals from the 40s and 50s into the triple digits.

Leo Kubiak, who started his professional basketball career with the NBL's Waterloo Hawks in 1948, says most current NBA fans would hardly recognize the game that was played in the 1940s:

The game then was very methodical, slow compared to the games now. You brought the ball down the floor and then you set up a play of some kind. The fast break was not that often pulled, unless it was wide open for you. Now you've got to be big, strong, you need to jump, and most of them can drop the ball in the basket. If the 3-point [shot] had been in existence in our time, the scores would have been a lot higher.

But most of all, according to Kubiak, the greatest changes occurred off the court in the business of basketball: "There were no agents, and the players didn't negotiate contracts, because they just wanted to play."[6]

Basketball salaries of the era were good but far from what would be paid just a few decades later. In the late 1940s, a typical contract for the six-month season might have equaled or slightly exceeded the $2,500 to $4,000 that an average middle-class factory worker could earn over a full calendar year. Top players had the opportunity to claim even more. Standard agreements also included weekly meal money, which itself exceeded the pay of some lower-wage workers.

Still, most players held other jobs during the summer. They were often supporting families, who moved across the country when a season began and back home after it ended. Those fortunate enough to have offers from multiple clubs considered nonbasketball factors like the day jobs available at companies often associated with their prospective teams.

Perhaps most challenging for players of that era was the fact that their contracts were not guaranteed. Teams held the right to cancel a contract for any reason by paying five days' salary. On the other hand, a player unhappy with his circumstances could move to another city only by asking for a release or a trade; free agency was nonexistent. Basketball players—like their counterparts in other sports—were bound by a reserve clause that gave teams the right to retain their rosters indefinitely. As stated in a standard NBL agreement, at an appointed date ahead of the next upcoming season, "the Club may renew this contract for the term of that year, except that the salary rate shall be such as the parties may then agree upon, or in default of agreement, such as the Club may fix."[7]

Other noticeable differences from postwar professional basketball compared with later eras include teams in the NBL—and later the early NBA—not being separated by the long distances that current teams face. Clubs of the 1940s and '50s also played a shorter schedule than the modern league. However, travel by car, bus, and train was equally, if not more, strenuous for players of that earlier time. Most arrived at road games by car when possible or train when necessary, in cramped quarters, especially for the tallest members of a club. Air travel was out of the question for most teams. A week-long four-game road swing from one side of the league to the other by car and train was challenging, to put it mildly.

Take, for example, this Waterloo itinerary from November 1949. The Hawks left northeast Iowa for Chicago by train at 6:45 on a Friday morning. Arriving shortly after noon, the team had a five-hour layover before boarding another train for an overnight trip to Rochester, New York. After playing a game there on Saturday night, the team was aboard another train for a fast Sunday trip to Syracuse and another game that evening. Pulling out of the Syracuse station around midnight allowed the Hawks to stop in Anderson, Indiana, by 10:00 a.m. Monday for the trip's third game—roughly ten hours later—in that city. Heading home at 11:00 Tuesday morning, the team could expect to arrive in Waterloo twelve hours later. Three games, five days, and more than 2,000 miles. Additionally, in this instance, Waterloo was scheduled to play at home on Wednesday evening, then travel to Denver on Friday.[8]

Travel may have been more strenuous, but training regimens were far more casual at that time. Off-season preparation might consist of players being encouraged to wander the golf course for a few rounds or avoid alcohol in the weeks before fall practices began. Formal workouts often started less than a month before the beginning of a season and just a few weeks ahead of the first exhibition games.

Injuries, of course, still posed a serious threat to career longevity—perhaps even more so than today. Ligament or tendon damage could be catastrophic in the time before those tissues could be surgically repaired. NBA teams were not obligated to help an injured player beyond what could easily be done to bring him back to the court. Contracts from the NBA's 1949–50 inaugural year, for example, required teams to pay anyone suffering a season-ending injury until the end of the schedule "but in no event beyond the season."[9]

Another aspect that modern NBA fans might have trouble imagining was the early league's difficulty attracting crowds. A consequence of this led to several teams, generally in small midwestern towns—the Waterloo Hawks, Sheboygan Red Skins, and others—being deemed a hindrance to prosperity by the owners of clubs in places like New York, Philadelphia, and Boston. Large-market team owners shunned the small-timers in an effort to convince fans that the then-fragile league had only the most notable players, in the most famous venues, representing America's most important cities.

Yet despite the treatment that Waterloo and other smaller towns received from the NBA, Leo Kubiak still looks back fondly on those days: "To me, it was such a beautiful time in the lives of the players because you were playing basketball and getting paid for it."[10] Kubiak—with his teammates and their opponents—helped establish the NBA that aspires to grow across the globe in the twenty-first century. They did it, in part, in Waterloo.

ORGANIZED PROFESSIONAL BASKETBALL

In the summer of 1947, when Bob Calihan stepped off a train in Waterloo, he could see right away that the town was crazy about its local sports. The Waterloo White Hawks baseball team was in the middle of an unlikely championship year. That summer, the Class B affiliate of the Chicago White Sox would barely qualify for the play-offs before thrilling Waterloo by taking the league pennant.

But Calihan wasn't there for baseball; he was there for professional basketball, on a scouting trip for the Chicago American Gears. He wasn't looking for players. Gears owner Maurice White had sent him in search of a city that could field a team in the new Professional Basketball League of America (PBLA).

With former DePaul standout George Mikan under contract for White's squad, the Chicago businessman already had a player who, a couple of years later, would be described as basketball's version of Babe Ruth.[1] The Gears had won the National Basketball League championship months earlier, which meant that White could also boast of having the league's best team. Yet despite building a championship organization over just three seasons in the NBL, his American Gears were not making money.

After first making millions of dollars as a military contractor, then enjoying nearly immediate on-court basketball success, White was dissatisfied with league leadership. Having built a business manufacturing parts for naval ships, he believed he deserved a chance at the NBL's helm. He wanted to grow professional basketball into a game worthy of the national attention that baseball, football, and hockey received. Unfortunately, he may have been his own biggest obstacle. White's often abrasive personality strained relationships with other owners and made his ambitions to be league president impossible, as explained by former American Gears player Dick Triptow:

> [White] seemed to be a constant thorn in their sides and they let him know in no uncertain terms, this would not be possible. Even under ordinary circumstances, the League owners had difficulty operating smoothly, and White's presence did not make it any easier.
>
> When he was not chosen as president, White became disenchanted.[2]

White's interpersonal difficulties were not confined to NBL owners. The American Gears' boss routinely attracted talented individuals, then put them in awkward positions. He drove Mikan into a six-week holdout in the middle of the 1946–47 schedule by asking him to take a 50 percent pay cut and releasing the star player's brother from the team. In another instance, White suggested that team adviser Ray Meyer—head coach at DePaul University—be dangled in a cage above the basketball floor to gain a different view of on-court tactics. White even designed, then scrapped, a bonus structure that would have paid players a few dollars for every field goal, free throw, and assist they contributed during Gears games.

Many of White's eccentricities could be traced to alcoholism. It was well known that he was a heavy drinker and would act carelessly while bingeing. Players told stories about him coming to practices drunk and betting heavily on team scrimmages or, during games, ordering his coaches to make lineup changes as he watched from the stands.[3]

Meanwhile, White publicly blamed the NBL's other owners for their supposed greed, positioning himself as an altruist with basketball's best interests at heart as he set out to form his own league, the Professional Basketball League of America. "There is no reason why pro basketball cannot take rank with hockey as a top professional indoor sports attraction, but to achieve this goal the club owners and sponsors must have purely unselfish motives," he explained, adding that "the Professional Basketball League of America will strive for the triple goal of attracting the highest type of athlete into the sport, presenting the athletes with the opportunity to enter an attractive graduate career, and having assembled these high type athletes, to present professional basketball of the highest caliber."[4]

The specific reason Bob Calihan was dispatched to northeast Iowa is lost, but there are several possibilities. Waterloo's population had multiplied by a factor of five from the turn of the century and, during the 1940s, no city in the state added more new residents on a percentage basis. Good industrial jobs attracted the newcomers. Approximately 17,000 workers earned $40 million annually from the city's factories, making enough disposable income to support local entertainment options during the final years before television saturation.[5] The city also had an almost ideal venue, missing only a basketball court. The National Dairy Cattle Congress Hippodrome on Waterloo's west side could seat more than 8,000 people, a capacity larger than many of the active professional basketball arenas in the Midwest at that time.

Perhaps Waterloo came to White's attention through the Chicago White Sox, who were not only affiliated with the local White Hawks but had owned and managed the minor league team since 1939. By the end of the 1947 baseball season, White Sox management was impressed enough with the city's support for the team that it backed a major expansion of the White Hawks' Municipal Stadium, providing the community with a $25,000 interest-free loan so 2,000 seats could be added for the following spring.[6]

In other words, Waterloo was a viable PBLA outpost for a number of reasons, especially considering that White wanted to create a league that would have been the largest confederation of teams in any professional sport at the time. The ambitious industrialist and would-be league builder envisioned a circuit with thirty-two clubs during its inaugural season. By August 1947, when Waterloo was officially awarded a franchise, the anticipated roster of cities had been cut to twenty-four. When the season began in October, the number had been reduced even further to a still-ambitious sixteen teams. The league footprint stretched toward St. Paul and Grand Rapids to the north, Birmingham and Atlanta to the southeast, and Houston, Oklahoma City, and New Orleans to the south and west.

Initially, the PBLA—and by extension White—was to own each of the sixteen member teams. Eventually, as the league prospered and local owners surfaced, the PBLA office hoped to divest each franchise. In the meantime, several of White's associates were installed in the league's executive positions. Harry Wilson, a writer for the *Chicago Herald-American* and one of the promoters of the annual World Professional Basketball Tournament in Chicago, was also brought on staff. Although White was behind all significant decisions, lawyer and banker Holland Pile was named figurehead commissioner. Pile had attended the University of Kansas when James Naismith was still part of the faculty, but a wire service article about the new commissioner and his responsibilities described him as "a white-haired giant of a man whose acquaintance with basketball never passed the nodding stage."[7]

In the same story, Pile unwittingly expressed one of the PBLA's greatest challenges while praising the enthusiasm for sports in each of the league's member towns, remarking, "All are ready for professional basketball of the highest major league caliber. Oddly enough, all except Chicago are entering major organized professional basketball for the first time."[8]

●

Basketball was played in Waterloo as early as the mid-1890s, just a few years after it was invented. One of the earliest teams in the community, organized to represent the First Presbyterian Church, traveled twenty-five miles from the city's east side for a game against a church team from nearby Independence. At the turn of the twentieth century, the sport came to Waterloo's two public high schools: Waterloo East was the first to reach a boys high school state championship game in 1922, but Waterloo West was the first to win a title in 1925.

The city's most notable basketball success had come at the Amateur Athletic Union (AAU) level during the Great Depression. A company team of Rath Packing employees consistently earned distinction among the state's leading industrial league clubs, winning five state championships, including four straight from 1931–32 to 1934–35, and appearing at the AAU National Tournament twice. Clarence Iba, later the head coach at the University of Tulsa, played for the Rath team in 1932–33.

In the years after World War II, more than 65,000 people lived in the northeast Iowa community straddling the Cedar River. The seat of Black Hawk County, Waterloo had been established nearly a century earlier. During World War II, the town became well known throughout the country thanks to the service and sacrifice of the Sullivan family. In 1942, the "Fighting Sullivans"—five brothers raised on the city's east side—had died together aboard the USS Juneau during the Battle of Guadalcanal. Their parents, Thomas and Alleta, and sister, Genevieve, became powerful speakers in the drive to support the military with funding from war bonds. Rationed foods like meat and dairy products had been limited for public sale during the war so that adequate quantities could be shipped to soldiers and sailors. Americans were also asked to conserve other resources, like gasoline, for the war effort. They could find inspiration to persevere through these relatively modest inconveniences compared to the ultimate sacrifice made by Waterloo's Sullivan brothers.

Before and after the war, Waterloo was also important to the Midwest thanks to its two largest industries: meat packing and tractor manufacturing. Rath Packing's Black Hawk meats were distributed across the continent—including Canada and Mexico—from the company's east side headquarters; its business volume placed it among the largest packers in the nation. On the opposite side of the river, John Deere's agricultural machinery rolled off assembly lines to farms across the country. Workers could produce three hundred tractors a day. More than a hundred other companies also manufactured their products in the city.

Following the war years, factories throughout the United States could not easily meet the swell of demand for goods. As a result, many products and services were hard to find. Home construction in Waterloo and elsewhere, which had virtually stopped during the war, exemplified the shortages of the era, which persisted into peacetime. "Every able local carpenter who is willing to work has a job and with a statewide shortage of carpenters, it will be necessary to go outside the state to secure these craftsmen," wrote the *Waterloo Courier* in 1947, continuing:

> Ironically enough, one large general contractor pointed out yesterday, workers do not come to Waterloo, even though employers are begging them to, because there is no place for them to live.
>
> Yes, these very workers are needed by the home building contractors to erect the homes they would be living in eventually, to say nothing of other new homes generally on demand.
>
> . . . The demand is heavy now for all essential construction work, both heavy (industrial) and light (homes and small business places), [and] the available [labor] supply is drastically short . . . and is getting tighter than ever daily.[9]

Yet the problems of an overheated economy in postwar America were relatively minor compared with the previous fifteen years of depression and world war. Waterloo's transition back to postwar normalcy was exemplified by the city's pride in its White Hawks. The club, like all teams in the Three-I League, had suspended operations during the war.[10] When the White Hawks returned to the diamond for a second season during the summer of 1947, Waterloo was captivated by their dramatic pennant run. Led by the strong pitching of Johnny Perkovich and Howie Judson, the team stole the league pennant in September. More than 200,000 fans attended games at Municipal Stadium during the regular season and the playoffs, one of the best figures in minor league baseball. The large number of fans represented a point of racial and ethnic unity as Waterloo residents from all backgrounds supported their team.[11]

However, the community had never fielded a professional basketball team. As a result, there was only limited interest in the sport at the pro level. The Chicago American Gears' NBL championship in 1947 had been described in just two sentences and a total of forty-five words by the local paper.[12] Residents were cautious about embracing their new and initially unnamed basketball team. *Waterloo Courier* sports editor Al Ney noted this sentiment in an October 1, 1947, column: "While many are taking the 'we won't believe it until we see it' attitude, the league office in Chicago insists there is no doubt that a team will operate here."[13]

Waterloo sports fans had reason to be optimistic about the man chosen to serve as the team's head coach: Harry "Swede" Roos, a thirty-four-year-old player with professional basketball experience stretching back to the 1930s. Roos had played industrial league basketball and softball on Chicago's South Side during the early 1940s; he eventually went to work for the American Gear and Manufacturing Company, where he met Maurice White. Roos served as captain of the last amateur American Gears team, which qualified for the AAU National Tournament in Denver, Colorado, during the spring of 1944.

With White's basketball ambitions turning toward the NBL for the 1944–45 season, Roos was put in charge of building the first Gears professional roster. After recruiting many of his eventual teammates and opening the season as player-coach, he transitioned to a full-time coaching role in the middle of the 1944–45 campaign. He remained in a similar capacity for 1945–46, although DePaul's Ray Meyer directed many of the Gears' practices, leaving Roos in more of a managerial position. After a year away in Los Angeles, he returned to White's service, tasked with assembling a basketball team in Waterloo.

To help generate interest in the new PBLA, clubs were encouraged to fill out their rosters with local stars. In Waterloo's case, Roos urged local baseball heroes Johnny Perkovich and Howie Judson to join the team. Both had healthy basketball credentials: Judson was a former guard at the University of Illinois, while Perkovich had been a successful prep player at Chicago's Tilden Tech High School.

Unfortunately, both baseball players turned down the offer to play professional basketball for fear of injuring themselves or otherwise hurting their chances of advancing within the White Sox organization. Undeterred, Roos eventually found his "local" star by signing 6-foot-9-inch center Noble Jorgensen, who had spent two seasons at the University of Iowa. Jorgensen had transferred to the Hawkeye program from Westminster College in Pennsylvania, where he had been an All-American in 1943. As Iowa's starting center in 1946–47, he averaged 9.4 points per game, using an accurate hook shot to good advantage. Standing taller than many of his contemporaries also made him a formidable defender. After college, he played briefly for the Pittsburgh Ironmen of the Basketball Association of America.

The PBLA's emphasis on local players also led to the acquisition of Dick "Looper" Lynch and Emil Lussow. The 6-foot-4-inch Lynch had led Loras College in Dubuque to a string of small-school successes; Lussow, meanwhile, was a solid basketball player and an even bigger football star across town at the University of Dubuque.

However, Waterloo's best player wasn't from Iowa; he came to town straight from the Chicago American Gears, a member of their 1946–47 championship team. Balding and displaying a toothy smile, 6-foot-3-inch Price Brookfield had actually been the first player on the new organization's roster. The twenty-six-year-old's relocation to the Cedar Valley was inspired in part by his hope to play basketball and simultaneously attend Iowa State Teachers College (today the University of Northern Iowa) in nearby Cedar Falls to pursue his master's degree.

Brookfield was a native of Dalhart, Texas. As an undergraduate, he started college at West Texas State, averaging more than 14 points per game in three years of varsity play. In 1942, he earned All-American honors and helped the small school earn a bid to the National Invitation Tournament (NIT) at Madison Square Garden. The war provided an extension of Brookfield's college basketball career. He joined the U.S. Navy and was assigned to train at Iowa State University in Ames. Wartime eligibility rules allowed him to play for the Cyclones, whom he led in scoring during the winter of 1943–44, when the team won the Big Six Championship and reached the National Collegiate Athletic Association (NCAA) Final Four.

Brookfield's wartime service experience was common to athletes of his generation. Waterloo's PBLA roster also included navy sailor Nick Vodick, former airman Otto Kerber, and Jack Spehn, who had gone to the Philippines with the Army Signal Corps. Dick Lynch had served in the army, too. Like Brookfield, many athletes were enrolled at new colleges after enlistment. The military relied on these institutions to provide training for its exponentially expanding forces, and athletics provided a means to promote fitness and morale.

Stars in other sports suited up for service teams as well. Arguably some of the best basketball, football, and baseball of the era were played by squads of military men. Meanwhile, many small colleges disbanded their athletics departments for the duration, and some professional leagues went dormant. At one point, the NBL was reduced to just three teams for an entire season.

By the autumn of 1947, however, the shortage of athletes and teams was long past. Brookfield, Jorgensen, and more than half a dozen others seeking a place on the Waterloo team were working out at the YMCA by mid-October. An $8,500 portable basketball court was being delivered from Chicago. The PBLA spent another $2,000 on baskets and glass backboards to be sent to the Cattle Congress facility.[14] Contractors were still doing the final work on the showers and locker rooms during the days leading up to the opening tip.[15]

The club nickname was another question settled alarmingly late. A number of creative monikers were suggested in a naming contest. The Hippos, Bulls, and Steers were all offered in homage to the Cattle Congress Hippodrome. The Aqua-Louies was a (perhaps too) clever play on Waterloo, as was the Waterloopers. The Napoleonites referred to the Battle of Waterloo, but that prospective namesake hardly conjured up images of victory. Ultimately, as had been and continues to be the case for teams based in the seat of Black Hawk County, a variant of Hawks was picked, and the squad was dubbed the Pro-Hawks. The announcement wasn't made until halftime on opening night after the players had come out of their recently completed locker rooms with simply "Waterloo" scripted across their jerseys.

To stir enthusiasm for the opening game, a large advertisement in the *Waterloo Courier* reminded fans:

WATERLOO HAS JOINED THE MAJOR LEAGUES

We feel it fitting that this city, which long has ranked as major league in population, major league in industry and business and major league in civic achievement, should have that classification in professional sports.

Our team and those of the 15 other clubs who are members of the Professional Basketball League of America have secured what we judge to be the nation's top coaches and players. We believe that ours will be the best professional basketball presented anywhere in the nation. Major league means tops, the best, and that's us.

Merely saying so does not make us "major leaguers," however. We want you to pass judgement upon us. Our first game at the Hippodrome will be played Monday, October 27th against St. Paul. See you there.[16]

A few more than 1,600 fans followed through on the suggestion.

●

When the PBLA solicited sponsors to place ads in the Waterloo basketball game program, the league estimated a stately first-year attendance figure: 155,000 for the thirty-four-game home slate. In terms relative to the population, every Waterloo resident would have needed to attend at least two games to reach that number. The mark would have required the 8,200-seat Hippodrome to be more than half full, on average, during a schedule that included more games on working Mondays and Thursdays than any other nights of the week.

The league's pitch for sponsors came to community businesses by mail. Andy George, a local boxing and wrestling promoter, was hired to manage business affairs and serve as the team's representative in the community only two weeks before opening night. George needed to convince the city's sporting public that the games would be worth the premium ticket prices. The ninety-cent outlay for general admission was substantially more than the cost of seats at White Hawks baseball games. Even under those circumstances and with a downpour outside on October 27, George would not publicly admit any disappointment related to the opening night's attendance.

As for the first game at the Hippodrome, both the Pro-Hawks and the St. Paul Saints played like teams that had started practicing only a few weeks earlier. However, parity came with poor shooting by both sides. Although the matchup was not crisp, it proved exciting. St. Paul swung from a halftime deficit to a 32–30 lead at the end of three quarters. Both teams executed more effectively during the final ten minutes, with Noble Jorgensen contributing the majority of his 13 points in the last period as the teams exchanged the lead. At the end of regulation, the score was tied, 47–47, forcing overtime. The Saints' Bruce Hale, formerly a member of the Chicago American Gears like Swede Roos and Price Brookfield, contributed a field goal in overtime. Hale finished with a game-high 14 points, boosting the visitors to a 55–49 win in a game termed both "ragged" and "thrilling" by the *Waterloo Courier*.[17]

Roos gave his team the next day to rest, but no combination of recovery and preparation would have been adequate to ready the Pro-Hawks for their second opponent five days later: George Mikan and the Chicago American Gears. Despite the dispersal of Brookfield, Hale, and other players to several of the PBLA's new entries, the championship Gears team of the previous season was generally intact. In addition to Mikan, veteran outside shooter Bobby McDermott still served as player-coach. Bob Calihan, Maurice White's original emissary to Waterloo, remained in the starting lineup. Stan Patrick and Dick Triptow had been Gears since Roos assembled the original Chicago roster for the 1944–45 NBL season.

Mikan's celebrity helped the Pro-Hawks bring a 50 percent larger crowd out for the Saturday matchup, but the 2,450 attendance figure was still shy of what was expected, especially for the league's premier attraction. The Gears left little hope for a Waterloo upset. McDermott stacked up 24 points, and Mikan added 22 in a game that was effectively settled at halftime. Jorgensen led the Hawks with 12 in the 82–56 rout. As one observer put it, the Gears "demonstrated pro basketball as it should be played—excellent teamwork, phenomenal shooting, and great passing. Waterloo demonstrated just the opposite."[18]

Following a close loss two nights later, Roos suited up during the next practice, then again for Waterloo's first road game on November 5. The Pro-Hawks' coach led the team with 9 points against the Tulsa Ranchers, but Waterloo's second overtime loss of the season left the club at 0–4. A week after Mikan and McDermott had attracted a respectably sized audience, just 850 people moved through the Hippodrome lobby to see the winless Hawks against the Outlaws of St. Joseph, Missouri, in the fourth home game on the Hippodrome schedule.

Waterloo's prospects for ending its losing streak did not look good early; at the midpoint, the Pro-Hawks faced a 12-point deficit after making just four first-half field goals. However, a third-quarter rally brought Waterloo within a basket. Brookfield contributed 10 of his game-high 13 points in the period. The home team pulled ahead in the fourth quarter, limiting the Outlaws to just 5 points and rolling to a 45–36 victory.

Waterloo's first win may have boosted team morale, but it did not lead to greater attendance at the Cattle Congress grounds two nights later. The Omahawks from Omaha dashed to a big lead in the second quarter, then held on. The 63–61 final score was overshadowed by a fourth-quarter fistfight between Waterloo's Otto Kerber and Omaha's Fred Gran.

Although 1–5, the Pro-Hawks could justly feel that they were only a player, or a few practices, or a turn of fortune away from winning with regularity. Four of their five losses had been in games with margins of 5 points or less at the end of regulation. They hoped that facing the Omahawks a second time—albeit in Nebraska—would lead to a different result later that week.

However, the rematch with Omaha was never played. Before embarking on a Wednesday evening road trip for the Thursday game, the PBLA sent unexpected word that the matchup was canceled. The next morning, a telegram arrived for Andy George from Chicago:

> Effective Nov. 13, 1947, league and teams therein are disbanded. All games scheduled that date and thereafter are canceled. Proceed to refund all tickets purchased for games hereby canceled. AP and UP carrying press release. Players and coaches being notified by letter of their release and availability to other professional basketball organizations. Take immediate steps to marshal all basketball equipment and paraphernalia assigned to players and otherwise under your management and prepare to wind up affairs of your team . . . your cooperation in this matter will be greatly appreciated.[19]

Swede Roos was sick to his stomach. He had relocated his family halfway across the country for a job that had evaporated in less than two months. Others reacted with similar regret. Dick Lynch had decided to join the team in lieu of accepting a high school coaching offer. Jack Spehn had surrendered three seasons of NCAA eligibility at the University of Detroit for just six PBLA games. Price Brookfield had to set aside his dreams of landing a spot in the White Hawks outfield as well as his aspirations to take graduate classes in Cedar Falls.

The situation was the same for other players across the league. Several PBLA coaches spurned the league's admonishment to return railroad tickets, instead cashing them in, along with anything else of value, and dividing the proceeds among their rosters. Some players considered lawsuits. Uncertainty prevailed for all but one team. On the assumption that the PBLA would fail, the rival NBL had made a dispersal contingency for American Gears players. Mikan—the biggest prize in every sense—was to become a member of the league's new Minneapolis club, the Lakers.

Detailing the decision to disband the PBLA, attorney James Brooks told reporters, "The league attendance has not been up to expectations, and it is good business judgement to terminate the league before further financial deficits are incurred."[20] Initial published reports put that deficit at $600,000 as of November 12 when the project was halted. Subsequent estimates ranged from a smaller loss of $200,000 to more than $1 million.[21]

Waterloo Courier sports editor Al Ney empathized with the players but had little sympathy for the league organizers regardless of their losses: "One league official [had] pointed out 'All we need is somebody to see that the lights are on and the seats are sold. Chicago will handle everything else' . . . Maybe the Chicago men know what Waterloo sportsmen were talking about when they warned against expecting too much here or in any other town, considering the half cracked way they did things."[22]

The PBLA's disintegration was the most visible public episode in Maurice White's unraveling. He was soon also out of the manufacturing business on which he had founded his fortune. By the mid-1950s, White was living in rural Wisconsin, battling the Internal Revenue Service and operating a refrigerated trucking business. The government claimed he had incorrectly reported his taxable income throughout World War II. In 1958, White died at age fifty-seven with nothing remaining of the wealth that had backed his outsize ambitions.

Meanwhile, three Pro-Hawks were fortunate enough to make their way from the dismal circumstances of the PBLA's mid-November failure to an unlikely championship celebration in April. The Portland Indians of the Pacific Coast Professional Basketball League were foundering in the middle of their 1947–48 schedule when Roos, Jorgensen, and Kerber arrived in Oregon. Roos took over as coach, and the Indians rallied to qualify for the playoffs. Led by Jorgensen's strong pivot play, Portland prevailed in the best-of-five league finals against the Seattle Athletics, three games to one. After the Indians' last victory, the Pacific Coast circuit — like the PBLA — was also shuttered, leaving Kerber, Jorgensen, and Roos once again without a team for the second time in five months.

While those former Pro-Hawks were becoming accustomed to the Northwest in January, the Waterloo community secured a tangible remnant from its failed basketball season. The portable floor and hoops, which had cost the PBLA more than $10,000, remained in the Hippodrome. The league initially asked for $9,000 to leave the equipment permanently. However, in early 1948, the city's Junior Chamber of Commerce negotiated a $4,000 deal as league assets were being dispersed by a Chicago bankruptcy court.[23] The Jaycees hoped that bringing regional high school tournaments to the Hippodrome would yield a return on their investment. Their purchase, coupled with another acquisition by a former Cedar Falls native, soon gave Waterloo a second chance at big league basketball.

THE REAL MAJOR LEAGUE THING

In the summer of 1948, seven months after the Waterloo Pro-Hawks and the Professional Basketball League of America disbanded, Des Moines–based boxing and wrestling promoter Paul "Pinkie" George was looking for a location for the National Basketball League team he had acquired. For a time, Iowa's capital and largest city seemed to be the obvious choice. In the years after World War II, Des Moines had grown rapidly and could even boast a distinctive skyline of big office buildings, highlighted by the golden dome of the capitol. The city was a hub for more than just state politics; it was a regional center for agriculture and home to substantial insurance, banking, and manufacturing businesses.

Waterloo was his second choice. George was quoted on several occasions as saying that the Cattle Congress Hippodrome might be a good location for his team to play some exhibition games. Perhaps a handful of winter contests there would count toward the NBL standings, while the majority of the home schedule would likely be on a Des Moines court. If basketball proved to be a success first in central Iowa, he reasoned, Waterloo might have its own NBL club the following year. However, the Cedar Valley did have a few factors in its favor, as George analyzed the situation.

For starters, George had spent much of his adolescence in Cedar Falls. Born to Greek immigrants in Massachusetts in 1905, the oldest son of the Georgakopoulos family made his way with his parents and siblings to northeast Iowa, at some point abbreviating and anglicizing their surname. Living near Iowa State Teachers College, George attended the on-campus high school there before stepping through the ropes for much of the 1920s as a flyweight professional boxer. By 1930, he was a fight promoter, scraping out a living during the Great Depression by sometimes accepting used glass pop bottles in lieu of tickets, then cashing them in for the meager refund.

After the challenging days of the Depression passed, George managed two boxers who each eventually had the chance to meet the most renowned fighter of the era, Joe Louis. George reignited the career of Johnny Paychek—who had been carrying guest luggage as a bellboy in a Des Moines hotel—sending him on course for a 1940 heavyweight championship fight against Louis in Madison Square Garden. For a time George, an unimposing midwesterner with a broad forehead, prominent ears, and a boxer's nose, also arranged fights for Lee Savold, who went from being an overweight Minnesota bartender to the British Boxing Board of Control's recognized champion. Savold fought Louis in New York while holding that British title in 1951, as both men neared the end of their careers.

George was also in a natural position to promote professional wrestling, first in Iowa, then throughout the region as that sport grew in popularity. By the mid-1940s, he was president of the National Wrestling Alliance, unifying promoters across the country. At one time, he arranged more than two hundred wrestling cards annually. Championship matches, female grapplers, "midgets," and sometimes even alligator wrestling boosted ticket sales at his events. George's connections with sporting venues in an array of cities brought him into contact with owners and other prominent figures in professional basketball.

By 1948, the NBL could claim to be the oldest surviving professional basketball league in America and the most successful circuit of its kind in the sport's history. Prior to the NBL, during the early 1930s, the game's best professionals played outside the jurisdiction of any league. The New York–based Original Celtics were professional basketball's first great team, with stars like Joe Lapchick, Dutch Dehnert, and Nat Holman. During the Great Depression, they toured extensively, playing one-off games that attracted substantial crowds due to the Celtics' name and reputation.

The Celtics and other traveling squads competed against local community teams that were often sponsored by large companies. A loose confederation of these clubs, primarily from Ohio, Indiana, Michigan, and the Chicago area, formed the Midwest Conference in 1935. Its teams initially played roughly a dozen league games in the middle of much larger schedules against touring and nearby independent teams. In 1937, members of the Midwest Conference rebranded themselves the National Basketball League.

That moniker belied a league that always remained regional in nature. Operating with Chicago as an informal hub, the NBL found success and longevity in medium to small cities. Oshkosh and Sheboygan, Wisconsin, became established during the late 1930s and were ultimately long-standing outposts in the league. Akron, Ohio, and Fort Wayne, Indiana, were regularly represented in early NBL seasons and were successful markets. Meanwhile, big cities like Chicago, Detroit, and Cleveland each had several attempts in the NBL, most of which were abandoned by their owners within a season or two.

The league could boast a level of competitiveness higher than any other and placed at least one team in the championship game of the World Professional Basketball Tournament every year from the time the Chicago event began in 1939. The National Basketball League survived the Depression and World War II, but by 1948 it was imperiled again amid a standoff with the rival Basketball Association of America (BAA). The BAA had been formed in 1946 by the owners of large arenas, generally in the eastern U.S., who hoped that professional basketball would fill their buildings on nights when hockey teams and other sporting attractions were idle. Drawing barely more than a million fans in its first season, the BAA did not deliver the windfall its founders expected and lost four of its eleven charter members before its second season. The BAA might have had the biggest markets and most impressive venues — Madison Square Garden, Boston Garden, Chicago Stadium, Detroit Olympia, and more—but the NBL still had the sport's best athletes. The bidding war for players that ensued hurt the chances for either league to survive and proved to be a major hardship for the financially limited, small-market owners of the NBL.

In May 1948, the BAA went beyond raiding NBL players, instead absconding with four whole teams. The most valuable prize was the Minneapolis Lakers, reigning NBL champions and owners of the sport's star attraction, George Mikan. The Lakers' championship series opponents, the Rochester Royals, also defected. Longstanding NBL members the Fort Wayne Zollner Pistons and the Indianapolis Kautskys, both named after their team owners, also switched allegiances. "There will be no respect of player contracts and open war on signing players now," declared an angered Leo Ferris as he assumed the interim presidency of the NBL's remaining teams.[1]

The NBL was reduced even further as two other 1947–48 members went out of business. Left with five returning clubs, the league was happy to welcome Pinkie George and a new crop of Iowa basketball fans. Meanwhile, the central Iowa promoter became increasingly dissatisfied with Des Moines as the base of his basketball operations. Sensing a lack of local enthusiasm for the project, in which he had already invested $25,000, he approached NBL leaders about switching locations. "You don't have to sell sports too much here," George said of the Cedar Valley. "Just tell the people where and what it is going to be, and if the attraction is worth anything, they'll be there."[2]

On August 16, 1948, the NBL—by then back to seven teams—agreed to the change, albeit by a 5–2 vote, which suggested some hesitancy about Waterloo's suitability. George elaborated on his decision during his announcement to Waterloo media and city leaders, noting that the community had made a determined lobbying effort throughout the summer: "I decided they were right. They showed me facilities here are better than in any other city in Iowa. . . . I'm a Cedar Falls boy, and I'm proud to be able to bring a major league team here."[3]

Although he didn't mention it at the time, George knew he had someone on hand to monitor the basketball project when his more established boxing and wrestling enterprises required attention in Des Moines and elsewhere. Andy George was Pinkie's younger brother by fifteen months. Andy had helped make the most of Waterloo's short-lived experience in the PBLA, serving as the team's manager of business affairs. He was also a local sports promoter in his own right and a local war hero, although the specific details of his service were not widely known in the community.

Wearing glasses and a thin mustache, the dark-haired younger George brother had spent one year at Iowa State Teachers College, then went to work as a machinist and beer distributor; he also arranged boxing and wrestling matches. He enlisted in the army in May 1943 at age thirty-seven. Although he was initially assigned to a field artillery unit in Colorado, his heritage and ability to speak, read, and write Greek led to his transfer. By October, he was preparing for foreign deployment with the Office of Strategic Services, the wartime entity that evolved into the civilian Central Intelligence Agency during the late 1940s.

First in Cairo, then in Italy, George served primarily in an OSS message center. He decoded secret, handwritten communications from agents of the Balkan resistance movements who sought to dislodge and push back occupying Nazi forces. In early 1944, he was on the ground for several months during operations in Yugoslavia and Greece, sustaining a lower back injury that led to recurring painful episodes for years to come. George earned two bronze stars for his service and had advanced with Allied forces into Austria when conflict in the European theater ended in 1945. Supervisors gave him superior marks for emotional stability and—despite his age—physical ability. One commanding officer, Captain Henry Eldredge, called him "an excellent man," noting in his service record that George "gets along well with people, follows orders, and possesses a very good attitude."[4]

Family ties aside, Pinkie George clearly had a reliable lieutenant in Waterloo.

In order for Waterloo's second attempt at professional basketball to be successful, it was essential to distinguish the new club and the National Basketball League from the failure of the previous fall. "Don't mention that fly-by-night affair in the same breath with the NBL," remarked Pinkie George. "This is established major league basketball, with established major league stars and practically every college All-America player of last season added . . . this is the real major league thing this time."[5]

Whether by intent or coincidence, the player-coach George hired to manage Waterloo on the court could hardly have been a better embodiment of the case he sought to make. Charlie Shipp had played in the NBL when it was still known as the Midwest Conference. Before that, his basketball exploits had gained wide attention while he was still in high school. In 1933, during the final game of the National Catholic High School Championship, Shipp contributed 15 points in a 31–10 Indianapolis Cathedral victory over St. Rita of Chicago. Like many other top professional players during the Depression, he chose to turn his basketball skills into a modest but immediate paycheck rather than a college scholarship.

Shipp's first job—simultaneously as a professional basketball player and in a factory—was with his hometown U.S. Tires team in Indianapolis during 1935. By 1937–38, in the rebranded NBL, he was with another tire company and part of a rivalry with far greater competitive implications off the court than on it. Akron was home to a pair of early company-sponsored NBL squads: the archrival Goodyear Wingfoots and Firestone Non-Skids. After winning a crosstown 1938 playoff series, Shipp's Goodyear club went on to claim the NBL Championship over the Oshkosh All-Stars, with considerable credit due to Shipp for his defensive play against NBL leading scorer LeRoy "Cowboy" Edwards.

Following one more season in Akron, Shipp departed for Oshkosh and $150 per month with the All-Stars, trading his day job with tires for work at Wisconsin Axle. The All-Stars were NBL champs in 1941 and 1942, also claiming the World Professional Basketball Tournament for good measure in '42. Involved in war industry and at the head of a growing household, Shipp remained on the home front during World War II. In the war's final year, he changed cities, teams, and industries again, becoming a member of the Fort Wayne Zollner Pistons and helping that organization to a league title, plus two more top finishes at the World Pro event. Adding a stint with the Anderson (Indiana) Packers, by the time Shipp arrived in the Cedar Valley he had played thirteen professional seasons and had been chosen for All-League honors seven times.

Shipp was a capable scorer. Using a two-handed set shot (much like a free throw stroke, to which some players of the period added a slight hop as they released the ball), the muscular, long-armed guard was accurate from a considerable range. In that low-scoring era, he contributed more than 5 points per game throughout his career; his highest scoring average was 7.5 in 1941–42. However, his greatest virtues were resolute defense and tenacious competitiveness, exemplified in two crucial efforts for Oshkosh during 1941–42.

In the last game of the 1942 NBL Finals, Shipp was assigned to guard league MVP Bobby McDermott, who had averaged 19.5 points per game to that time in the series. Shipp shut out McDermott and the All-Stars prevailed, 52–46, to repeat as NBL champions. Days later, during the championship game of the World Professional Basketball Tournament in Chicago, Shipp contributed 7 points in a 43–41 win over the Detroit Eagles; moreover, he was the only Oshkosh player on the court for all forty minutes of the game. He and his All-Star teammates were given a hero's welcome by 4,000 buoyant fans when their train rolled into the Sawdust City before dawn the following morning.

One mark against Shipp was his tendency toward occasional temperamental outbursts. During his time with U.S. Tires and the Goodyear Wingfoots, he was involved in more than one on-court fistfight with members of the barnstorming all-black New York Rens. In another incident around that time, after fouling out of a game in Indianapolis, Shipp "threw the ball at the unprotected head of the referee, the leather smashing directly into his face."[6]

Perhaps the most notorious moment in his career came in 1946, while he was a member of the Zollner Pistons. By that time, Shipp and McDermott were teammates. A dice game involving the two guards during a train ride back to Fort Wayne turned into a brawl, significant enough that team management was forced to trade Shipp to the Anderson Packers and release McDermott, who then found his way to the Chicago American Gears.

Pinkie George was willing to see Shipp's missteps in a positive way. "He's a good gamble," George noted. "After all he's been given the rap for a lot of things . . . he'll be sure to know when some of his players try to pull his leg."[7] For his own part, Shipp set out the barest of guidelines for his players, as described by *Waterloo Courier* sports editor Al Ney: "that (1) they act like major leaguers, (2) they stay in shape, (3) they hustle all the time and (4) they do not enter taverns when the training season or regular season is in progress."[8] "I think he wanted to be one of the players," remembered Leo Kubiak, a first-year professional in 1948–49. Shipp "knew the game of basketball, but it just seemed he could have been a lot tougher on the players."[9]

By late August, the team had officially been dubbed the Hawks and began to build a roster. Rookie guards Kubiak and Jack Spencer had wrapped up their NCAA careers the previous spring at Bowling Green and Iowa, respectively. Rollie Seltz, a former All-American at Hamline University in Minnesota, had been Shipp's teammate in Anderson. The most significant experience on the Waterloo roster—other than that of Shipp himself—came from the defunct Toledo Jeeps, who had finished fifth in the NBL's Eastern Division during 1947–48 before disbanding. Several former Jeeps players, including former All-Americans Harry Boykoff and Dick Mehen, switched over to the Hawks' black and gold colors. Dale Hamilton also came from Toledo. After Shipp, Hamilton was Waterloo's most-seasoned professional and served as a semiofficial playing assistant coach.

Not all the former Toledo Jeeps whom the Hawks attempted to

acquire were excited about the opportunity to play in Waterloo. Outside shooter Fran Curran had been the captain of Notre Dame's basketball squad before his stint in Toledo. After purchasing his NBL rights, the Hawks spent more than half the 1948–49 season trying to coax or compel the forward to honor his Jeeps contract in northeast Iowa. However, Curran preferred to join the Rochester Royals in the Basketball Association of America and never reported to Waterloo.

By January 1949, the Hawks convinced a Toledo court that Curran had breached his contract. Judge Thomas O'Connor imposed an injunction, which team officials believed would force Curran to leave the Royals and either play for Waterloo or not at all. However, the former Fighting Irish star had learned more than basketball at Notre Dame: his law degree gave him the means to outmaneuver the state court decision in Ohio while he was living and playing basketball in New York. The Hawks eventually gave up the issue when it became evident that their legal victory was a hollow one.

Meanwhile, players reported for their first practice on October 1. The league announced its schedule a little more than a week later, and the Hawks began a ticket sales campaign. General admission prices were pegged at eighty-five cents, just slightly below the level suggested to have been out of bounds for the PBLA the previous fall. To put this in perspective, George arranged for reporters to talk with Leo Ferris, now the league's vice president and owner of the Moline, Illinois, Tri-Cities Blackhawks. "There's one thing about which I don't agree with Pinkie—that's his price of tickets," Ferris noted, about to startle his interviewer. "We get a minimum of $1 and a top of $2.50 in Moline, and that's not high in the league. . . . He has to draw 33 percent more than we do to break even. Your prices here will be among the lowest in the league."[10]

Basketball tickets appear reasonable in light of other prices during the era (and blushingly modest beside NBA ticket rates of later generations). In the late 1940s, bacon processed at Waterloo's Rath Packing Company was available at grocery stores across the city for as little as thirty-five cents a pound. A quart of milk cost sixteen cents, and a twelve-pack of beer sold for $1.35. At a time when most dinners were eaten at home, potatoes could be purchased, ninety-eight pounds at a time, for less than four dollars. As for durable goods, a modest home in Waterloo might have sold for $3,000 to $4,000, comparable to a typical annual middle-class wage. On average, a new car cost a little more than $2,000.[11]

The Hawks' first basketball and business test of the season came on October 21 against Tri-Cities at a relatively neutral court in Tama, forty-five miles southwest of Waterloo. Harry Boykoff, the 6-foot-10-inch center, led the Hawks with 12 points, and Waterloo held a halftime lead before falling, 47–38. Most of the seven hundred people in attendance were on hand to see a pair of former Iowa Hawkeyes: Waterloo's Jack Spencer and Tri-Cities' Murray Wier.

The importance of exhibition games to the financial health of a professional basketball team in the 1940s should not be understated. A well-conceived schedule of these friendly matchups could easily make the difference between profit and loss. Professional basketball was a novel attraction in smaller communities, and proper advance publicity could draw a large percentage of a town's sports fans to their local gym for a single game. Even into the postwar years, some of the sport's most famous players and teams spent entire winters playing only exhibition games.

In the 1930s and '40s, the Harlem Globetrotters played top-caliber competitive basketball. Formed in 1927 (in Chicago, not New York), the Globetrotters' reputation was already well established by 1940, when they won the World Professional Basketball Tournament. The authentic Globetrotters' success as a team and a business led to the formation of several counterfeit all-black "Globe Trotters" teams traveling across the country by the 1940s.

Waterloo arranged to tour with one of these squads, organized by promoter Bobby Grund. In late October 1948, the Hawks went dashing through Iowa with the Famous Globe Trotters, taking to the court on a near nightly basis. Their ramblings included stops in Marshalltown, Newton, Centerville, Humboldt, and Denison before concluding at the Cattle Congress Hippodrome. Indicative of the complexities of race in sports during the time—and of Grund's effectiveness as a promoter—nearly every newspaper preview in the rural Iowa communities focused glowingly on the strengths of the Globe Trotters' black roster rather than on details of the white All-Americans who played for the Hawks.

Covering more than six hundred miles and playing six times in a week, Waterloo won every game. The closest margin of victory was 20 points in the final matchup as the two tired teams went up and down the floor in front of a Sunday crowd of 1,200. All told, more than 6,000 fans (3,000 in Centerville alone) turned out for the series. By adding a few more preseason games, including another neutral-court loss to Tri-Cities in Dubuque, the 1948–49 NBL Hawks had played more exhibition games together before opening night than the PBLA Pro-Hawks had managed during their aborted regular-season schedule a year earlier.

●

The National Basketball League consisted of nine teams by the time the first jump ball was contested in the fall of 1948. The Hawks' rivals in the Western Division were the well-established Oshkosh All-Stars and Sheboygan Red Skins; the Moline-based Tri-Cities Blackhawks, opening their third campaign in the league; and the Denver Nuggets, who like the Hawks were new to the NBL. The Eastern Division included the Syracuse Nationals and the Anderson Packers, both returning from 1947–48, plus the expansion Detroit Vagabond Kings (named for a sponsoring camper trailer manufacturer) and Hammond Calumet Buccaneers of northwest Indiana.

The schedule was composed of sixty-four games per team, eight against each opponent. The Hawks looked ahead to four home and four road matchups against each club, with one significant inequitable exception: seven of eight games against Syracuse were to be away from the Hippodrome. This was attributed to Waterloo's home schedule being entirely comprised of favorable Sunday and Wednesday dates, which apparently made it difficult for the NBL's easternmost team to reach the Cedar Valley. Ultimately, Waterloo was left with twenty-nine home games and thirty-five on the road.

Over 2,500 fans—more than had attended any single home game the previous autumn—came to the Hippodrome for the season opener against Sheboygan on the first Sunday evening in November. Prior to the featured matchup, they watched the local John Deere Tractorettes women's basketball team fall to the Marshalltown Gasoline Alley Girls in a close game, 27–23. Auditorium president and local radio personality R. J. "Mike" McElroy spoke to the crowd before the game began, as did Pinkie George. Waterloo mayor Bailey Barnes tossed up the ceremonial first jump ball.

When the game began in earnest, Hawks center Harry Boykoff drew whistles quickly. In the early minutes of the second quarter, he was sidelined with three fouls, shifting Dick Mehen into the pivot. Trailing by 3 points after one period, Waterloo pulled within 2 at halftime in a game that was close from start to finish. Waterloo and Sheboygan traded the lead during the third quarter, but fouls continued to accumulate for the home team, putting Mehen over the limit with five while more than ten minutes remained. Fortunately for Waterloo, the Red Skins struggled at the free throw line, missing a sequence of nine consecutive attempts. However, concern continued to mount when Boykoff fouled out early in the fourth quarter.

Despite the Hawks' lack of size on the floor, 5-foot-10-inch forward Rollie Seltz provided the offense that Waterloo needed to stay with Sheboygan. Seltz finished with 17 points, including a basket and a free throw that put the Hawks in position to later take the lead for good when player-coach Charlie Shipp sank a shot from the corner, making the score 56–55 with five minutes remaining. Adding to the lead slightly, the Hawks then methodically kept the ball away from the Red Skins for most of the final two and a half minutes. It was 63–61 with eight seconds remaining when Waterloo's Dave Wareham went to the free throw line for two shots after an intentional foul. Wareham, a Loras College alum, made the first free throw, and under the rules of the era Waterloo declined the second shot in order to keep the ball. Inbounding successfully, the Hawks held on to win the opener 64–61.

The victory was a true team effort. Nine of ten Waterloo players finished with at least 1 point, with Mehen, Boykoff, and Seltz all in double figures. Bob Lowther, a 6-foot-5-inch Louisiana State product who had been an All-American javelin thrower in addition to playing basketball, was lauded for filling the lane late in the game and tipping in a key bucket at a crucial moment for his only field goal. Sheboygan's Mike Todorovich led all scorers with 20 points. Former Waterloo Pro-Hawk Noble Jorgensen, who had returned from Oregon to join the Red Skins, played a minor role with 3 points for the visitors.

The heavy non-regular-season schedule Waterloo had played in October extended into November as the team traveled to Eau Claire and La Crosse, Wisconsin, and split a pair of exhibitions against Oshkosh on the two nights following the official opener with Sheboygan. Thus, the ten-man Hawks squad was on the court for the fourth time in four nights when they played their second regular-season league game against Denver on Wednesday, November 10. Despite fatigue and overtime, Waterloo shook out a 51–48 victory against the winless Nuggets, with Shipp scoring in the final minute of regulation to tie the game, then recording the go-ahead bucket early in extra time.

With two immediate home wins, the schedule looked promising; four of the Hawks' next five games were to be at home in the Hippodrome. Waterloo's Cattle Congress auditorium was located amid a complex of barns and other fair buildings covering more than eighty acres, close to the Cedar River near the western outskirts of the community. The grounds around the Hippodrome had hosted the National Dairy Cattle Congress, which felt akin to a state fair and had brought farmers to northeast Iowa from most of the nation's forty-eight states, since 1912. Improvements to the facilities had been made as the event returned annually.

Ahead of the 1948 Cattle Congress, the campus underwent $56,000 in improvements. The investment included the introduction of seven acres of lighted parking for the fair, which ultimately also benefited Waterloo basketball fans. By the early weeks of the 1948–49 season, the Hawks were also making their own enhancements to the interior of the Hippodrome: a new scoreboard was ready for the game against Denver, and a furnace to heat the building's lobby would make the facility much more comfortable during the basketball season's winter months.

The basketball court and glass backboards purchased from the bankrupt Professional Basketball League of America by the Junior Chamber of Commerce were installed in the center of the auditorium floor, surrounded by more than 5,000 permanent seats escalating in rows that reached nearly to the ceiling. Box seats were available for a premium, as were chairs on the floor and on short risers alongside the court. Adjacent to the boxes at regular intervals, half a dozen steel girders on each side of the building rose vertically to support the roof, creating an obstructed view for some in the general admission seats beyond.

Breaks in the grandstands behind each basket allowed teams to get to their respective dressing rooms at one end of the building and opened toward a large exterior door at the other. Round fixtures hung above the floor to light the court, and a big electric fan at one end of the building circulated the air. Some opponents claimed this unit was only turned on to disrupt the visiting team when shooting at that end of the court. However, the fan may have been a necessity due to the haze that clouded the building on game nights from the hundreds of smokers in attendance. The Hawks eventually had to ban smoking in the seating sections, relegating those with the habit to the lobby during breaks in the game.

In this atmosphere, the Hawks continued to build upon a schedule that regularly kept them at home in Waterloo during the early weeks of the season. By the end of November, they had a league-best 9–1 record. Seven of their first ten games were played at the Hippodrome, all resulting in wins. The home streak included a 5-point victory over the Oshkosh All-Stars to break a tie at the top of the division, a robust 9-point Thanksgiving Eve decision over the Eastern Division–leading Syracuse Nationals, and a narrow 2-point result against the Tri-Cities Blackhawks to cap that holiday weekend in front of 7,536 fans. An inventory of the Cattle Congress parking lot that night turned up license plates from fifty-seven of Iowa's ninety-nine counties in addition to thirteen other states.[12]

The Hawks were particularly creative with stalling and ball control tactics during the Tri-Cities game, protecting a lead for most of the fourth quarter. Shipp took stalling to a new level with one late stoppage in order to save a time-out for his winded ball club. Recounted by *Courier* sports editor Al Ney, "as the teams lined up for a free throw shot, Shipp waved his arms and said [to the referee] 'Jim (Enright), I think that's five fouls on me . . . guess I have to go out.' Enright of course stopped the play. Shipp rested as Enright checked the fouls with the official scorer. By the time Enright found that Shipp only had three fouls, the Hawks coach was rested and ready to continue play."[13]

Rest would prove harder to find when December began. Eighteen Waterloo games were scheduled for the month, with a dozen away from home.

●

Harry Boykoff was the Hawks' star player. The twenty-six-year-old was 6 feet 10 inches tall, the biggest body on the floor for Waterloo when the 1948–49 season began. Pinkie George spent $10,000 for the right to purchase Boykoff's $10,000 Toledo Jeeps contract, essentially paying for the star center twice. The team's tallest and most expensive player came to northeast Iowa with greater renown as a college star than any of his teammates.

Boykoff grew up in the basketball-playing Brooklyn neighborhoods of Brownsville and East New York, not far from Jamaica Bay and a few miles east of Ebbets Field. Childhood friends Art Fronczyk and Sid Tanenbaum respectively went on to college basketball scholarships at Long Island and New York University (both were among the leading programs in the country at the time). Max Zaslofsky played briefly in college before achieving greater success in the Basketball Association of America and, later, the National Basketball Association. Boykoff became a star at St. John's University with diminutive neighborhood "Mutt and Jeff" partner Hy Gotkin. St. John's was coached by Joe Lapchick, a former center whose height had been considered far above average at 6 feet 5 inches a generation earlier.

"Joe Lapchick deserves credit for making a player out of me," Boykoff recalled later. "When I came to St. John's, I soon found out that I didn't know much. There were other tall guys around. Lapchick showed me how to roll on a pivot play. He taught me how to move around."[14]

Injuries limited the dark-haired, long-armed, shot-blocking Boykoff early in his college career, but he began to gain attention as a sophomore. One of his first notable performances came in the closing days of 1942 against Tennessee. Facing future Waterloo teammate Dick Mehen, Boykoff swung the Redmen from a 13-point halftime deficit to a 52–41 win at Madison Square Garden. At the Garden less than two months later, he set a then-arena record with a 45-point effort against St. Joseph's. The season ended with St. John's sweeping to the 1943 National Invitation Tournament championship; Boykoff led all scorers during the three-game event and was named tournament Most Valuable Player as well as an All-American.

Previously excluded from military service because of his height, Boykoff sneaked into the army before his junior year, overcoming the height limitation by putting his size-13 feet beside the scale on which he was supposed to stand for his official measurement. He achieved the rank of sergeant and trained green artillery units at West Point. After World War II, Boykoff returned to St. John's, became the first player in school history to record 1,000 career points, helped the team to two additional National Invitation Tournament appearances, and earned additional All-American honors. He also set another Madison Square Garden scoring record—54 points— during a 1947 game against St. Francis. Following graduation, he was the center for the 1947 College All-Star team that defeated the World Professional Basketball Tournament Champion Indianapolis Kautskys in an exhibition game ahead of the 1947–48 season.

Upon becoming a professional himself, Boykoff chose the Jeeps and the NBL instead of his hometown New York Knicks and the BAA in part because, in addition to his salary, the Toledo club promised him a home for his family and an off-season job. For a brief time, he worked as the city's tallest milkman. An accountant by trade, Boykoff had an NBL-record 219 personal fouls counted against him during his season in Toledo. Despite the dubious total and a lack of speed, he was still recognized on the league's All-Rookie Second Team as he tallied 9.7 points per game.

Through ten 1948–49 games in Waterloo, Boykoff was averaging just shy of 13 points per contest, second only to Mehen. Back in his home state, Boykoff put in a game-high 18, but the Hawks lost their first game of December, 68–59 on the road against the Syracuse Nationals. League coaches, players, and media voted the rematch the next evening the best NBL game of the season.[15]

Waterloo sprinted to a 19-point lead by halftime and still maintained a double-digit margin late in the fourth quarter. The aggressive Nationals committed a number of late fouls as Waterloo tried to stall. The Hawks declined the resulting free throws in favor of keeping the basketball, but Syracuse eventually converted enough turnovers into baskets to be within 1 point during the waning seconds. A traveling call against Leo Kubiak gave the home team the ball for a final possession, from which a wild long shot resulted in a rebound basket by Syracuse's Jim Homer with four seconds to go. The late field goal completed the comeback and gave the Nationals an unlikely 72–71 win.

Back at the Hippodrome two nights later after making the long train trip from Syracuse, Waterloo faced the Oshkosh All-Stars, with whom they shared a virtual tie at the top of the Western Division. Before a meeting weeks earlier, player-coach Charlie Shipp had called his former club the roughest team in the league: "Year in and year out, under Coach Lon Darling, Oshkosh plays rough, tough basketball and doesn't pull any punches when it fouls."[16]

Darling had backed the All-Stars as a semiprofessional squad as early as 1929; the team moved to the NBL in 1937. An agricultural supplies salesman with an entrepreneurial penchant, he had earned the money to finance a basketball club by starting his own seed company after his former employer went out of business. Although Darling had never played basketball, he was interested in sports of all kinds, and basketball corresponded with the months when his seed operation was slow. By 1948, the former high school dropout had coached the All-Stars to a pair of NBL championships (among five consecutive trips to the league championship series) and one World Professional Basketball Tournament title.

Like Waterloo, the city of Oshkosh had been founded nearly a hundred years earlier. With 40,000 people by 1948, the town on the western shore of Lake Winnebago was smaller than Waterloo but similarly benefited from large industry. It was the home of Oshkosh B'Gosh work clothes and travel gear made by Oshkosh Trunk and Luggage. Drivetrain components for motor vehicles were assembled by Wisconsin Axle, and an array of wood products originated in the city.

What Waterloo had but Oshkosh lacked was a large indoor sports venue. The All-Stars played in a number of local school gyms—South Park Middle School notable among them—with capacities of 1,000 to 2,000 people. Darling addressed this problem as well as the challenge of an already small market by playing a substantial portion of the schedule on neutral courts in all corners of Wisconsin and sometimes beyond state lines. Fans in these wayward locations may not have known the words to the team's "On, You All-Stars" fight song, but they were often willing to meet the price of admission.

Despite Oshkosh's good start in 1948–49 and the club's long history of success, the forty-five-year-old Darling considered that his team might be better coached by a former player. A pair of late November losses may have influenced his decision to resign near the end of the month. However, if Darling had doubts about his ability to coach the All-Stars, his players did not share them. Unanimously, they asked him to return to the bench after less than a week and, thus confirmed, Darling and the All-Stars prepared for the first of three consecutive games against the Hawks.

Waterloo claimed the opening matchup, taking the low-scoring game with a fourth-quarter push. The victory materialized even though Shipp had been ejected early in the second quarter when a wrestling match with opposing forward Alex Hannum led to jabs being thrown. Shipp was later fined fifty dollars by the league for the incident. The next night in Appleton, Wisconsin, it was the All-Stars who celebrated a comeback win. Then, playing for the third time in three days in a third city, Oshkosh cruised to a 15-point decision in Elgin, Illinois, taking over first place in the division as a result.

The losses to the All-Stars were the beginning of a six-game losing streak that eventually dropped Waterloo to third place and only one game above .500, with a record of 10–9. During this stretch, the Hawks suffered their first home loss at the hands of the lowly Denver Nuggets, who followed up by defeating Waterloo twice more in the thin Rocky Mountain air. Within a week's time, the Nuggets had doubled their season win total, all thanks to matchups against Waterloo.

As for business, the Hawks' average attendance was more than 3,100 fans per home game, just short of the mark needed to operate with a break-even cash flow through nearly two months of the season. With the organization in this relatively secure financial situation, Pinkie George decided to make his exit. The departure came under the pretext of a heart condition that was affecting his health. The nearly forty-four-year-old George had been living in Waterloo and focusing on basketball for months while his wife, son, and more established promotional activities remained in Des Moines. George gave his interest in the franchise to his brother, Andy, and to Shipp. "I consider that this move creates an opportunity for both Charlie and Andy," he said after the change was announced. "I wish them the best of luck, with full confidence that they'll give the fans the best results possible in all phases of the operation."[17]

The new owners had the opportunity to begin without the debts incurred by bringing the club to Waterloo. *Courier* sports editor Al Ney noted that Pinkie had absorbed a $20,000 to $25,000 loss by walking away without selling the team to his brother and Shipp. He had also passed up the chance to mitigate his losses by selling the Hawks' top players to other teams.

"The club is solvent only because Pinkie assumed costs," Ney wrote. "The Hawks will have to pay for themselves at the gate. Neither Shipp nor Andy makes any pretext of having the cash to throw into a money losing venture. It will be up to the fans of Waterloo to support the club at the gate—even when it is in a losing slump."[18]

Losses on the court and at the box office were affecting other NBL teams and were about to change the look of the league midway through the season.

3

FOR THE SAKE OF LEAGUE PRESTIGE

Bennie Schadler's trip to Waterloo was slow, even by the two-lane-highway standards of 1948. Starting out early from Benton Harbor near the Michigan-Indiana state line, the second-year professional basketball player made his way to join his new team by circling around the southern shore of Lake Michigan, then navigating through Chicago. Winter storms on the final Sunday before Christmas prolonged the ride. The hills that he crept up and down on either side of the Mississippi River in western Illinois and eastern Iowa seemed all the steeper when glazed with ice. Finally, just after 7 o'clock in the evening, he wheeled into one of the many snow-covered spaces in the Hippodrome parking lot.

After meeting with Andy George and Charlie Shipp inside the arena, Schadler signed his contract and officially became the newest member of the Waterloo Hawks on December 19, an hour before tip-off against the Oshkosh All-Stars. Waterloo's co-owners told the forward that he need not feel obligated to be on the bench after his long and trying trip. "I'd like to get into uniform if you don't mind," Schadler replied.[1]

More than 1,800 fans battled the weather to see the game. As Waterloo-Oshkosh games had been earlier in the month, the matchup was aggressively physical from the outset, and Waterloo led only 10–5 at the conclusion of a low-scoring first quarter. Oshkosh started the second period with a 10–0 run and took an 8-point lead into halftime. Dick Mehen and Harry Boykoff were held without a field goal prior to intermission.

Facing the possibility of a seventh consecutive loss, Shipp sent his new #21 to the scorer's table to begin the third quarter. The Hawks' lineup covered the spectrum, with Schadler at 6 feet and Leo Kubiak at 5 feet 11 inches in addition to the towering Boykoff and Mehen. The variable components clicked, and Waterloo was back within 2 points by the start of the fourth quarter. From there, the deficit stretched briefly before narrowing again to 5 as Oshkosh center Gene Englund fouled out with a game-high 17 points and 2:01 remaining.

Mehen cut the All-Stars' lead to 3, then after a quick takeaway, assisted on a Schadler layup that brought the Hawks closer than they had been since early in the second quarter. Waterloo swiped possession again after a tie-up by Kubiak. Down 1 point but with the basketball, the home team worked the front court until Schadler came free near the foul line, hoisting a shot that circled the entire rim before falling through. The All-Stars had more than one opportunity to retake the lead with attempts from close range in the final ten seconds, but the ball stayed out, and Waterloo came away with a 47–46 win.

Although Mehen had led Waterloo with 13 points to help end Waterloo's losing skid, the unexpected 6 contributed by Schadler were the story of that snowy Sunday. The speedy, short-haired 6-footer had attended Northwestern, serving as captain of the Wildcats' basketball team in 1944–45 and 1946–47. Between those two seasons, he spent a year in the U.S. Navy. After returning from the service, Schadler was Northwestern's Most Valuable Player in his senior year. He and Boykoff were briefly College All-Star teammates prior to their respective professional rookie campaigns in 1947–48. Using primarily one-handed, over-his-head hook shots, Schadler spent that season in the Basketball Association of America with the Chicago Stags. He moved on to the National Basketball League's Detroit Vagabond Kings during the summer of 1948 and had led Detroit with team-high scoring in two November meetings with Waterloo.

The twenty-four-year-old became a Hawk when the Vagabond

Kings went bankrupt. Detroit's 2–17 record was hardly the club's most significant problem. The Vagabond Kings had been playing in a Catholic school gym seating around a thousand. Making matters worse, on many dates when it might have been possible to reach that modest capacity, the facility was unavailable. Kings players reportedly went unpaid for much of the season.

The Detroit club had cast one of two votes against Pinkie George's plan to locate the Hawks in Waterloo. At the time, George had clairvoyantly been quoted as saying, "Waterloo will be playing NBL ball when Detroit is out."[2] That statement proved true sooner than expected, and the league replaced Detroit with one of the most remarkable teams in basketball history.

The New York Rens preceded the Harlem Globetrotters as the first great all-black touring basketball club. Initially organized in 1923, "Ren" had quickly become shorthand for Renaissance in reference to the Renaissance Casino in Harlem, where the team played occasionally. For most of their existence, the Rens barnstormed across the country—during the height of their success, they even traveled in their own private Pullman railcar—playing and winning more than a hundred games per season. The team reflected the complex and contradictory relationship between race and basketball—and sports in general—at that time. As with the traveling Negro League baseball clubs of the same era, white communities would turn out to see the Rens play but rarely socialized with them or even provided basic accommodations after the game ended.

The Rens had already been part of the professional basketball landscape for well over a decade when they won the first World Professional Basketball Tournament in 1939. In 1948, they also played in what proved to be the event's final championship game, finishing as runners-up to the Minneapolis Lakers. William "Pop" Gates had been a youngster with the '39 Rens and appeared in all ten World Professional Basketball Tournaments. In late 1948, he led the redubbed Dayton Rens into the NBL as player-coach. The all–African American team was unique in the otherwise white league. Dayton was chosen as the Rens' home city, but the squad actually played home games in several Ohio towns. The league was mainly concerned with filling the game schedule in other NBL markets on dates orphaned by the Vagabond Kings. The Rens were also anchored to the bottom of the Eastern Division standings, inheriting the record left behind by Detroit and thus entering league play fifteen games below .500.

Forty-two-year-old NBL president Ike Duffey presided over the necessary alterations to the 1948–49 schedule. Days after the Dayton addition was secured, Duffey was on his way to Waterloo to oversee a ceremonial transfer of the Hawks from Pinkie George to the new ownership tandem of Andy George and Charlie Shipp. The timing was convenient: Duffey owned the visiting Anderson Packers.

Like Lon Darling in Oshkosh, Fort Wayne's Fred Zollner, and Maurice White of the Chicago American Gears, Ike Duffey was a businessman who had decided to start a basketball team. This was far from the meatpacking millionaire's most outlandish aspiration. In the 1950s during semiretirement, Duffey talked his way into becoming the supposedly ceremonial president of the money-losing Central Indiana Railroad, which operated near Anderson. By one Associated Press account, he could soon be found at work "with the section crews, straightening rails and killing weeds. He even help[ed] load hogs, and [flag] the crossings."[3] Within two years, Duffey had turned the short line into a profitable operation, and for years afterward he would travel across the Midwest to baseball games and other events in a private railcar.

With his railroading days still in the future, Duffey focused his energies on basketball from the time that his Packers—literally, the front of their jerseys read "Duffey Packers"—entered the NBL in 1946–47. During that initial season, Anderson battled to a record of 24–20. The next year, the team was 42–18, outdistanced only by the Minneapolis Lakers and the Rochester Royals, who went on to meet each other in the league championship series.

Representing the small town northeast of Indianapolis—also home to General Motors' Delco Remy subsidiary and the Gospel

Trumpet Company, a large religious publisher—the Packers not only played on a high school court, they were led on game nights by a former high school coach. Murray Mendenhall had transitioned directly to professional basketball after spending more than two decades at Fort Wayne Central High School. At the end of the 1947–48 season, the league had named him Coach of the Year. During the 1948–49 season, Mendenhall's roster was boosted by the addition of his son, Murray Mendenhall Jr., whom he had coached to a state title in 1943 and who had gone on to play for Rice and Indiana Universities.

The senior Mendenhall won by coaching a slashing, driving, high-tempo game. In contrast, Waterloo under Shipp—who had previously played for Mendenhall in Anderson—preferred a methodical, controlled game. In their meeting three days before Christmas, Waterloo's strategy proved more effective, resulting in a 50–45 Hawks win. Dick Mehen played all forty minutes, finishing as the night's top scorer with 17 points. Meanwhile Duffey, who had spoken to a group of Waterloo business leaders earlier in the day and emphasized his responsibility to put the league's interests above his team, suspended one of his own players for receiving a technical foul and fined another twenty-five dollars for "indifferent play."[4]

Waterloo's consecutive wins versus Oshkosh and Anderson—the respective division leaders—gave the Hawks reason for early holiday cheer, but the remaining December results had the opposite effect. The team's game count was lightened by schedule revisions, but Waterloo still finished the month with five consecutive losses, including one to the All-Stars and two more against the Packers. In Anderson on December 30, it was Shipp's turn to run afoul of Duffey. After he received a double technical foul at the end of the third quarter, Shipp's ejection led to a loud courtside confrontation with both the referee and the league president. As a result, a 4-point Hawks lead disintegrated into a 12-point loss during the final period. After opening the season with nine wins in ten tries and owning first place in the division when December began, Waterloo was two games below even at 12–14 as the month ran out. Although they had dropped to fourth place, the Hawks still entered 1949 in contention for the playoffs and only four and a half games out of first place.

●

Bennie Schadler's debut with the Hawks occurred near the end of a period when the Waterloo roster was evolving. Of the ten players who appeared on opening night, four were gone before Schadler arrived. Gordon Flick and Dave Wareham—both rookies from small Iowa colleges—were the first to depart amid the personnel upgrades as the Hawks gathered veteran castoffs from other professional teams. Bob Lowther was traded to the Minneapolis Lakers. Jack Spencer had been loaned permanently to the independent Cedar Rapids Raiders while the Hawks were in the midst of their first December losing streak. For good measure, center Ray Ellefson was both acquired and then released within a three-week span just before Christmas.

Waterloo's more permanent additions supplemented the team's size, experience, or both. Guards Les Deaton and Bill Brown—both standing over 6 feet—came from Sheboygan and Oshkosh, respectively. Although Deaton had spent more than a year in eastern Wisconsin, he was a central Iowa native and a graduate of Simpson College in Indianola; he would later return there to serve as head basketball coach. Brown had played at the University of Maryland and—like Schadler—made an important contribution to a Waterloo win during his debut when the Hawks hosted his former team early in December.

Waterloo's final move was to acquire National Basketball League nomad Elmer "Al" Gainer just after the New Year. Following an All-American college career at DePaul in 1941, the 6-foot-7-inch center went on to play against Charlie Shipp in the 1942 NBL Championship series as a member of the Fort Wayne Zollner Pistons, then with him in 1946–47 on the Anderson Packers' roster. Gainer's other notable stops before arriving in Waterloo included the Chicago American

Gears during their inaugural season, the Sheboygan Red Skins, and the Baltimore Bullets of the Basketball Association of America.

The Hawks lost Deaton for much of January and February after he broke his ring finger during practice. Meanwhile, Shipp was put under doctor's orders to cut his own playing time beginning in late December due to a gallbladder problem that consistently made him ill. The misfortunes of Waterloo's player-coach during the latter part of the season led to additional minutes for Schadler, Brown, and the Hawks' other reserves. Shipp's health troubles compounded when he broke out in a rash covering much of his body, which was attributed to a wool allergy. His most uncanny hardship came while nursing a sore, blistered toe. Hoping to relieve the pressure on his foot, he strategically cut a hole in one of his old sneakers. However, when he pulled on the footgear, he painfully discovered that some discarded fishing tackle had found its way into it, leaving him hobbled to an even greater degree.

January began with games against the Red Skins, first in Waterloo, then in Sheboygan, on consecutive nights. Besides battling on the court, the Hawks were also chasing their opponents in the standings, opening the series fourth in the Western Division, two and a half games behind the third-place Red Skins. Waterloo cruised to a 9-point win in the Hippodrome matchup but fell by 3 the next evening. The defeat was the twelfth consecutive road game to go against the Hawks.

Waterloo's meetings with Sheboygan provided a reunion for Schadler and Max Morris, former college teammates on Northwestern's football and basketball teams. Morris had just returned to the Red Skins after completing the 1948 professional football season as a receiver with the Brooklyn Dodgers of the All-American Football Conference. Both Schadler and Morris had been selected in the National Football League draft—Schadler in 1945 by the Detroit Lions prior to his turn in the navy, Morris in 1947 by the Chicago Bears following his first season in the AAFC with the Chicago Rockets. Although Morris went on to wear both cleats and high-tops professionally, another former multisport Wildcat of the era achieved greater notoriety. During the 1943–44 academic year, Schadler's Northwestern football and basketball teammate had been Otto Graham, whose contributions to the Rochester Royals' 1945–46 NBL Championship were a footnote to his Hall of Fame career as a quarterback for the Cleveland Browns.

In the late 1940s, baseball was the more likely vocation for multisport professional basketball players. Although there was some overlap with spring training near the end of basketball season, talented athletes found ways to manage the challenge, at least for a while. Two members of the 1948–49 Hawks had previously earned baseball paychecks. Rollie Seltz had given up his baseball aspirations by the time he came to Waterloo after playing for several years with various minor league affiliates of the St. Louis Cardinals. The shortstop peaked during a stint in the International League with the Rochester Red Wings. Meanwhile, Leo Kubiak's only season in a minor league baseball lineup came during the summer of 1948. The Cleveland Indians assigned him to Green Bay in the Wisconsin State League, thus providing him with an opportunity to antagonize both Sheboygan and Oshkosh with a bat and glove as well as a basketball all in the same year.

With 7 points against Oshkosh when the All-Stars visited the Hippodrome on January 9, Kubiak was not the primary Hawks player to torment the division leaders, but he played his role during a big Waterloo victory. Harry Boykoff, Dick Mehen, and Seltz were all in double figures during the 62–39 win. The Hawks never trailed in the affair. At one stage during the third and fourth quarters, they reeled off an 18–0 run.

January continued to be favorable for Waterloo. Three days after defeating Oshkosh, the Hawks topped the NBL-best Packers by 6 points, despite a poor start that included a 10–1 deficit in the opening quarter. The Hawks missed their first nineteen attempts from the field yet still won. Adding more home court victories, Waterloo went 6–3 during the month, benefiting from a favorable schedule: seven of nine January games were at the Hippodrome. Strong performances in friendly surroundings were a trend across the NBL in 1948–49; through January 11, league teams collectively won 69.5 percent of their home games, and the percentage was even higher in the Western Division.[5]

The Hawks might have added another January home win if not for bad weather. A Sunday game against the Hammond Calumet Buccaneers had to be postponed when the visitors could not complete their trip to Waterloo. Battling icy roads, the Hammond players decided in Freeport, Illinois, that the drive was too dangerous to continue.

Travel in general, besides being one of the most costly budget items for NBL teams, contributed to the difficulties of winning on the road. Packed tightly into a couple of cars and taking turns at the wheel, Waterloo players drove themselves to away matchups in Sheboygan, Oshkosh, Moline, and Hammond. The Hawks were never caught in a serious accident, despite sometimes dangerous road conditions. However, other basketball clubs of the era were occasionally in consequential collisions. While commuting between games with four Sheboygan teammates, Noble Jorgensen was injured in March 1950 after an overnight head-on wreck during a snowstorm. That fall, another group of professional basketball players in transit was involved in a crash that killed a Missouri woman.

More expensive train trips were reserved for distant opponents. While those accommodations were comfortable in relative terms, tight schedules did little to reduce the stress of travel. With three or four games packed into some weeks, it was common to arrive for a game—whether away or returning home from the road—just hours before the opening tip. Long-distance rail expeditions also typically involved changing trains at hubs like Chicago or driving from Waterloo to a distant train station to use a more direct rail line.

The Denver Nuggets were the only 1948–49 NBL team to consistently fly to games. In the early days of passenger plane travel, the Nuggets faced unique challenges with this strategy. They were without center Ward "Hoot" Gibson during one late January loss at the Hippodrome because he refused to fly. Gibson's phobia was strong enough that he was reduced to taking trains by himself and meeting his teammates in opposing cities. Had he gone directly to Denver's next scheduled destination after Waterloo, Gibson would have still found himself alone; a snowstorm prevented the Nuggets from flying out of the Cedar Valley for at least two days, forcing them to miss a matchup against Oshkosh.

The Hawks, meanwhile, ended their road losing streak on February 3 by defeating the Tri-Cities Blackhawks in Moline. Three days later, when Waterloo visited Syracuse, the matchup was settled in overtime by a 79–75 score in the Nationals' favor. Every free throw was important, a fact that was further magnified when Rollie Seltz missed a potential game-winning technical foul shot with two seconds remaining in regulation. The disappointment in Syracuse left Waterloo with a 20–18 record and third place in the tightly bunched NBL Western Division. The Hawks were two games behind Tri-Cities, with the Oshkosh All-Stars wedged in between. Sheboygan sat half a game behind Waterloo in fourth place.

Third place bore special importance during the 1948–49 NBL season: the top three teams from each division qualified for the playoffs. Division winners were to be rewarded with a first-round postseason bye, while the second and third seeds were scheduled to meet for a best-of-three series. The semifinals and championship rounds would be played in a best-of-five format. As February continued, there was little doubt about who would qualify from the four-team Eastern Division, with the Dayton Rens struggling to overcome the early futility of the Detroit Vagabond Kings, whom they had replaced. In practical terms, four of the Western Division's five teams had the opportunity to win the playoff bye, while also facing the alternative prospect of being left out of postseason play. Only the Nuggets seemed too far adrift to contend.

●

The second and third weeks of February proved to be disastrous for Waterloo, as the Hawks lost seven times in a twelve-day span. Three of those defeats were by 1 point. The skid included two games versus the Sheboygan Red Skins and one each against the Oshkosh All-Stars and Tri-Cities Blackhawks. The streak ended on February 23 thanks to a game-winning shot by Shipp with seven seconds to go against the Hammond Calumet Buccaneers. That 63–61 home win left Waterloo four games under .500, six and a half games out of first place, and three games short of the final playoff berth. Just a little more than five weeks remained on the NBL schedule.

The slump-busting win against the Buccaneers drew a paltry crowd of 1,065. Against the same opponent two nights later in a game rescheduled due to earlier travel difficulties, attendance nearly tripled to 3,001, although expectations had been set for an even larger audience. Many on hand were there to see a preliminary matchup between Waterloo East and Waterloo West High Schools. Both games started slowly: the prep affair included just 19 combined points at halftime before West pulled away to a 40–30 victory. Later during the featured matchup, the Hawks were held without a converted shot from the field for the first five minutes but ultimately coasted to a win, 65–52.

Dick Mehen contributed 15 points, but it was the only time during a span of nine games from February 20 through March 7 that the big forward did not lead or share his team's top scoring honors. Instead, Harry Boykoff paced Waterloo with 20 points. Still, approaching the final month of the season, the 6-foot-5-inch Mehen was the Hawks' offensive centerpiece with 13.6 points per game. Shooting while holding the ball above his head—combining a unique technique with a height that few players could defend—Mehen had an average that put him in contention with Don Otten of the Blackhawks and Gene Englund of the All-Stars for the NBL scoring lead.

Mehen turned twenty-six before the 1948–49 season. A dark-haired high school standout in Wheeling, West Virginia, he had followed his older brother, Bernie, to basketball stardom at the University of Tennessee. The Volunteers suspended athletics in 1943 due to the war, and the younger Mehen joined the Army Air Corps, spending almost three full years in the military, including eleven months of overseas duty. After his service, he returned to Tennessee, gradu-

ating with a degree in education. He began his professional basketball career in 1947–48 with the Toledo Jeeps.

In early February 1949, Mehen had set the single-game Waterloo
scoring mark at 27 points in a win against the Dayton Rens. That
night, he shot over 68 percent, while no other Hawk contributed
more than two field goals. Typically a 70 percent free throw shooter,
Mehen might have reached 30 points against the Rens, except for a
1-for-4 showing at the foul line. The Hawks would need him to be at
his best in all aspects if a charge toward the playoffs was to be successful.

The late weeks of the NBL schedule were unfavorable for Waterloo. Eight of the Hawks' final eleven games were to be on the road.
The first matchup during the late stretch was in Sheboygan, providing Waterloo with an opportunity to move to .500 and putting the
team within one game of the Red Skins for the final playoff position.
However, a 21-point Sheboygan fourth quarter keyed a 63–57 Red
Skins win. The result was the first of four ill-timed Hawks losses.
Waterloo finally broke the streak with a win in Syracuse against
the Nationals on March 10, but the team remained two and a half
games behind Sheboygan with little opportunity to erase the difference. The Hawks were hurt further when arrangements could not be
finalized to reschedule a game at home against the last-place Denver
Nuggets and another on the road versus the Dayton Rens, both of
which had been postponed by bad weather.

Considering the difficulty of winning on the road, the Hawks delivered a respectable 3–5 record in their last eight games away from
the Hippodrome. Those results included two victories at high altitude in Denver, the first in overtime on Elmer Gainer's decisive
basket during the final minute. By now, however, Waterloo needed
timely results in other league games. Instead, Sheboygan continued
to stay out of reach.

In the Hawks' precarious playoff circumstances, the team feared
crowds might slacken and took desperate steps to maintain attendance. This nearly led to the cancellation of a matchup against the

Tri-Cities Blackhawks just before game time, as the *Waterloo Courier* related:

> When Andy George, president of the Waterloo Hawks, informed Leo Feris, Tri-Cities general manager, that no radio rights for the game had been granted, Ferris turned to an associate and ordered him to tell the Blackhawks players to "get in the bus; we're going home."
>
> After a heated exchange of words, George granted the Tri-Cities station permission to broadcast "because I can't disappoint the fans and Ferris knows it."
>
> George had announced to Waterloo stations earlier in the week that no broadcasts would be allowed Sunday because, he said, "We want to test attendance interest in Sunday afternoon basketball." [Earlier Sunday games had been played in the evening.] . . .
>
> Faced with either cancelation of the game or granting the broadcast right to the one station, George decided to have the game go on. . . .
>
> After the game another heated argument between George and Ferris ended with George requesting a police officer to escort Ferris out of the Hawks' office. . . .
>
> George at first had threatened to hold up the $500 check for playing the game, then turned it over to Ferris "because I didn't want to be guilty of violating any NBL rules myself."[6]

Only a meager crowd attended the game. It ended 50–49 with a winning Tri-Cities shot from between the top of the key and the center jump circle with five seconds remaining.

As the final week of the season began, the Hawks were out of play-off contention. On the other side of the NBL, Hammond's status added to Waterloo's disappointment; although the Hawks' record was eight games better, the Buccaneers would qualify for the play-offs due to the league's unbalanced divisional structure. It may have been some consolation when Mehen received recognition on the All-

NBL First Team. The Waterloo forward received more votes than any other player in ballots cast by league coaches, players, and media. At season's end, his average was 0.4 point per game behind Don Otten for the league scoring title.

The schedule ended on the final day of March. Due to changes brought about when the Dayton Rens replaced the Detroit Vagabond Kings, the Syracuse Nationals returned to the Hippodrome for only the second time during the season. Fewer than 1,700 attended, but those fans saw some unexpected excitement before tip-off. "A rat that ran around the outside of the court and even chased one woman up on a chair helped the crowd loosen up," explained *Waterloo Courier* sports editor Al Ney.[7] Fans maintained their energy during the exciting game that followed and on two occasions, Ney wrote, Charlie Shipp "looked up from the bench wondering how 1,650 fans could make that much noise."[8]

The Hawks appeared to be headed for a disappointing finish; late in the final quarter, the Nationals went on a 7–0 run to swing from a 4-point deficit to a 3-point lead. Just over a minute remained when a Mehen field goal brought Waterloo to within 1 point. The basket gave him 29 for the game, a new team-best for one night. However, a free throw miss by Shipp still left Waterloo behind by 1. On the Hawks' final possession, the game was in the hands of Rollie Seltz. Waterloo's third-leading scorer—behind Mehen and Boykoff—made the final shot of the season with six seconds to go, yielding a 69–68 win and the hugs of his teammates. The Hawks ended the year 30–32, in fourth place and four games shy of qualifying for the playoffs.

Although the NBL regular season was over, one of the best-attended basketball games at the Hippodrome was held three days later. Wellsburg, a town of just over six hundred people thirty-five miles west of Waterloo, had won the 1948–49 girls six-on-six high school basketball championship. In front of 4,500 Cedar Valley fans, the Wellsburg girls clobbered the Texas champs from Seagoville—located on the outskirts of Dallas—35–19, with 18 points coming from star forward Lorraine Boekhoff.

The crowd attending that matchup of top girls teams nearly

doubled Waterloo's NBL attendance average for the season. At 2,400 fans per game, the Hawks were short of the mark needed to avoid a financial loss by about 400 fans per night. Yet there was optimism for 1949–50; many other NBL clubs had suffered far greater losses in their inaugural seasons.

Toward the end of the campaign, Shipp announced that he would drop the player portion of his player-coach title while remaining on the bench. Editorializing in the *Courier*, Al Ney acknowledged the positives from Shipp's first season as a coach, noting that "he made a pretty fair ball club out of a gang of nice guys who weren't in particular demand around the circuit."[9]

Shipp and many of his players made arrangements to stay in Waterloo and anticipated off-season jobs. Harry Boykoff and Bennie Schadler planned to use connections with large companies to pass the summer working elsewhere as executives. Dick Mehen expected to visit his brother in Toledo and the rest of his family in West Virginia.

Meanwhile, in the NBL playoffs, the division-winning Oshkosh All-Stars and Anderson Packers put their first-round byes to good use. Both advanced to the best-of-five final series. Anderson prevailed in the championship round, winning the first two games by first 4- and then 2-point margins in Wisconsin, then completed the three-game sweep in Indiana. No one realized at the time that the clinching victory made the Packers the NBL's final champions.

Less than a year after four teams had switched from the National Basketball League to the Basketball Association of America, anyone with an interest in the sport's professional operations anticipated the end of the 1948–49 season to see what would happen next. Through the addition of strong clubs and some of the game's top players, the BAA had gained greater notoriety but not economic prosperity. Owners in both leagues feared what probably awaited them during the summer of 1949. An open market for new stars and subsequent bidding battles seemed likely to exacerbate financial strains. Additionally, instances like Fran Curran's skillful elusion of Waterloo in court suggested that even teams with a legal right to a player's services might not be able to keep a determined league jumper from pursuing more money or other advantageous circumstances.

In the context of a potential battle over St. Louis University senior Ed Macauley, Al Ney speculated on how leverage might be lost to players if the league war continued:

> There is a draft rule within the NBL designed to protect the lower ranking teams, but the war for players between the NBL and the Basketball Association of America takes the teeth out of the draft. . . .
>
> This is the way it will work in all probability.
>
> Denver will get first choice in the draft and under its plan of players sharing in the profit probably wouldn't be able to get Macauley, who will want a good sized guarantee.
>
> Hammond will get next choice and won't be able to afford Macauley. Waterloo will get next choice and ditto unless things change or the club decides to put all its dollars in one basket-getter.
>
> That leaves the five strongest clubs in the league taking cracks at Macauley.
>
> Denver, Hammond or Waterloo could claim him and then dicker with him, but all three probably would realize that they couldn't meet or better the BAA's bid for Macauley.
>
> Then the question would be should those three clubs draft Macauley knowing they can't land him and thus keep him away from rival NBL clubs or should they pass him on to higher ranking and more sound financially teams in their own league?
>
> Needless to say, the teams have no choice but to pass him in the draft and hope that the NBL can land him for the sake of league prestige and drawing power when the team that signs him is on the road.[10]

Rumors suggested that Indianapolis (renamed the Jets) and the Fort Wayne Zollner Pistons were regretting their departure for the BAA. Printed reports claimed that both teams were negotiating a return to the NBL.[11] Expansion during the NBL off-season had all but been promised. The Phillips 66 Oilers were a strong Oklahoma-based Amateur Athletic Union team, ready-made to fill the wide gap between Denver and the rest of the circuit. Des Moines, Omaha, and Kansas City also offered the possibility of a westward drift. Milwaukee, Grand Rapids, Rockford, and Cedar Rapids all fit within the existing geographic footprint, and other candidate cities offered additional possibilities. NBL leaders aspired to grow from a nine-member loop to at least twelve.

Meanwhile, the BAA's concern for its future manifested itself in a mid-February appeal by Maurice Podoloff. The BAA president indicated an interest in negotiating standard terms for the transfer of players between the two leagues and arbitrating other points of contention. It is not clear precisely what Podoloff had in mind, but the rules that governed the relationships between professional baseball teams in different leagues were mentioned as a comparable framework. Within a week of that statement, NBL commissioner J. Doxie Moore had responded that his league was not interested in any peace talks.

The thirty-eight-year-old manager of NBL affairs had been an Indiana high school basketball star just a few years ahead of Waterloo's Charlie Shipp. While Shipp advanced in the game as a professional, Moore chose to attend Purdue as both a basketball and a football player. At the school, John Wooden was among his basketball teammates. By the late 1940s, Wooden — who became a star player in the pre-NBL Midwest Conference — was just beginning a legendary coaching career at UCLA, while Moore was serving as NBL commissioner.

Moore had worked at high schools in Indiana and Illinois until the early years of World War II, when his enlistment in the armed forces brought him to Iowa. The navy assigned Lieutenant Moore to Iowa City, where he instructed future pilots in hand-to-hand combat and coached basketball, football, wrestling, and soccer service teams at the preflight school there.

Out of the military after the war, Moore briefly became the head coach of the Sheboygan Red Skins. By the summer of 1948, he was off the bench and had stepped into the vacant NBL commissioner's office. Following his first season in that role, Moore would be among the executives who forever changed the landscape of professional basketball during the summer of 1949 as the NBL-versus-BAA question was finally settled.

EVERYBODY'S BALL CLUB

As evening arrived on a seasonable Wednesday in May 1949, one by one or in small groups businessmen gathered at the Elks Lodge on Waterloo's east side to discuss the fate of the city's professional basketball team. Many of them had another civic concern of even greater immediacy. The following night, across town at the Cattle Congress grounds, as many as 6,000 John Deere employees were expected to take part in a union vote. A two-year labor deal had expired in April. Members of the United Automobile Workers in five other midwestern Deere factories had already authorized their leaders to call for a strike if necessary. After a month and a half of slowly progressing contract negotiations, now the local UAW chapter would decide whether to take a similar step. The first work stoppage at the Waterloo plant in a generation (if it happened) would lead to difficult times for many families and businesses. Just a year earlier, Waterloo had seen a violent strike at Rath Packing, and uncertainty about the Deere labor impasse would worry many in the community until the company and the union reached a formal agreement.

City and business leaders gathering at the Elks Lodge faced a question of civic pride rather than one of economic necessity. Iowa Basketball Inc., owned by Andy George and Charlie Shipp, had lost between $5,000 and $10,000 operating the Waterloo Hawks in 1948–49. Without the personal resources to easily cover the deficit, much less operate through the beginning of a new season, George and Shipp did not intend to put a team on the court in the fall. Other National Basketball League clubs were in similar straits; although the Tri-Cities Blackhawks could boast a $75,000 profit, most other teams had struggled through the season. Even the Oshkosh All-Stars were facing dire times, despite having reached the league championship series.

Fortunately, the Elks Lodge conclave included men of means representing some of the city's strongest companies. They were proud of the big league prestige they thought Waterloo had earned from having a professional basketball team. In addition, they were interested in keeping the Hippodrome active beyond the annual Cattle Congress fair each autumn. Hawks games had generated income that allowed the venue to operate throughout the winter for other community events. The building was beginning to be referenced as Waterloo Auditorium, and a city-funded effort was under way to make improvements in coordination with Cattle Congress organizers. The men at the Elks Lodge studied the numbers and concluded that just a few hundred additional fans at each home game would have been enough to erase the team's operational deficit. As their meeting ended, they finalized a plan to keep professional basketball in northeast Iowa.

The following day, the *Waterloo Courier* sports page devoted three columns below the fold to a stock subscription form for an entity that would become known as Waterloo Basketball Inc. Those gathered at the Elks Lodge had resolved to buy the Hawks and operate as a for-profit civic corporation. Anyone with an interest and at least ten dollars (most of one day's wages for a typical Deere or Rath line worker) could buy a share of the team and, as the document stated, "insure continuation of Waterloo's representation in the National Professional Basketball League."[1] Three Waterloo banks also committed to making similar forms available to their depositors.

Basketball backers hoped to sell 3,000 shares. Roughly half the money would go to George and Shipp, thus purchasing the Hawks' equipment, player contracts, and other assets. The remainder would be used to operate the business until ticket and sponsorship revenue began accumulating at the start of the new season. Before the first newspaper reader or bank customer had inked the slightest mark on a stock purchase form, fund-raising was nearly half-completed. The initial Wednesday night gathering had concluded with commitments of more than $13,000 from attendees.

Waterloo media was firmly behind the effort. R. J. "Mike" McElroy was the operator and principal owner of local radio station KWWL. In addition, he was a leading member of the city's commission to improve and operate the Hippodrome and thus had an interest in seeing professional basketball continue there.

The *Courier* also lent its support, encouraging fans to invest with a long-term outlook. Sports editor Al Ney urged:

> There'll be some rough years through which the fan-owners and the fans who don't own stock will have to stick with a poorer ball club than they would like to have.
>
> There'll probably be other years when things will go great and everybody will be trying to buy up some stock. Through thick and thin the stability of the civic venture in the NBL will rest with the fans more than ever before.[2]

Ney was not above adding some humor related to the community ownership model, noting about the shareholders: "They'll probably be figuring out just what each owns. For $10, for instance, a guy might figure he owns Dick Mehen's big toe."[3]

Robert Cass was charged with managing the drive to find investors, large and small. Part of a family that successfully operated the Iowa Warehouse Company, Cass had retired in 1947 at age forty-five. The former University of Iowa varsity cheerleader had a history of backing local athletics. In the spring of 1949, Cass was the commissioner of the Iowa Intercollegiate Athletic Conference, composed of thirteen small private schools scattered across the state. He also served on the board of directors that oversaw the Waterloo White Hawks baseball team, sat on the local school board, and was an active member of a variety of clubs, including the Elks.

From his Campbell Avenue home on Waterloo's west side, Cass oversaw the stock subscription effort, which added more than $1,500 in the first week. Before the end of May, retailers in Grundy Center,

La Porte City, and other surrounding communities had volunteered to collect pledges, and more than $20,000 had been committed. Pinkie and Andy George each bought small stakes, seeking to help the team they had started without bearing the entire load. Chuck Comiskey, president of the White Hawks and namesake grandson of the Chicago White Sox founder, also bought ten shares, noting in the letter that accompanied his hundred-dollar check, "I believe the idea of the town taking over the franchise is a very good civic move . . . the Waterloo professional basketball franchise will be a going concern."[4]

By the second week of June, the fund's total of cash and commitments added up to more than 90 percent of the initial $30,000 goal. Organizers set a ten-day deadline to raise the remainder. They sought to complete the ownership transfer ahead of NBL meetings scheduled for early July. Cass explained, "The committee believes that 10 days more will give every fan a chance to say yes or no to the effort. . . . We've exhausted practically all of our business firm prospects and now it's going to be up to the individual fans."[5] Any doubts about those fans were allayed a week and a half later, when an updated count put the effort at $35,900.

The first shareholders meeting was held at the Elks Lodge exactly six weeks to the day after the small but resolved group of businessmen assembled to consider professional basketball's fate in Waterloo. Late-arriving subscription forms boosted the fund-raising figure nearly another $2,000. Of the 377 individuals and entities that purchased stock, 92 were represented at the meeting, which was also attended by NBL commissioner Doxie Moore. The shareholders elected a thirty-three-member board of directors, including several prominent community figures: Mayor Bailey Barnes, president of Rath Packing R. A. Rath, John Deere's top Waterloo executive Gust Olson, Chuck Comiskey, and an array of other business leaders and entrepreneurs. Chris Marsau was chosen as president; Mike McElroy was installed as first vice president.

Like Cass, Marsau was a broad backer of local sports and athletes. Six feet tall, the forty-five-year-old with receding dark hair had been born in Dysart, south of Waterloo, eventually coming to the city and beginning a four-decade career at Rath Packing during the 1920s. In 1943, Marsau was appointed to the Waterloo Recreation Commission, an entity he continued to serve until shortly before his death in the late 1980s. He was also a member of the White Hawks board and was voted exalted ruler of the Waterloo Elks in 1945.

Marsau understood that the community nature of Waterloo's basketball project required an optimistic outlook. When he heard late in the 1949–50 season that a recently arrived player had been griping about the team's amenities, the Hippodrome, and other aspects of playing for the Hawks, he took the player aside. After Marsau repeated the litany of complaints, which had not been printed in the newspaper or stated anywhere near a microphone, the rookie asked the team president how he had heard. Marsau revealed that the young man who shined shoes at the Hotel Russell-Lamson — to whom this player had voiced his resentments — was one of the team's 377 shareholders.[6]

With the team's investors behind him, Marsau was in Chicago less than a week after he had been elected president of Waterloo Basketball Inc., representing the Hawks at meetings that would help alter the future of professional basketball.

●

During the previous summer of 1948, the Basketball Association of America had coaxed teams in Minneapolis, Indianapolis, Fort Wayne, and Rochester to switch leagues. In the process, the BAA acquired many of the sport's most notable players without having to offer unsustainably large salaries or fight protracted legal battles over contract jumpers. BAA president Maurice Podoloff later remembered, "I believed that the only way I could save our league was the addition of what I considered star players. . . . That wasn't a merger, it was a raid."[7]

By 1949 — as the Waterloo Hawks were in the midst of their ownership change — the National Basketball League was planning to make sure another coveted collection of new stars didn't land in the rival association. The University of Kentucky won consecutive NCAA tournament championships in 1948 and 1949. In between, a handful of Wildcats helped the United States to a dominant gold medal performance during the London Olympics. Three BAA clubs drafted four top Kentucky seniors in 1949, anticipating that Alex Groza, Ralph Beard, Wallace "Wah Wah" Jones, and Cliff Barker would help them win more games and draw more fans.

The NBL made a more attractive proposition. Rather than scattering the Wildcats' stars in a draft, league president Ike Duffey offered the Kentucky quartet their own franchise in Indianapolis. The opportunity to continue playing together and potentially make even more money by owning any profit the club might generate won them over. Although putting all the Kentucky players on the same team did not improve the rosters of the NBL's existing clubs, league leaders reasoned there would be a boost in attendance for each team when the college and Olympic champions visited. In addition, by locating the team in Indianapolis and securing the right to play in Butler University's Fieldhouse, the arrangement all but doomed the BAA's Indianapolis Jets, who had finished last in their league's Western Division during 1948–49. Fittingly, the new NBL club was dubbed the Indianapolis Olympians.

With this skirmish won by the NBL, the two leagues held simultaneous off-season meetings at the expansive Morrison Hotel in the Chicago Loop during the first weekend in July. One Associated Press report indicated BAA owners had come to the ominous conclusion that their league "must show an overall profit this coming season (1949/50), or else."[8] Other stories suggested another group of desirable NBL teams might be lured away to the BAA, along the lines of the previous raid. Whatever the intentions of the vying ownership groups, professional basketball was unstable.

Between the NBL and the BAA, twenty-one teams had completed the 1948–49 season. By July, seven of these clubs were uncertain whether they could continue into 1949–50. While the Minneapolis Lakers and Rochester Royals had thrived after moving to the BAA, half the teams on that loop had lost money or only broke even in 1948–49. Under these circumstances, the two leagues dispatched key representatives, including Duffey and Podoloff, to a joint meeting within the hotel, hoping to resolve some of their differences and perhaps even merge the two circuits.

The representatives outlined a possible four-point agreement during their executive conference: teams in both leagues would honor all player contracts held by other clubs, all disputes would be arbitrated, interleague exhibitions would be held, and any further discussions about a merger would be put on hold. The full body of NBL owners gathered to receive these terms; within fifteen minutes, they unanimously decided to reject the offer. The second point seemed to limit the NBL's legal remedies in the event that the first point was ignored. Meanwhile, language regarding interleague exhibitions was construed as a sly attempt by the BAA to draw crowds by hosting the Olympians while shunning less star-laden NBL teams. Still, the two leagues were closer to coming together than they had ever been.

Throughout July, conversations continued. Rumors of teams moving, folding, or jumping leagues persisted. By early August, another gathering was scheduled for New York, with six NBL organizations having committed to a merger with the BAA that would yield a single eighteen-team league. Waterloo leaders were concerned about the plan and initially abstained from a league vote. However, the financial realities of reducing travel expenses through efficiency, limiting player salaries through a more controlled procurement process, and capping the competition to attract fans in some markets took precedence. On August 3, the National Basketball Association came into being, with Waterloo as one of the eighteen members and Maurice Podoloff as president.

One syndicated account suggested that the BAA had dictated the terms of the merger.[9] However, *Milwaukee Journal* sports editor R. G. Lynch eschewed the notion that either league had truly gained a decisive edge: "The truth is that nobody won the war. Economic necessity drove the bitter rivals into each other's arms. The NBL, in fact, was so far from licked that it recently made a counterattack [by acquiring the Olympians], which no doubt had a good deal to do with bringing the BAA leaders to their senses."[10]

The Indianapolis Jets and the Providence Steamrollers, owners of the BAA's worst records in 1948–49, were abandoned, as were the NBL's Hammond Calumet Buccaneers and the all-black Dayton Rens. The Oshkosh All-Stars sought to overcome their challenges through relocation—perhaps to Milwaukee. The club's financial loss from 1948–49 was estimated at $50,000 to $70,000. Better business results in Oshkosh did not seem likely in 1949–50 with the limited capacity of the gyms there. Founder Lon Darling and other members of the club's board of directors sought both a bigger market and new investors to propel the team into a new season. However, arrangements could not be finalized, and the NBA canceled the All-Stars' membership in mid-September after the team failed to submit a $7,200 entry fee.

The absence of the All-Stars presented the new NBA with one of its first substantial problems. At one stage, the league had considered a format with two nine-team divisions. Whether or not clubs played across divisional lines during the regular season, league officials anticipated manageable circumstances for building a schedule, even with teams as far east as Boston and as far west as Denver. The loss of one team made the project more—not less—complicated. The NBA ultimately adopted a three-division format. When the final schedule was released in October, less than a month ahead of opening night, some teams were slated for sixty-two games, others sixty-four, while ten of the seventeen planned for sixty-eight.

In the team's opening night game program, the Hawks described the challenges of building the first NBA schedule as follows:

> Many problems have presented themselves in the making up of a working schedule which would best protect the interests of all teams concerned. In order to arrange this complex schedule it was first necessary to ascertain what nights were available in each respective arena or gymnasium. Next, each team was given preference of one or two nights which seemed to be the most logical in their community, so far as the public was concerned.
> Take into consideration available dates, preference of nights

and the problem of travel connections from N.Y. to Denver and you have a faint idea of the problems confronting officials upon the merger of the two leagues. Trial and error methods were employed to get at the problem, with each league team offering suggestions, objections and assistance.

The '49–'50 schedule, while by no means perfect, represents a terrific amount of work. Due credit is extended to President Maurice Podoloff and his staff for an excellent job.[11]

Waterloo was one of three teams with sixty-two scheduled games. All sixteen of the NBA's other clubs would visit the Hippodrome at least once during the Hawks' thirty-one-game home calendar. Waterloo's Western Division rivals for berths in the twelve-team playoffs were to be the Indianapolis Olympians, Anderson Packers, Tri-Cities Blackhawks, Sheboygan Red Skins, and Denver Nuggets. The Central Division included the three surviving teams that had jumped to the BAA the previous summer—Minneapolis, Rochester, and Fort Wayne—plus the Chicago Stags and St. Louis Bombers. In the Eastern Division, the Syracuse Nationals joined the remaining BAA squads.

Despite the Hawks' shorter schedule, Waterloo fans could actually look forward to watching more basketball each night during 1949–50. After the marriage of the two leagues, a number of BAA rules were adopted, including twelve-minute quarters (NBL periods had been ten minutes), which extended regulation to forty-eight minutes. With the extra time, players were also granted an additional foul: relegated to the bench only after their sixth infraction, rather than the five that led to disqualification in college and the NBL. The NBL-BAA merger was a blending of strategy and style, not just teams and rules. BAA clubs were perceived to play a more open and higher-scoring brand of basketball than the defensive and methodical NBL squads.[12]

At the time of the merger—when professional players could still remember learning the sport using a ball stitched with football-like laces—basketball was still in the midst of major refinements. The game's history had included an era when a single designated shooter took all his team's free throws, when there was no three-second lane violation, and when teams made their way to midcourt after each field goal to restart play with a jump ball. By the late '40s, all these customs had been swept away. Other rules like goaltending, which had been implemented in response to the emergence of bigger centers like George Mikan, Harry Boykoff, and Amateur Athletic Union sensation Bob Kurland, had been in effect only for a few years.

One observer shared his impressions of professional basketball during the era, after seeing an exhibition during the postwar period:

> Fans who are accustomed to the collegiate and high school variety of basketball watched with awe as the pros demonstrated some deft ball handling and floor play.
>
> They saw, too, a brand of basketball that incorporated all the major features of football. The rugged style is more or less typical of the professional habits in the sport.[13]

More changes were still in the future. In 1951, the NBA would double the width of the lane from six to twelve feet, forcing large-bodied centers to be more active under the basket in order to avoid a three-second call. Jump shots would gradually supplant set shots as the preferred shooting method from a long distance. The underhanded free throw technique would eventually be replaced by the overhead style. The three-point line was a distant innovation, more than a generation away.

Two of basketball's most frustrating problems, high foul counts and late-game stalling tactics, were on the cusp of being remedied, but not before the 1949–50 season. In the late 1940s, teams often combined to accumulate more than a foul per minute. Rules of the time yielded only single free throws when a player was fouled outside the act of shooting.

"Fouling was the only way for a trailing team to get the ball back," noted sportscaster Marty Glickman. "Give up one point for a chance at two. The leading team would do the same. As a result, there was a parade from baseline to baseline and the final minute of play was almost interminable."[14]

One attempt to fix this action-sapping problem involved restarting play with a jump ball after a converted free throw during the closing minutes. However, a team foul limit, resulting in two free throws once that limit was exceeded, eventually proved more effective.

Meanwhile, stalling by maintaining possession with no attempt to score was perceived to restrict late-game excitement and the chance for fans to see a late comeback. Some players of the era would claim that superior skill was required to avoid turnovers and keep the ball from a desperate opponent. However, professional basketball became arguably more fan-friendly and undoubtedly higher-scoring with the arrival of the twenty-four-second shot clock. Both the twenty-four-second rule and the foul limit would be implemented in 1954, five seasons after the NBL-BAA merger.

●

The Waterloo Hawks added to both their roster and their front office after the demise of northwest Indiana's Hammond Calumet Buccaneers. Waterloo's executive board invested $6,000 to buy all the Hammond players' contracts. Although many Buccaneers veterans could not be persuaded to join the Hawks—in those cases, they either retired or Waterloo resold their rights to other teams—the deal led to the acquisition of a sizable rookie crop. Meanwhile, days after making the purchase, the Hawks added to their operations staff by salvaging Loren Ellis from the Buccaneers to serve as Waterloo's new business manager.

Ellis had signed many of the young Buccaneer players in preparation for a 1949–50 season that never arrived for the organization. Like Waterloo during the summer of 1949, the Hammond franchise was fund-raising in order to continue operations; at the time of the merger, the team was still in the midst of an investor drive, and the NBA decided to proceed without them. Ellis had been with the Buccaneers only since the beginning of May. Prior to that, he had been the athletics director at nearby Valparaiso University after serving as the school's basketball and football coach. Ellis' strong basketball record with the Crusaders had included eighty-seven wins over six seasons; perhaps the most notable victory was against DePaul and George Mikan in January 1944, during the first of two years in which the Blue Demons reached the National Invitation Tournament final.

With contract or draft rights to as many as forty protected Hawks players, Charlie Shipp prepared for practices to begin in early October, while Ellis made arrangements to fill the Hippodrome. Season tickets ranged from thirty dollars for the auditorium's more than 2,000 reserved chairs to fifty dollars for box seats. Nine Waterloo companies with employee credit unions offered interest-free, ten-week installment plans so members could afford season tickets more easily and make payments through payroll deductions. Books of ten ticket vouchers for $7.50 went on sale the same day practice began; team leaders set an optimistic goal of selling 5,000 of these. Single-game tickets starting at fifty cents for children and eighty-five cents for adults were to be the cheapest in the NBA.

"This is everybody's ball club here in northeast Iowa," noted Ellis. "We don't want to break anybody who supports the club and enjoys the games by charging high prices. Thirty dollars for a season's reserved seat is the best bargain ever offered in major league basketball."[15]

Meanwhile, Shipp expected much of the 1948–49 team to return. Rules of the era provided Waterloo with the right to sign all players who had been under contract the previous season. Dick Mehen had been given a new agreement with a sizable raise almost immediately after the 1948–49 season concluded, even while the Hawks' ownership situation was still in question. Had the transfer to Waterloo Basketball Inc. not occurred, selling Mehen's rights to another club could have provided Shipp and George with enough cash to cover most—if not all—of their losses.

Harry Boykoff did not have a signed contract when he returned for his second season in Waterloo, but the big center still practiced and appeared in the Hawks' first exhibition game. At the same time, he participated in a series of six negotiation sessions, which finally led to an agreement. However, the team could not successfully come to terms with holdout Rollie Seltz. By mid-October, Seltz was dealt to Anderson for $1,000, on the condition that the Packers would be able to sign him. Bill Brown and Bennie Schadler planned to leave professional basketball and were both waived.

Practices were initially held in Cedar Falls at Iowa State Teachers College. Rookie Don Boven—one of the top players acquired from Hammond—had been on the campus before as a visiting football player with the Western Michigan Broncos. The 6-foot-3-inch Kalamazoo native had delayed attending his hometown college, instead serving in the U.S. Army as a gunnery sergeant during the final years of World War II. Boven's service put him on the beaches of France just days after the 1944 Allied invasion. He remained near the front lines and saw combat through the end of the war.

When he returned to Western Michigan, Boven won two letters for football and was also part of the Broncos' baseball roster, but he earned distinction as the best basketball player to attend the school through that time. His 1,099 points—including some against Ellis' Crusaders—were a Western Michigan record. By accumulating 367 of them as a senior during the program's mediocre 1948–49 season, Boven led the Mid-American Conference in scoring and earned All-American recognition. Rarely afraid of confrontation, the former Bronco was involved in several on-court shoving matches—and even fistfights—during his time as a professional.

NBA rules allowed the Hawks to carry a roster of twelve players from the beginning of the season through the end of November. After that point, the squad could number between nine and eleven. Having spent his entire adult life on the court, Shipp could not see himself as anything but one of the players; he reconsidered his decision to retire and activated himself once again as player-coach. He was joined by returnees Dick Mehen, Harry Boykoff, Dale Hamilton, and Leo Kubiak. Boven led a group of rookies including Wayne See, Al Miksis, Gene Ollrich, and Jack Phelan. After substantial efforts, Hammond holdover Stan Patrick was convinced to join Waterloo for his seventh season of professional basketball. Jake Carter, another former Buccaneer, was on the season-opening roster but never played for the Hawks. Waterloo residents welcomed their 1949–50 team with a Hawk Day parade through downtown as the regular season was about to start.

A schedule thick with home games to open the year suggested an opportunity to begin well. Following a 3–1 exhibition slate, the first meaningful matchup was scheduled for November 2 at the Hippodrome against the New York Knickerbockers. On the eve of the opener, *Courier* sports editor Al Ney speculated about the implications of hosting the team representing America's biggest metropolis. To Ney, it was clear that the larger cities did not appreciate Waterloo being in their league:

> It is no secret that the larger cities expect Waterloo to fold after this year. Directors of the club here refuse to work on that basis; in fact, they have long range plans for pro ball here, but could suffer a severe setback if fans don't welcome the sport with open arms and pocketbooks. . . .
>
> Crowds will have to average about 4,000 per game here to pay the bills. . . .
>
> Waterloo could easily wind up better off financially than four or five other clubs in the 17-team league, but the "big cities" have strictly the "show-us" attitude now.[16]

By the time the Hawks were preparing to host New York during the first week of the NBA season, Ney had been the *Courier*'s sports editor for more than four years. The oldest of five children, he was raised just blocks from the University of Dubuque, eventually attending college there and writing for the school's student newspaper. After graduating in 1942, Ney quickly became the top sports writer for his hometown paper, the *Dubuque Telegraph-Herald*, before bringing his "Sports Alley" column to Waterloo in 1945. The twenty-nine-year-old would witness the Hawks host all of basketball's top professional stars that winter, as well as observing firsthand some of the key moments in the young league's history.

The Knicks had defeated the Chicago Stags one night earlier, 89–87 in overtime. Their western trip was made in the comfort of a private railroad car as far as Cedar Rapids, and they bused from there to Waterloo. The New York entourage included Marty Glickman, tasked with delivering live play-by-play radio coverage back to listeners in the East. When the traveling party arrived, they found a refinished court highlighted by a large *W* in the center circle and surrounded by nearly five hundred chairs, with boxes and bleachers beyond. Pennants representing all seventeen NBA clubs hung above the seating sections. In their orange and blue uniforms, the Knicks prepared to face the white-clad Hawks, whose jerseys included piping and lettering with the gold and black colors revered by University of Iowa Hawkeye fans.

A crowd of 3,695 attended. Some had just piled off the buses looping continuously between downtown and the Cattle Congress grounds. Men took their seats in coats and ties while chomping through fifteen-cent Rath hot dogs in buns from Waterloo's Altstadt and Langlas Baking Company. Youngsters with their programs and pens hoped for autographs after the game. Some of the women on hand—especially those sitting close to the court who wore memorably short skirts that revealed a considerable length of nylon stocking—were perhaps hoping to catch the attention of the players they had come to see. The city's black community, although more fond of the increasingly integrated minor league baseball played by the White Hawks, was also represented with a scattering of fans around the auditorium.

The meeting was a reunion between Boykoff, the Hawks' star, and Knicks coach Joe Lapchick. The former St. John's mentor had once predicted that Boykoff would become the greatest basketball player in history, and Waterloo's center had been wooed by the Knicks before he chose the NBL.[17] It was a tough start for Boykoff and the Hawks. Although Waterloo opened an early 7–2 lead, a 13–2 Knicks run swung New York in front and on the way to a first-half edge as large as 15 points. Turnovers and shooting troubles tripped up the home team.

After trailing by 11 at halftime, Waterloo rallied, thanks to a surge led by Kubiak with 7 third-quarter points. Boykoff lifted the Hawks to a 45–44 edge with just under three minutes remaining in the period. However, Vince Boryla helped the Knicks recover and stay out of reach during the late stages. He ended the affair with a game-high 19 points—all but 4 scored during the second half—and New York claimed its second win of the season, 68–60. Boykoff topped the Waterloo stat sheet with 15 points, 10 coming in the final twenty-four minutes. Kubiak added 11.

Although the loss was not what they wanted, the Waterloo organization could nonetheless be pleased with the effort. Just as important, attendance was up more than 46 percent compared with the first home game a year earlier. NBA head of officials Pat Kennedy, who had refereed the game, even offered an endorsement of sorts, saying, "The lighting and the floor here are terrific. I'm pleasantly surprised."[18]

Four days later, the Hawks were back on the court hosting another of the former Basketball Association of America teams from a major East Coast city.

●

Since being founded in 1946, the Boston Celtics had never finished above .500. The squad's best record in the BAA had been 25–35 during 1948–49, and each winter the Celtics trailed the New York Knicks and Philadelphia Warriors in the final standings. Although Boston Garden president and Celtics co-owner Walter Brown held a prominent place in the BAA and was an important figure in the NBL-BAA merger, his hopes of both fielding a winning team and playing in front of a consistently full arena had been thoroughly frustrated.

The 0–2 Celtics followed the Knicks' Chicago-to-Waterloo route for a Sunday evening matchup against the Hawks during the first weekend of the season. The game was only tied once, 3–3, before Waterloo seized control. By halftime, the Hawks owned a 12-point margin and stayed ahead by double digits most of the night. Forward Stan Patrick led a group of ten contributing home players with 14 points.

The final score of Waterloo's first NBA win: Hawks 80, Celtics 66.

The creation of the NBA brought demands for more extensive media coverage when teams from major cities traveled to the smaller former-NBL communities. Sports writers from the *Waterloo Courier* were requested to write multiple accounts of the same contest so that competing large-market newspapers could print game stories different from those of their rival dailies. Western Union installed a telegraph line at the Hippodrome for visiting teams unable to travel with a radio contingent. Ahead of the Hawks' next game with the Denver Nuggets, Al Ney described the procedure for sending back live details, which required one of Western Union's local employees to "tap out a Morse Code play by play from court side. The report, including each pass or as close to it as possible, will be transcribed by an operator in Denver and he will hand the play-by-play to the Denver announcer for airing."[19]

The account in the telegraph stream crossing the wires to Colorado must have singled out Leo Kubiak in particular; Waterloo's second-year guard missed just one shot from the field and sank all four of his free throws to lead the Hawks with 20 points in an 80–65 result. Undoubtedly, he also added a few marks to a new statistical tabulation that had not been tracked in the National Basketball League. During the 1949–50 season, the 5-foot-11-inch guard—unflatteringly nicknamed Little Leo—would lead the Hawks in assists.

Due to his stature, Kubiak developed an effective one-handed jump shot at a time when the technique was not widely popular. He was also an aggressive defender. Passed over for service in the armed forces during World War II when a heart murmur was discovered during his military physical, he instead attended Bowling Green State University in northern Ohio. As the Falcons' senior captain in 1947–48, Kubiak starred on a team that qualified for the National Invitation Tournament. It was the third time that Bowling Green was invited to the NIT during Kubiak's four seasons at the school. He had played in all sixty-two Waterloo games as a professional rookie during 1948–49, and his 7.4 points per contest ranked fourth on the squad, helping earn him a place on the NBL's honorary

All-Rookie Second Team. Despite being limited to just 3 points during Waterloo's fourth game of the season—an 89–59 road drubbing by Fort Wayne, for which the Hawks arrived only two hours before tip-off against the Pistons—Kubiak was still the club's early-season scoring leader.

Waterloo's next game put two of the NBA's most exciting undersized stars on the court against each other: Kubiak and Murray Wier of the Tri-Cities Blackhawks. From the beginning of the previous season, the Waterloo Hawks' progress had been measured against their rivals to the south and east. NBL basketball had come to Moline, Illinois, midway through the 1946–47 season when the foundering Buffalo Bison were transplanted from western New York to Wharton Field House. The multiuse arena, owned by the Moline school board and one of the largest in Illinois outside Chicago, had a capacity similar to the Hippodrome. After initially struggling for profitability, Tri-Cities attracted approximately 3,500 fans per game by the 1948–49 season. The fast evolution of the team's business success suggested what might be possible with persistence in the Cedar Valley.

The Tri-Cities—Moline and Rock Island, Illinois, plus Davenport, Iowa—shared connections with Waterloo beyond basketball. The "Hawks" variant in both team names was derived from the Sauk Indian leader Black Hawk, whose people had lived at the confluence of the Rock and Mississippi Rivers, near where Rock Island was founded. The name was eventually bestowed on the Iowa county that is home to Waterloo. Both cities had major farm implement plants. John Deere managers in Waterloo answered to executives at company headquarters in Moline. Meanwhile, Deere's competitors, International Harvester and J. I. Case, operated their factories nearby in the Tri-Cities, leading Moline to be called the Plow City.

Professional basketball animosity was ensured for the two communities before a ball was ever tossed up between their respective Hawks. In 1948, the Blackhawks had been one of the two NBL organizations to vote against Pinkie George's plan to relocate his NBL team from Des Moines to northeast Iowa. Eventually, Waterloo's first exhibition game was held against the Blackhawks, and later the largest crowd to attend a professional contest at the Hippodrome had crammed into the auditorium in 1948 on another night when Tri-Cities visited. Many individual Hawks and Blackhawks players reportedly even held on-court grudges against their counterparts.[20] However, the rivalry was about to find a new focus with a Tri-Cities coaching change, made two days before Waterloo traveled to play the Blackhawks for the first time in 1949–50.

In the decades of professional basketball that followed, Arnold "Red" Auerbach would gain renown as the greatest coach and executive of the NBA's early decades. After graduating from George Washington University, Auerbach had coached high school teams in the Washington, D.C., area during his early twenties, then enlisted in the navy near the beginning of U.S. involvement in World War II. Returning to civilian life, he took the helm of the Washington Capitols at just age twenty-nine during the BAA's inaugural year and led that team to a pair of regular-season division championships, as well as an appearance in the 1949 BAA finals. However, a contract dispute prevented him from extending his stay with Washington. Shuffled out of professional basketball, Auerbach landed temporarily at Duke University, where he prepared to serve as an assistant coach during the 1949–50 season.

The Blackhawks' poor start brought Auerbach to Moline on a two-year, $25,000 contract. His first NBA victory—after 115 BAA regular-season wins—came against the Waterloo Hawks during his November 12 debut. Amid eighty-three fouls called on the two clubs, Dick Mehen, Don Boven, and Jack Phelan each departed during the third quarter, costing the Hawks much of their inside depth. Leo Kubiak led all scorers with 17 points, trading baskets with Murray Wier during the fourth quarter as Tri-Cities pulled away to a 99–89 final.

Waterloo's defeats against Tri-Cities and earlier to Fort Wayne represented the beginning of a five-game losing streak. Some of the results were close—including separate 2- and 3-point decisions against the Sheboygan Red Skins—and others were not, like a 106–74 affair while visiting the Indianapolis Olympians. The skid ended at home and at Auerbach's expense a little over a week after the Hawks' trip to Moline. Jumping to an 11-point halftime lead and shooting better than 50 percent from the field, Waterloo overcame Tri-Cities' second-half efforts to press by finding Harry Boykoff in the middle of the forecourt, then letting the big center feed teammates dashing to the basket for layups. Stan Patrick benefited from several of these assists, finishing with a game-high 21 points, 17 during the final two quarters, during the 75–62 win.

On the bench beside the court, Auerbach drew reactions from the Hippodrome crowd as he barked at the lone official working the game, Jocko Collins, and fumed about Charlie Shipp. The Hawks' player-coach—nearly four years older than his sideline-bound counterpart—was antagonizing one of Tri-Cities' young players, as described in Al Ney's postgame story:

> During the second half Mac Otten, 6-7 rookie forward, went into the game for Tri-Cities and immediately got into an elbowing match with Waterloo's Jack Phelan.
>
> Shipp stepped over to the Tri-Cities bench and yelled at Auerbach: "Are you going to let that go on?" Auerbach ignored Shipp, so Shipp went into the game.
>
> He called Otten's actions to the attention of the official and "nudged" Otten when he could. Three fouls were called on Otten in quick order as Auerbach . . . screamed.[21]

It was the first of several incidents that led to increasing anticipation for the Blackhawks' visits to Waterloo. More than once during future games against Tri-Cities, Hawks management needed to ask for calm over the public-address system in order for play to continue. A uniformed police officer was occasionally stationed near the visitors' bench to ensure that the verbal exchanges between Auerbach and the fans would not turn physical. By the end of the season, Hippodrome fans were waving rubber chickens at Auerbach. With an average attendance of more than 4,100 during the three remaining Hawks-Blackhawks games played in Waterloo, Cedar Valley fans evidently looked forward to Auerbach's sideline rants and the chance to taunt him.

5

I WANT TO PLAY BASKETBALL

Three months after being hired by the Hawks and only two weeks into the 1949–50 National Basketball Association schedule, Loren Ellis resigned as the Hawks' business manager and left Waterloo. Little explanation was given for his abrupt departure other than an intent to move south. Settling in Florida, Ellis eventually returned to college coaching at Stetson University. With Charlie Shipp in charge of the Hawks' basketball affairs, the change had little impact on Waterloo players or results. Meanwhile, the board of directors moved quickly to fill the vacancy with a man who had achieved great success just across the Cedar River.

William "Perk" Purnhage was an able, brilliant baseball salesman. In 1946, the Chicago White Sox enlisted the southern Indiana native, recently mustered out of the Army Air Corps after World War II, and assigned him to their Class D affiliate in Cordele, Georgia. The small-town team smashed its attendance record despite suffering through a season that ended eighty-seven games under .500.

As that summer concluded, a south Georgia sportswriter en-dorsed Purnhage, saying, "It seems certain that he has what it takes, and it's about time the baseball world 'perked' up and watched this fan-building, money-making man from the banks of the Wabash."[1] A year later, Purnhage was promoted to the Waterloo White Hawks. The club won the Three-I League championship while attracting more than 200,000 fans to Municipal Stadium during the regular season and playoffs. Purnhage's astounding success in Waterloo led the *Sporting News* to honor him as the 1947 Minor League Executive of the Year, and the White Sox promoted him again, this time to Memphis.

Portly and round-faced with a wide nose, a dimpled chin, and a shock of long and strategically arranged dark hair in the center of his high forehead, the middle-aged Purnhage was back in Iowa by 1949. Hired by the Pittsburgh Pirates to bring more fans to their affiliate's ballpark in Davenport, he boosted attendance from under 46,000 to over 133,000 in one season. After purchasing an ownership stake in the Davenport club, Purnhage had the flexibility to set his own schedule and accepted the offer to moonlight with the Waterloo basketball squad. With the move, Hawks leaders simultaneously improved the team's front office while reducing their costs: the arrangement with Purnhage acknowledged the time he would devote to baseball and thus provided a smaller salary than Ellis had received.

Almost instantly, Purnhage extended box office hours and set up a pep band, high school cheerleaders, and other attractions on game nights at the Hippodrome. He added seats closer to the action by moving the team benches to the baseline under the baskets. This allowed approximately sixty additional fans to sit beside the court on the sideline.

Purnhage implemented one of his favorite promotions almost immediately, declaring a November 23 game against the Rochester Royals to be Ladies Night. General admission tickets for women were pegged at thirty-five cents, and nylon stockings were handed out as door prizes. Almost 1,500 women were at the Wednesday night matchup—a 90–71 loss—with the game's total attendance 25 percent higher than the 1949–50 average at that point. Yet even with the popular promotion, the figure was still a few fans shy of the mark needed, at full price, to break even for the season. As to the basketball performance during that game, losing to Rochester dropped Waterloo to 3–8 and into a fourth-place tie in the Western Division with the Tri-Cities Blackhawks.

The following week, the Hawks fell by double-digit margins in three consecutive road games. The disheartening results suggested weaknesses within the Waterloo lineup. The prospect of reducing the roster loomed with an approaching, NBA-mandated December 1 cut deadline. Under these circumstances, the Hawks' twofold objectives were to slice costs and simultaneously improve the team. By trimming the roster from twelve to eleven, the organization anticipated a season-long savings of $6,000 in payroll and expenses. Meanwhile, players jettisoned by other NBA clubs created a pool of experienced talent that might help change the fortunes of the struggling club.

Waterloo began by adding former Sheboygan forward Paul Cloyd, a two-year member of the Red Skins. In 1947–48, he had been Sheboygan's second-leading scorer; the next season, he contributed a reduced but respectable 6 points per game. The Hawks also opened an effort to acquire Ward "Hoot" Gibson. Despite a fear of flying that had complicated his time with the Denver Nuggets, Gibson finished the prior season as the National Basketball League's fourth-leading scorer. Shuffled to the Tri-Cities Blackhawks before the 1948–49 schedule ended, at 12.8 points per game he had earned recognition on the All-NBL Second Team. Originally from the Des Moines area, the 6-foot-5-inch center had played basketball only during his sophomore year at Des Moines Roosevelt High School but still became an All–Missouri Valley Conference star in college for Creighton. He was a member of Denver's Amateur Athletic Union team prior to the Nuggets' transition to the NBL during the summer of 1948.

Two other new Hawks landed in a different way and just in time for a November 30 matchup against the Fort Wayne Zollner Pistons, as *Waterloo Courier* sports editor Al Ney reported:

> Jack Smiley, former member of the famed Illinois University Whiz Kids, and veteran Bob Tough arrived at Waterloo Auditorium just a half hour before game time. The game was held up for 10 minutes to give them some warmup time. . . .
>
> Both Smiley and Tough agreed to contract terms by telephone before leaving Fort Wayne and then signed shortly before going on the floor. Neither quibbled about salary. Said Smiley: "I probably could make more money in my trucking business in Fort Wayne, but I want to play basketball."

They barely had time to get their ground legs before being ready to play. Both had been air sick and neither had eaten since noon.

The new Hawks arrived in Chicago from Fort Wayne by one chartered plane at 4:30 p.m. They left Chicago aboard a Waterloo owned chartered plane 15 minutes later and arrived here at 7:20 p.m. Twenty-five minutes later they were at the Auditorium and ready to dress for the game after the contract signing.

Original plans to have the two planes meet at Moline, Ill., had to be changed at the last minute because of weather conditions.[2]

Under the circumstances, Smiley delivered a solid performance with 7 points. Both late arrivals had played in Fort Wayne the previous year, but new coach Murray Mendenhall, formerly the Anderson Packers' boss, did not find a place for them in 1949–50, making Waterloo's 95–71 win versus the Pistons on the final day of November all the more satisfying. The disjointed pace of play must have been a relief to Smiley and Tough as referees called eighty fouls during the contest. Fort Wayne's Bob Henry actually fouled out during the opening quarter, followed by the Hawks' Leo Kubiak in the second. All totaled, seven players were disqualified; the group also included Dick Mehen, but not before the Hawks' veteran recorded 30 points.

To make room for the new additions, Waterloo parted with first-year players Gene Ollrich and Jack Phelan as well as veteran Dale Hamilton. Amid the moves, guard Wayne See kept his place on the team; See and Don Boven were the squad's only two remaining rookies. By the beginning of December, the 6-foot-3-inch See was working into a starting role. Although he averaged only about 4 points per game at that stage of the season, his strong defensive play and rebounding made an impression. Ellis had called him "one of the most promising rookies in the entire professional basketball field."[3] The former business manager's departure from the organization did not alter the Hawks' regard for See.

Just two generations removed from his pioneer ancestors, who settled in northern Arizona when it was literally the Wild West, See enrolled in Flagstaff's Arizona State Teachers College (now Northern Arizona University) in 1941. He left the school soon after and went to work briefly in the state's copper mines before joining the marines, serving much of World War II aboard the *USS Massachusetts*. "Being on a battleship was probably the safest place in all of the fleet, because the Japanese warplanes and ships had a hard time against those battleships," See remembered. "They were built to float unless you hit a bad storm. We manned the guns—the major artillery—the Marine Corps manned those when we were on the ship."[4]

See returned to college following the war at the insistence of his former basketball teammates, who drove through a snowstorm to make their case in person and brought him back to campus. While establishing himself as the school's star basketball player, he also took a spot as an end on the Lumberjacks' football team, although he had never previously played that sport in organized competition. As a muscular, broad-shouldered, twenty-three-year-old sophomore in 1946–47, See led the school to twenty basketball wins and an appearance in the National Association of Intercollegiate Basketball's small-school national tournament semifinal. It was the first of three times he was recognized as Most Valuable Player of the Border Conference.

In December 1949, See was perhaps better prepared than any of his Waterloo teammates for the Hawks' next road trip. Since he had spent much of his life at altitudes comparable to Denver, thin air would not have caused any difficulty for him. However, the Hawks had to contend with a problem bigger than low oxygen during their two-game visit with the Nuggets. Harry Boykoff had broken multiple ribs the previous week and was unable to play effectively. Although Denver had just one win prior to its games against the Hawks, Waterloo fell twice during the excursion to the Rockies. With the Hawks' edge in the standings over the Nuggets reduced to only two games, Waterloo risked dropping to last place in the NBA.

New cities and unfamiliar styles were an adjustment for players and coaches during the first season of NBA basketball. The merger was just as challenging for the third team on the court each night: the referees. In 1947, the haphazardly organized Professional Basketball League of America had hired Hon Nordly and Leonard Raffensperger to officiate the first pro game in Waterloo. At the time, Nordly had served as the basketball coach at Iowa State Teachers College in nearby Cedar Falls for a decade. Raffensperger, meanwhile, coached basketball and football at Waterloo East High School and later would go on to direct the Iowa Hawkeyes football team. No concerns were recorded about possible partiality of these two local referees, and the visiting St. Paul Saints won that inaugural game in overtime anyway.

Unlike the PBLA, the National Basketball League and subsequently the National Basketball Association chose to operate with a roster of roving officials to avert any charges of hometown favoritism. In the inaugural 1949–50 NBA season, a staff of thirty-six referees traveled to the league's seventeen cities, working in pairs. They balanced the responsibilities of their full-time jobs against assignments and itineraries just as grueling as those of the teams. Although the NBA covered their expenses, each referee received just forty dollars per game, less than college officials in many prominent conferences at the time.

"Their schedule was as tough as ours," remembered Mike Todorovich, who spent the NBA's first season with the St. Louis Bombers and Tri-Cities Blackhawks. "And they didn't travel together, either. They traveled all alone, so it was a lonesome journey for them. They had a tough route."[5] However, in the heat of the season, there was little sentiment in favor of referees. Players, sportswriters, and fans worried that tightly officiated games might ruin professional basketball. "This can't go on," editorialized a *New York World-Telegram* column, adding:

The incessant whistles shrieked again in an unbearable concert at the Garden last night. . . . It was another fine house — 15,145 paid. But instead of rewarding this turnout with good fast basketball, the pros put on a free throw contest. In 48 minutes there were 98 free throws attempted in a game Syracuse won 77–74 over the Knicks. . . . The score on fouls alone was New York 38, Syracuse 37.[6]

Even NBA president Maurice Podoloff publicly expressed frustration about officials and officiating, saying that "something must be done immediately to improve both. Officials must recognize that the public comes to see the players perform, not the officials, who should discharge their duties without attempting to overshadow the players."[7]

An anonymous referee responded to the criticism later that winter, writing in a *Sport Magazine* article, "Referees are not at fault for the messy state of the rules. Nor are we to be blamed for excessive whistle blowing. We're doing what the rules require . . . the confusion isn't lessened in the least by the rock-'em and sock-'em style of the west as opposed to the fancy-pants style of the east."[8]

Officiating problems became so bad that representatives of the league's seventeen teams voted in early December on a variety of rule changes to be implemented on a trial basis. The alterations included a jump ball after converted late-game free throws, plus positioning defensive players nearest to the basket on both sides of the lane during free throw situations, thus lessening the likelihood of a foul while rebounding. Meanwhile, Podoloff reiterated to referees that a degree of contact was to be both expected and allowed within the game. He also reminded them to use standardized officiating signals, rather than the more ostentatious indications for which some had become known.

Jim Enright was one of the more flamboyant referees, although his antics generally drew positive reports in the *Waterloo Courier*, which compared him favorably with comedian Lou Costello. Stocky and shorter than nearly all the players on the court, he would gesture demonstratively what had been done to earn a foul. Enright was also known for hollering warnings to players loudly enough that fans several rows from the court could hear the often humorous instructions. Not above self-deprecation, he was once heard to ask for the ball by saying, "You and you, give the ball to the little man for a jump."[9]

Away from his whistle, Enright's regular job did not take him far from the court. Although this would be unimaginable in later decades, he was also a sports reporter for the *Chicago Herald-American*, which gave him a degree of authority different from that of most journalists writing about basketball. Enright's role as a writer and insider may have had more of an impact on the sport than anything he did with his whistle. In fact, longtime DePaul coach Ray Meyer credited Enright with convincing him to accept the job with the Blue Demons.[10] Meyer had been an assistant coach at Notre Dame, and when George Mikan followed him to DePaul after a failed Fighting Irish tryout, NCAA and professional basketball were changed forever.

Bob Austin was another well-known referee in Waterloo. Born in Davenport and educated there at St. Ambrose College, Austin had been part of Waterloo's Rath Packing Company Amateur Athletic Union basketball teams of the 1930s. Following service in the U.S. Navy during World War II, he returned stateside to work as a professional baseball umpire and football official as well as a basketball referee. Many other officials had similar ties. Referee shortages occasionally became problematic when baseball spring training began or football and basketball schedules overlapped in the fall. In both 1948 and 1949, Austin may have been particularly glad to come indoors for basketball after working as the back judge in consecutive National Football League championship games, the first played during a blizzard and the latter in a torrential rainstorm.

The travel troubles of some NBA referees during the winter of 1949–50 became a story that exasperated Waterloo civic leaders. Though railroad routes connected the city to Chicago directly, it was often more convenient for referees departing from Chicago to commute on a train line passing well south of Waterloo. Nationally syndicated New York sports columnist Hugh Fullerton had a laugh at Waterloo's expense when he described the instructions league executives allegedly gave officials traveling to Hawks games.

"The National Basketball Association has just issued a 'directive' to officials telling them how to get to Waterloo, IA," Fullerton wrote. "It says, roughly, to take a train to Tama, IA, go to 'a nearby feed store' and ask for Mr. Soandso, a farmer who'll gladly drive them to Waterloo for six bucks ($10 for two) and a free ticket to the game."[11]

The Chamber of Commerce defensively volleyed back, "Waterloo is not just a hick town," noting that the city ranked among the leading manufacturing hubs in the western United States. The chamber's letter to Fullerton also swatted at New York, then in the midst of a serious water shortage, telling him, "If you will visit us at Waterloo, we will promise to give you all of the pure, fresh drinking water that you need and at least one bath a day without rationing."[12]

Fullerton ultimately had the last word in a column that appeared a few weeks after the original item:

> Further report on the midnight ride of Paul Revere, as relayed by one of the NBA officials who has made that hazardous tour from Tama to Waterloo, Iowa, once too often. . . . The gent who provides transportation, it seems, has purchased a brand new (in 1937) car. . . . "Well, sir," says the ref, "a step on the brake was enough to start the horn blowing without waiting for midnight [this is a reference to a much-maligned movie of the era, *The Horn Blows at Midnight*], but not slow down this hot rod's progress; the lights blinked out no fewer than four times in 42 miles; the gas fumes were so strong I refused to light a fresh cigar; and the rattles to his new chariot were so loud and solid it was impossible to listen to the car radio. . . . Hereafter I'm using the regular taxi service."[13]

Waterloo was not the only midwestern NBA city to be scorned by a New York columnist around this time. The *New York Times*' Arthur

Daley sized up the circuit this way: "We now have in the same league two such thriving metropolitan centers as New York and Sheboygan. The New York arena, the Garden, can accommodate 18,000 for basketball. The Sheboygan one bulges at the seams when 2,300 are in the joint [an inaccurate figure that may have confused Sheboygan with Oshkosh]—with a $2 top, too. It's too silly for words."[14]

Big city fans were not impressed with the smaller-market teams either. When the Hawks and other former NBL clubs appeared as visitors in 1949–50, they typically did not attract large audiences. The smallest crowd to arrive for an Olympians game in Indianapolis through early December turned out on a night when Waterloo was on the schedule. Hawks trips to six other cities drew below-average attendance. Teams in the biggest NBA markets plotted to play Waterloo on neutral courts as the undercard of league double features, rather than booking limited home dates in their busy arenas for an opponent that wouldn't draw a respectable crowd.[15] As 1949 changed to 1950, these were the circumstances under which the Hawks prepared to play in the league's largest venues and face many of the NBA's biggest stars.

●

Stan Patrick measured the distance to the basket. Fifteen feet from the Hippodrome rim, his toes were just off the free throw line. Anderson Packers player-coach Howie Schultz had just fouled out with seconds remaining in a game tied at 75–75. Converting the free throw would leave the Hawks with just moments left to defend the Western Division's leading team. Waterloo was in a position to win for the third time in five tries and move within two games of the Sheboygan Red Skins for third place. Patrick lifted his shot toward the hoop, and 2,781 fans gazed as the ball floated up and forward.

Just off target, it fell away.

The Packers had opened a 4-point lead in the first twelve minutes and staked out a 40–33 advantage by halftime. During the third quarter, Waterloo rallied back into a tie. In the final period, Patrick repeatedly scurried up the court, scoring in transition to keep the game tight. He had 10 points during the fourth quarter alone and a total of 13 at the end of regulation. With overtime required after his missed free throw, Patrick added an early basket to help the Hawks pull ahead to an 81–77 advantage. However, free throws undid the Waterloo effort again. This time, a series of fouls against the home team allowed the Packers to parade to the line and, ultimately, to an 87–83 victory.

Other than player-coach Charlie Shipp, no Hawks player had more professional experience than Stan Patrick. Harry Boykoff and Dick Mehen were more renowned, but the twenty-seven-year-old forward was just as capable. Prior to the Anderson game, Patrick's field goal percentage of 45.1 stood second in the NBA, behind only Mehen's 47.9 percent. Persuading the 6-foot-3-inch veteran to join the Hawks after the Hammond Calumet Buccaneers disbanded appeared to have been worth the effort; as of early December, Patrick ranked as Waterloo's fourth-leading scorer with more than 9 points per game. His importance grew as the Hawks began to run the court more while Boykoff was limited by injury.

Originally from Chicago's South Side, Patrick made his way to Santa Clara University in 1939, then enlisted in the navy in 1942; he was released from service after one year on a medical discharge. Unable to play basketball for the Broncos, who had suspended athletics for the duration of World War II, Patrick returned to his home state and joined a depleted University of Illinois squad. Entering 1943–44 as the only player in Champaign with NCAA experience, he led the Fighting Illini in scoring and was named the team's Most Valuable Player.

Starting his professional career with the Chicago American Gears in 1944, Patrick had set a then-single-game National Basketball League scoring record with 38 points on the final night of the 1944–45 season. He was named the league's Rookie of the Year, remaining with the Gears through their 1946–47 championship and subsequent disintegration in the failed Professional Basketball League of America.

After Waterloo's unfulfilled comeback effort against Anderson,

Patrick was held largely in check during the Hawks' next game. The veteran was limited to just 3 points while Waterloo rallied from 18 down before finally succumbing to the Philadelphia Warriors, 73–70. Don Boven took Patrick's mantle as top Hawks scorer during the rough game, contributing 15 points. Boven's night might have ended prior to the final whistle had the officials seen him send an elbow into the face of Joe Fulks just after the Warrior forward had swung and hit Boven in the midsection. Fulks, who ended with a game-high 20 points, was the first professional with a consistently effective jump shot and the biggest star in the Basketball Association of America prior to the arrival of George Mikan.

Two nights later, Waterloo was at Philadelphia Arena, but not to meet the Warriors. Instead, the Hawks prevailed, 77–75, in a neutral-site game against the Baltimore Bullets. It was Waterloo's first win of the season away from the Cattle Congress grounds. However, the Hawks could not repeat the result in another neutral-site matchup during the two-game trip. Fulks had 30 points and the Warriors won by 9, 81–72, in front of 16,500 fans during Waterloo's only appearance at Madison Square Garden. Within a week, Waterloo was mired in a four-game losing streak that dropped its record to 6–19.

Prospects for a merry Christmas looked unlikely as the Hawks prepared to host the Indianapolis Olympians for the first time on December 25. The Olympians had already played twenty-eight games, more than any other team in the league at that point except for the Chicago Stags, and had exceeded expectations with a 16–12 record. Big crowds came to auditoriums across the NBA to see the former Kentucky collegians make their impressive transition to professional basketball.

Credited by Al Ney as being "the biggest single factor in the merger of professional basketball's two major leagues," teammates Alex Groza, Ralph Beard, Wallace "Wah Wah" Jones, and Cliff Barker each had Olympic gold medals.[16] They had won two NCAA championships together. Groza, Beard, and Jones had been recognized as All-Americans three times over. If the Olympians' dominance as a team in the NBA was not immediate, it appeared to be rapidly approaching. Individually, Groza entered the Christmas game as the league's leading scorer, just ahead of Mikan.

The Indianapolis players' experiment in ownership of their own franchise might have changed the business model for NBA teams. On the court, their potential to play and win together throughout the 1950s could have put the Olympians among the league's great early clubs. However, just two years after beginning their pro project, Groza and Beard had their careers shattered by a college point-shaving scandal. The two were convicted of accepting bribes from gamblers to fix winning margins within the point spread during their championship seasons at Kentucky. A federal judge banned them from basketball for three years. The NBA expelled them for life. Without the two stars, the Olympians' organization unraveled at the end of the 1952–53 season.

Ahead of the 1949 Christmas game, Waterloo's court problems were of a different nature that involved determination and the scoreboard rather than lawyers and judges. Dissatisfied with his team's efforts, Shipp put the Hawks through a grueling practice on December 24. The severe tactics appeared to have been ineffective: Waterloo trailed Indianapolis by 12 points in the final minute of regulation. Many fans were making their way from the auditorium to the parking lot and into the cold and snowy December air when the Hawks achieved a Christmas miracle, thanks to the Olympians' short bench and the application of convoluted NBA rules. As Ney recounted:

> Indianapolis no longer was able to put on the floor a five man squad without using a player on whom six personals already had been called. NBA rules, in that case, call for the addition of a technical foul every time a man with the foul limit commits another or each time a man already out of the game has to return. . . .
>
> The extra technical shot free throws, plus possession of the ball after the technical foul shots, gave the Hawks the chance they used to win.[17]

As Indianapolis fouls accumulated in the final minute, Stan Patrick, Leo Kubiak, and Wayne See all hit shots from the field while See and Hoot Gibson combined to make four free throws. Patrick had recorded just 2 points during the first forty-seven minutes. Trailing by 1 with just four seconds remaining, he went to the line hoping to tie the score with his second free throw conversion during the sequence. In this crucial situation, his shot was true, delivering overtime with the game tied at 84.

When the night began, 4,083 fans were in attendance. The auditorium's large sliding cattle door had to be opened to accommodate the returning contingent who had left when an Indianapolis victory appeared inevitable. Many were brushing the snow off their coats and not yet back in their seats when Patrick laid in the first basket of overtime, spurring a 13-point extra period. Waterloo finished on top, 97–93. Five Hawks reached double figures, led by Boven with 17 points. Among the Olympians who had fouled out, Groza watched in anguish from the bench after scoring 28 points.

Despite the dramatic win, Waterloo remained deep below .500 and well short of the average attendance needed to break even as a business. Still, the game was a reminder that amazing and unlikely comebacks were possible.

●

In the immediate aftermath of the Christmas rally, the Hawks suffered 7- and 2-point losses to the Chicago Stags and Sheboygan Red Skins, respectively. Despite the defeats, all the Hippodrome's nearly 3,000 reserved seats had already been sold for New Year's Eve. Anticipation had been building for weeks ahead of George Mikan's first appearance in Waterloo since 1947. The game against the Minneapolis Lakers held the promise of a financial windfall and, simultaneously, a problematic on-court challenge. Harry Boykoff was still the Hawks' best option to stop Mikan, but Boykoff had been playing for nearly a month without being fully healthy. The Lakers' star was averaging more than 27 points per game. By comparison, Dick

Mehen was pacing Waterloo at 16 per night, still among the league's highest scorers yet far behind Mikan's pace.

Charlie Shipp had intended to retire as a player the previous spring but then reconsidered. However, his status was changed to full-time head coach on the afternoon of the Lakers' visit. The Hawks' board of directors had abandoned hope that having Shipp on the floor would add more veteran experience while providing a two-for-one salary savings. Business manager Perk Purnhage announced the new strategy, saying the board "did not feel Charlie was getting the best out of the ball club while playing. We feel that as a bench coach Charlie will be in a better position to handle the team."[18]

Along with 5,322 fans, Shipp watched a performance that might have stirred memories of his own best defensive efforts during fifteen seasons as a professional player. Unfortunately, it was the Lakers' Jim Pollard who forced repeated turnovers and missteps by Waterloo. As the Hawks regularly gave up the ball, Mikan capitalized at the other end of the court. Four first-quarter fouls on Boykoff created a matchup problem that Shipp did not have the personnel to solve. Mikan was on the court for all but four minutes and ended the game with 35 points in the 88–68 Laker drubbing.

The beginning of 1950 brought no better tidings. Waterloo's winless run quickly stretched to eight games as the Hawks lost five times during the first eight days of January. There were second-half collapses, as in an 82–70 neutral-court affair with the New York Knicks, during which Waterloo faltered after holding a 3-point lead at halftime. Hot shooting nights by opponents sank Waterloo when, for instance, the Washington Capitols converted nearly 47 percent of their attempts in a 101–83 thrashing. Rarely was there a close game. During the span, a 73–69 home loss to Sheboygan was the only contest settled by fewer than 12.

In late December, the *Courier*'s Al Ney actively tried to rally community sentiment for the Hawks as enthusiasm flagged under mounting losses, noting that it took years to build a contending team. "Win or lose," he lobbied, "NBA games offer the best in basketball here in

Waterloo. Someday, if the Hawks do come through in a year or two, the fame of the city for basketball will know no bounds, and those who keep it here today will be proud if that comes to pass."[19]

Yet the problems on court that led to losses were exacerbated by lower-than-expected attendance figures, and vice versa. Shipp hoped to improve his roster with a $2,500 purchase of veteran Leo Mogus from the Philadelphia Warriors. The board rejected the move out of fear that the expense could not be recouped. Not surprisingly, a $5,000 reported asking price for the Tri-Cities Blackhawks' Whitey Von Neida proved too high as well. Meanwhile, Waterloo's investment in Boykoff was not yielding the return that had been anticipated. In addition to his injuries, the faster pace of the NBA in comparison with the NBL limited his effectiveness. While other teams expressed interest in acquiring Dick Mehen or Leo Kubiak, there was no market for Waterloo's big center.

At the ticket counter prior to the holiday week matchups against the Lakers and the Olympians, the Hawks had been $800 per night short of the amount needed for solvency, on average. While attendance had climbed for the high-profile opponents, fans and shareholders worried that the organization might still lose $15,000 or more by the end of the season. The operating reserves built up during the summer stock drive had nearly been exhausted. Ticket sales ahead of Waterloo's January 10 home game against the Syracuse Nationals were going badly. "It's not a good report for me to make to the noon meeting of the directors," Purnhage conceded on the morning of the game. "They still want to save major league basketball for Waterloo, so they're going over the up to date financial report at the meeting."[20]

Ney's hope for brighter days had also dimmed. He noted in a column prior to the Syracuse visit, "The Hawks have a not so nice eight game losing streak to bring home. It should be interesting to see the fans' answer—support for a loser or non-support and the probability of throwing in the towel after this season."[21]

A meeting with the Nationals seemed like an improbable pivot point for the campaign. Syracuse came to the Hippodrome with the

NBA's top record at 27–4. Center Dolph Schayes, in the middle of just his second professional season, was already among the NBA's leading scorers. Just two nights earlier, forward Billy Gabor had led the Nationals against the Hawks, contributing 19 points during an 84–68 result in western New York, a game that had been Syracuse's third win versus Waterloo in 1949–50.

The home rematch tipped off at 8:15 following the playing of an up-tempo, sixty-second recorded rendition of "The Star-Spangled Banner" over the auditorium speakers. The speedy pace of the anthem compared favorably to Boykoff's start. He dropped in 10 points during the opening quarter, on his way to outdueling Schayes throughout the contest. Waterloo engineered a 6-point lead at halftime. By the fourth quarter, the advantage stretched to as many as 14.

However, the gap began to wane during the final five minutes of regulation, thanks to a pressing Syracuse defense and a succession of Waterloo players reaching their foul limits. Dick Mehen and Don Boven were out with more than three minutes to play. Leo Kubiak took a seat with more than two minutes on the clock, and Hoot Gibson departed in the final minute. Only a succession of made free throws kept Waterloo in front until the lead completely evaporated, and regulation concluded with a 74–74 tie.

Boykoff scored the first basket of overtime before Syracuse swung in front by 1. The lead teetered back to the Hawks on Stan Patrick's first basket of the game. The teams eventually found themselves tied at 80, then again at 82. With 1:32 left in overtime, Patrick created room in the lane to lift a shot that fell through. Boykoff added a free throw before Syracuse's next field goal. Clinging to the 1-point margin, the Hawks watched as Gabor aimed to give the Nationals a new lead in the closing seconds, but his try was off target. One more free throw made the final count Waterloo 86, Syracuse 84.

Boykoff's 26 points led all scorers in the stunning victory. Free throw accuracy also played a part: Waterloo was 32 of 41, while Syracuse made just 24 out of 45 attempts. The Nationals were incredulous in the closing minutes. Player-coach Al Cervi repeatedly screamed at the referees. As the game ended, he kicked and then flung a chair, breaking it into several pieces. The Nationals' owner Danny Biasone, in the middle of his own outburst while sitting on the Syracuse bench, was warned by Hawks management that he might be escorted from the building by police. Although the win improved Waterloo to just 8–27, the Hawks looked forward to a well-deserved celebration as they left the court for the locker room. Any festivities would be brief; next on the schedule was a three-game, four-day trip to Anderson, Indianapolis, and Tri-Cities.

As the players dressed, Shipp and Jack Smiley were separately called to the team office. In the first meeting, Shipp learned from Purnhage that the board had decided that afternoon to relieve him of his duties. The win against the Nationals made no difference; in the team's strained financial situation, a nonplaying coach was untenably expensive. Stan Patrick and Bob Tough were also to be waived in a roster reduction. Shipp left the office dazed; unable to hold back tears, he returned to the locker room to say goodbye to his players. "Nothing ever hit me like that did," he said later. "I told the boys to stick with it and play good ball as they did for me Tuesday night."[22]

Smiley had not connected for a field goal during the game. However, he had converted nine free throw tries, many of them during the late minutes of regulation and overtime. While others were preparing to leave the team, Smiley was informed by Purnhage that he had been named the Hawks' new player-coach. Protesting at first, the twenty-seven-year-old, who had arrived in Waterloo only six weeks earlier, was persuaded to take on the responsibility when it became evident that the decision to fire Shipp would not be changed. Waterloo was four games out of a playoff spot and averaging just under 3,000 fans per home game. Including himself, Smiley would have nine players and twenty-seven games to settle the fate of the organization.

He set practice for 1:30 the following afternoon.

Price Brookfield was the most accomplished professional to come to Waterloo in 1947 after winning a National Basketball League championship with the Chicago American Gears. Iowa State Athletics Communications.

Center and former University of Iowa standout Noble Jorgensen joined the Waterloo Pro-Hawks of the Professional Basketball League of America for the 1947–48 season. Collection of M. Wayne See and Vicki S. Sidey, used by permission.

On the eve of its first game in October 1947, Waterloo's PBLA team still did not have an official nickname. Front row, left to right: Carl Bruch, Nick Vodick, Noble Jorgensen, Dick Lynch. Back row, left to right: Coach Swede Roos, Ollie White, Jack Spehn, Otto Kerber, Emil Lussow, Price Brookfield. *Waterloo Courier.*

(*above left*) Waterloo player-coach Charlie Shipp ahead of the NBL's 1948–49 season. Waterloo was Shipp's first opportunity to coach. Collection of M. Wayne See and Vicki S. Sidey, used by permission.

(*above right*) Harry Boykoff was a standout center at St. John's University and set several Madison Square Garden scoring records in college. Collection of M. Wayne See and Vicki S. Sidey, used by permission.

(*right*) During the NBL's final season, Dick Mehen received All-League First Team recognition and led Waterloo in scoring. Collection of M. Wayne See and Vicki S. Sidey, used by permission.

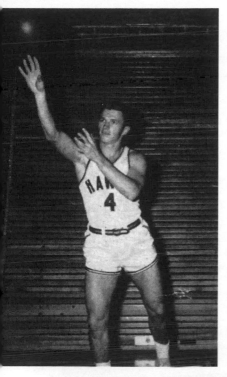

(*above left*) Leo Kubiak's time in Waterloo lasted longer than that of any other player. During the Hawks' 1949–50 NBA season, fans voted him the team's Most Valuable Player. Collection of M. Wayne See and Vicki S. Sidey, used by permission.

(*above right*) A midseason acquisition in 1948–49, Bennie Schadler had been both a football and a basketball star at Northwestern. Northwestern University Athletics.

(*left*) In 1944–45, Stan Patrick was the NBL Rookie of the Year. He won a championship with the Chicago American Gears and later came to Waterloo in 1949. Collection of M. Wayne See and Vicki S. Sidey, used by permission.

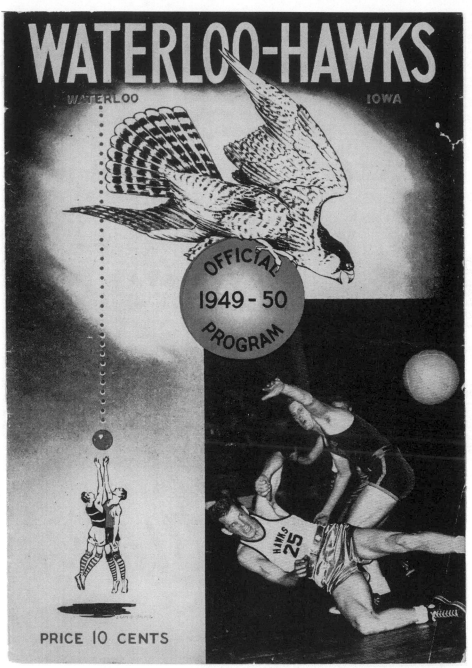

The cover of the Waterloo Hawks' game program for the team's first National Basketball Association game against the New York Knicks on November 2, 1949. Player-coach Charlie Shipp is featured on the front cover. Collection of M. Wayne See and Vicki S. Sidey, used by permission.

On December 31, 1949, the Hawks hosted George Mikan and the Minneapolis Lakers. Mikan is pictured in the center of this photo as Stan Patrick chases Herman Schaefer and Harry Boykoff guards Mikan. Minneapolis went on to win the NBA Championship in the spring of 1950. Clyde Artus, *Waterloo Courier.*

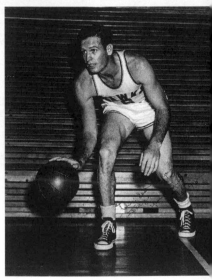

(*above*) Leo Kubiak eyes the basket on a driving layup attempt while avoiding Frank Brian of the Anderson Packers at the Waterloo Hippodrome, February 1, 1950. Clyde Artus, *Waterloo Courier*.

(*top right*) Don Boven served with the U.S. Army in Europe during World War II before returning to Western Michigan University. He was a professional rookie for the Hawks in 1949–50. Western Michigan University Athletics.

(*bottom right*) Wayne See, who served with the Marine Corps in the South Pacific during World War II, became a Hawks rookie when the Hammond Calumet Buccaneers did not survive the NBL-BAA merger. Collection of M. Wayne See and Vicki S. Sidey, used by permission.

(*left top*) Jack Smiley, one of the University of Illinois' Whiz Kids, was named Waterloo's player-coach in January 1950. Smiley brought the Illini's running, pressing style to the Hawks. University of Illinois Athletics.

(*right top*) After the Hawks' final game of 1949–50, the *Waterloo Courier* described Johnny Payak's December 1949 waiver acquisition from the Philadelphia Warriors as probably "the best $500 the Hawks spent all season." Marketing and Communications, Bowling Green State University.

(*left bottom*) Waterloo scored a major victory by beating the Boston Celtics to sign Bowling Green All-American Charlie Share in the summer of 1950. Marketing and Communications, Bowling Green State University.

(*right middle*) Impish Murray Wier, a former star for the Iowa Hawkeyes, became a teacher and coach at Waterloo East High School after retiring from pro basketball. Collection of M. Wayne See and Vicki S. Sidey, used by permission.

(*right bottom*) Buckshot O'Brien came to Waterloo from the Grand Rapids Hornets after the NPBL began to disintegrate in the middle of its inaugural season. He first played for the Hawks on January 4, 1951. His 422 points ranked sixth among the 1950–51 Hawks even though he appeared in only thirty of fifty-six games. Butler Athletics.

The 1950–51 NPBL season ended in confusion with the Waterloo Hawks and Sheboygan Red Skins both claiming to be the league's champion. Seated, left to right: Murray Wier, Coach Jack Smiley, Johnny Payak, Wayne See, Buckshot O'Brien. Standing, left to right: Pops Harrison, John R. Walker (the team's physician), Stan Weber, Ed Dahler, Buddy Cate, Don Boven, Joe Nelson, Chris Marsau. *Waterloo Courier.*

THE BAND DID NOT STOP PLAYING

Many Waterloo Hawks players were understandably dismayed when Charlie Shipp was fired. The morning after the win against the Syracuse Nationals, which was followed by the postgame announcement of Shipp's dismissal, Harry Boykoff and Dick Mehen brought the team's sentiment to the board of directors. Set for a tense encounter, Boykoff and Mehen opened by airing the players' stance. "Every player on the squad is against the change," Boykoff said. "We may not always have played good ball, but it's our fault, not Charlie's."[1]

Hawks managers denied that the decision was based on team performance. Waterloo's poor record was irrelevant, they argued; the future of professional basketball in the community was in jeopardy. The fundamentals of shooting, ball control, or defense were trumped by the fundamentals of business: balancing revenue and expenditures. The board's counterargument must have been convincing. The players left the meeting startled by the team's circumstances. "We learned from the board just how bad the financial situation is," said Boykoff. The lanky center who had studied accounting at St. John's continued, "We're professional basketball players, and we'll play for whomever the board designates . . . the board makes the decisions. . . . Smiley is our coach now."[2]

Jack Smiley spent his childhood a little more than an hour west of Chicago in the farm town of Waterman, Illinois. A waypoint on U.S. Highway 30, Waterman is a few miles down the road from Hinckley, site of the Harlem Globetrotters' first game in 1927. By the late 1930s, the 6-foot-3-inch Smiley was one of several notable basketball players from the small community. He was recruited by the University of Illinois, where he studied physical education while working his way from the far end of the long Illini bench into the varsity starting lineup. Illinois won consecutive conference championships in 1941–42 and 1942–43. Using quickness to mask limited size at the pivot, the Illini core of Smiley, Ken Menke, Gene Vance, Andy Phillip, and Art Mathisen pressed on defense and ran a fast break offense. A remark about their speed by WGN radio commentator Jack Brickhouse led to a lasting nickname: the Whiz Kids.

Their second season together at Illinois was concluding in early 1943 with the team on a thirteen-game winning streak; the 17–1 Whiz Kids were in a position to go far beyond the opening round of the NCAA tournament, where they had been upended a year earlier. Yet once again the end arrived prematurely, though this time it had nothing to do with a loss on the court. The U.S. Army drafted Smiley, Menke, and Mathisen, and before the end of March they had begun their service. With more than half the starters gone, Illinois chose not to participate in either the NCAA or the NIT tournament. As the school year ended, Vance also entered the army and Phillip became a marine.

Arriving at Camp Wallace in Texas during the spring, Smiley quickly earned a reputation on the base as a star right-handed pitcher. He was married there while preparing for combat in Europe. Shipped across the Atlantic and promoted to corporal, he served in an artillery unit as the Allied forces dislodged the Nazis from France, Belgium, and the Netherlands. Just before Christmas 1944, his 106th Division was right in the path of the last broad German offensive on the front. Thousands of men in the command were killed or captured—and Smiley was slightly wounded by an exploding shell—in what became known as the Battle of the Bulge. A participant in at least four other major engagements, Smiley would later recall bodies being taken from battlefields by the truckload, but he survived and was with American forces in Germany on V-E Day.[3]

Returning to the University of Illinois while raising a family after the war, Smiley played his final NCAA games in the spring of 1947.

Always regarded as a strong defensive player, he also had several high-scoring showings during his senior season, earning the Illini's MVP award as well as All-American recognition. He accepted a $10,000 offer from Fort Wayne to both play basketball for the Pistons and work for team owner Fred Zollner's auto parts company. After his two years in Fort Wayne followed by a brief stint with the Anderson Packers, the Hawks became Smiley's third professional team. He moved to the Cedar Valley with his wife, Joyce, three children, and a fourth on the way.

Smiley assumed the Hawks' player-coach responsibilities after just twenty appearances with the club. He brought the Illini's high-intensity offensive and defensive tactics to Waterloo. His players—although still his teammates—would note a level of discipline different from what Shipp had sought. "If you wanted to play basketball for Jack Smiley, you better play," remembered Wayne See. "If he'd have caught you drinking, you'd have been gone forever."[4]

A muscular figure with hair combed back into a curl from the top of his forehead, the Hawks' new on-court leader possessed a characteristic midwestern modesty. He was also direct, willing to speak frankly with both his team and the local paper. Sizing up the situation the day after Shipp's dismissal, Smiley ultimately decided to talk with his squad rather than running a full practice. The players agreed that they would work through the transition toward the best finish they could manage.

The roster Smiley inherited had been tweaked regularly during the ten weeks since the season opener. Of the twelve players Waterloo had chosen to begin the campaign, only five remained: Harry Boykoff, Dick Mehen, Wayne See, Leo Kubiak, and Don Boven. Several others briefly spent time with the Hawks before passing out of the lineup and out of town. Besides Smiley, the more permanent additions included Ward "Hoot" Gibson, who had claimed regular minutes despite running afoul of the team's curfew and training rules. His play was later characterized as having "a lack of any show of desire."[5]

Forward John Payak—a 6-foot-4-inch teammate of Kubiak's at

Bowling Green—had come to Waterloo after the Philadelphia Warriors waived him. He began playing off the bench in the final days of December.

Prior to the Hawks' impending road trip and Smiley's coaching debut, the team secured guard Gene Stump. The 6-foot-2-inch Chicagoan had overcome poor eyesight—eventually playing with early contact lenses—and won an NIT championship at DePaul. Blue Demons Coach Ray Meyer noted the humor Stump brought to the college program: "Stump, the joker of the team, would do his best to drive [George] Mikan crazy. He'd walk about ten steps behind him down a crowded street, then whirl suddenly, point to George, and exclaim to passersby, 'My, is that man tall!'"[6]

Graduating in 1947, Stump was the only DePaul player other than Mikan at that time to have recorded 1,000 career NCAA points. Following Stump's first two professional seasons with the Boston Celtics, the two former Blue Demons were reunited on the Minneapolis Lakers for the beginning of 1949–50. Stump was released after twenty-three games; although he was noted as an outside scorer, his shots had not been falling during his limited playing time.

Waterloo also hoped to find value with Smiley's fellow Whiz Kid, Ken Menke. The two shared similar backgrounds: each had spent time at Illinois, had gone to war with artillery units, and had been on the court with the Pistons. Their stories diverged when Menke took a high school coaching job in the western Illinois community of Galesburg. So that he could preserve his regular income and working hours while staying within the Waterloo budget, Menke's arrangement with the Hawks stipulated that he would appear only in home games—or on the road when practical—for fifty dollars per contest.

Opening a sequence of three road games in four days against the Anderson Packers, Waterloo had the opportunity to win Smiley's coaching debut. The score was tied 63–63 in the fourth quarter before the Packers rolled away on a 9-point run, eventually prevailing 80–69. The Hawks bemoaned the foul differential—twenty-seven called against Waterloo compared with just nine Packer infractions—that allowed Anderson to convert more than twice the number of free throws (twenty-eight) as the visitors even attempted (thirteen). However, the disparity in whistles may have legitimately resulted from the implementation of Smiley's aggressive pressure defense, which the team had not had much time to practice. Waterloo's new player-coach was willing to admit that he was not initially at ease with his new responsibilities, saying, "I was nervous, extremely so, about substituting in the Anderson game. I learned a lot in that one."[7]

At Butler Fieldhouse the next night, Alex Groza's 28 points, plus 23 from Wah Wah Jones, keyed a 16-point victory for the Indianapolis Olympians. It was a tough finish after Waterloo had held a 10-point halftime lead. The trip ended with an 84–80 defeat against the Tri-Cities Blackhawks. Menke found his first opportunity to appear with the team, recording three field goals in the Sunday matchup after driving north to the game from Galesburg.

After the Hawks returned home, shareholders were called to a meeting at the same Elks Lodge where Waterloo Basketball Inc. had been conceived eight months earlier. Nearly half attended to hear about the team's new direction and financial status from the board of directors. A petition to rehire Shipp was presented, allegedly signed by 3,000 fans, but it received comparatively little attention. The board's budget report suggested that the reshaped roster would cut the projected season-ending deficit by two-thirds to between $5,000 and $6,000. A booster game was suggested to further reduce that figure. Issuing new stock would be required to keep the team active in the following season, but overall the future of professional basketball in the community seemed more secure. To conclude the gathering, shareholders formally gave the board a vote of confidence.

Confidence in Smiley received a boost at the Hippodrome one night later.

Waterloo had fallen to the St. Louis Bombers by 12 points during a road game less than three weeks earlier. The home court rematch swung almost as far in the opposite direction: Hawks 80, Bombers 69. Smiley's concern about making substitutions was solved with wholesale changes. Starters Boykoff, Mehen, Kubiak, Boven, and Smiley himself all came off the court together to be replaced by the other half of the Hawks' roster. Both units kept St. Louis off balance. For good measure, the above-average crowd of 3,441 raised more than $450 for the March of Dimes, and a hundred area polio patients attended as guests of the local AMVETS post. The win was Waterloo's fourth against a former Basketball Association of America team.

●

Low attendance created difficulties across the league by the middle of the 1949–50 season. All Chicago Stags tickets were reduced to a dollar, down from as high as three dollars, to draw spectators. Rumors suggested that the Anderson Packers would be moved or sold as team founder Ike Duffey divested assets. However, a community effort raised thousands of dollars to ensure the Packers' short-term viability in the city. In a syndicated Associated Press story, owners of the St. Louis Bombers urged anyone interested in purchasing a professional basketball team to contact them.[8] By February, the Baltimore Bullets had been sold for $30,000.

Ten of the league's seventeen clubs were generating less than $4,000 each home game. In Waterloo, from preseason through the end of the calendar year, the Hawks had spent more than $60,000. Expenses ranged from payroll to Hippodrome rent. During the same period, ticket sales for Waterloo home games averaged just over $2,500 per night, ahead of only Baltimore and Anderson. Some team owners believed the assertion made by large-market sports columnists, who claimed that the small-town teams absorbed from the National Basketball League were not attractive to fans in bigger cities. Owners of the Rochester Royals and Philadelphia Warriors even formulated a plan to create a basketball minor league for 1950–51, to which Waterloo, Sheboygan, Anderson, and other less desirable outposts could be off-loaded. The Warriors' Eddie Gottlieb expressed publicly what other owners may have quietly been hoping throughout 1949–50: "Actually, we expected two or three teams to drop out by now, but apparently everybody is sticking the season out."[9]

Needless to say, leaders of the clubs to be discarded reacted bitterly to the plan. "The idea that Waterloo be part of a minor league is fantastic because Waterloo's operation will be much more sound than that in several of the larger cities next season," responded Hawks president Chris Marsau, taking a more restrained jab at eastern cities than had some of his peers. Tri-Cities Blackhawks owner Ben Kerner suggested that it was Rochester that should depart if the club was unhappy.[10]

From the league offices in the Empire State Building, NBA president Maurice Podoloff was, of course, more diplomatic. Publicly, Podoloff lauded the lower operating costs and rental fees that smaller cities enjoyed. Rather than removing teams like the Hawks, the president sought opportunities to enhance natural rivalries, although this generally meant rivalries between big cities: Philadelphia–New York, Washington-Baltimore, or Chicago–St. Louis. Throughout the winter, he spoke of dividing the league into sequestered divisions and even possibly solving the NBA's problems by adding teams rather than subtracting them. "It's those long jumps between cities that kill us," he argued. "If we can install clubs in some of the intermediate cities, we can form two geographically compact divisions next year and cut down on traveling expenses."[11]

Podoloff repeated these sentiments directly to Waterloo's board and management when he was on hand for Jack Smiley's second victory: 88–84 against the Denver Nuggets on January 21. The league president took the train to Waterloo and arrived in time to watch Johnny Payak lead the Hawks with 19 points. He also saw a Hippodrome crowd of more than 3,900 excited by a strong second-half performance, which yielded the team's third consecutive home win. After the game, Podoloff charmed Waterloo dignitaries with self-deprecation, sharing a remark made by a sports writer about his dual role as a basketball executive and president of the American Hockey League: "Belt high to a basketball player, as wide as any hockey player and with his chief qualification being that he has never played either sport."[12]

Hawks officials sent Podoloff back east with a toy John Deere tractor as a memento of his visit as well as the promise—either an unfortunate lapse of tact or a display of ignorance regarding their guest's heritage—that Rath Packing's New York distributor would deliver a ham to him. Podoloff's Russian Jewish family had immigrated to the United States when he was a boy.

After Podoloff returned home from Waterloo, pressure on both Smiley and the Hawks' budget continued to ebb during the final week of January. Waterloo topped Denver for the second time in five days, overcoming a bad first quarter for a 104–83 decision. It was the first time Cedar Valley fans had seen 100 points for the home team and, in fact, the first time Waterloo had ever reached that mark. Although losses in several intervening games left the Hawks 0–5 on the road under Smiley, he was 3–0 at home, with the club on a four-game Hippodrome winning streak.

Regarding team finances, the booster game scheduled at the January 17 shareholders meeting proved effective ten days later. Over 5,000 tickets were sold at a dollar each, with more than 3,000 people actually making their way to the Cattle Congress grounds to see the intersquad exhibition. Fans were treated to music by a local band, a preliminary game between Waterloo baseball and football players, and some humor.

The squad divided itself into two five-man teams: Boven's B-Os and See's Stinkers. See's group held a healthy lead when the game was stopped for a uniform change with five minutes remaining. Half the Hawks—Smiley, Dick Mehen, Harry Boykoff, Gene Stump, and Elmer Gainer—finished the night playing in women's dresses as the crowd laughed uproariously. The other half of the Waterloo squad returned to the court costumed as male movie stars. The team split $1,500 in cash and goods donated by local businesses.

Back to league play two evenings later, a game against Tri-Cities further enhanced Waterloo's financial situation, albeit at the expense of the home winning streak. The Sunday afternoon meeting was played in front of 4,264 fans. Although close throughout before ending 85–79 for the visiting team, the game was more notable for the continued antics of Blackhawks coach Red Auerbach, which Al Ney described in the *Waterloo Courier* the next day:

> The heated exchange between Auerbach and [Perk] Purnhage came in the third quarter as Waterloo rallied. With the count 43–40 Tri-Cities, the band played as a Tri-Cities player shot and missed the first of two free throws he was awarded. Auerbach sprang from the bench, ran to the opposite end of the floor and grabbed Referee Ed Bro. Auerbach screamed loudly that a technical should be charged because the band did not stop playing.
>
> Bro refused to call the technical but went to near the scoring bench where Purnhage was and told the Hawk Business Manager to quiet the band during free shots. Purnhage told Bro he wouldn't until officials also made Auerbach obey the rules and stay on the bench.
>
> An exchange of words ended with Auerbach's shouting a foul remark that could be heard into the grandstand.[13]

Bro had to step between the two men as it looked momentarily like Purnhage might swing at Auerbach. The Blackhawks' victory put their record seven games ahead of Waterloo for the final playoff berth in the Western Division.

Despite winning more often at home, Waterloo continued to face poor results away. By February 12, when the Hawks arrived in Syracuse, they had lost fifteen consecutive contests in opposing or neutral arenas. Syracuse Coliseum was a difficult place to challenge such a streak. The 7,500-seat building attracted hard-drinking crowds that were among the toughest in professional basketball. Nationals star Dolph Schayes described the environment: "Opposing players knew that when they came to Syracuse to play they were going to have to face a great team, hostile fans, and that goddamn cold and ice. I think that whole syndrome helped us win. It must have added at least a couple of points to our score, because we were almost invincible at home."[14]

Professional basketball had arrived in the community of 225,000 in time for the 1946–47 NBL season. The Nationals joined the league because the Rochester Royals did not want to go to Syracuse. When Danny Biasone could not convince the Royals to visit for an exhibition game, he purchased his own franchise in the league instead. Later, Biasone would champion an innovation that was vitally important to the league's eventual success: in 1954, he convinced other NBA owners to adopt the twenty-four-second shot clock.

Starting in 1948, Syracuse teams were built around veteran player-coach Al Cervi. The 5-foot-11-inch guard had dropped out of high school in Buffalo during the late 1930s and was one of the last players of the era to find professional success without going to college. After serving in the Army Air Corps during World War II, he returned to the sport with Rochester and won an NBL championship and a league MVP award. Cervi was noted for his bruising defensive style, his ability to intimidate bigger opponents, and his colorful (often blue) language.

Mild-mannered Schayes was the precise opposite of Cervi. Standing at 6 feet 8 inches, the muscular forward was a scorer and rebounder. Schayes was already attending New York University at sixteen, roughly the same age at which Cervi had left school. The Bronx native became an All-American and was one of the players wooed by both the National Basketball League and the Basketball Association of America. He chose Syracuse when the Nationals offered him a contract worth 50 percent more than the New York Knicks' bid. Under Cervi's influence, Schayes developed the toughness and tenacity to remain in professional basketball for sixteen seasons. "I'd never had that type of coach before, the kind that tried to make me more aggressive," Schayes remembered. "He actually had a lot to do with my becoming more aggressive, because that's the way he was . . . it rubbed off. You begin to think that way and your whole personality changes."[15]

The Hawks and the Nationals had already met for a variety of thrilling encounters in the less than two years of their rivalry. On this occasion, Waterloo scored first against the Eastern Division leaders, staying just ahead or tied until using a 7–0 run to make the score 14–7 during the opening quarter. Early in the second quarter, the Hawks were in front by 12, the first of two occasions Waterloo would lead by a dozen. With Syracuse closing just before halftime, the Hawks shocked the Nationals and 4,500 fans in attendance by forcing consecutive turnovers, resulting in 5 points during the fifteen seconds prior to intermission.

However, the game began to turn in the third quarter when Mehen left with a thigh injury, and Smiley fouled out before the period ended. That started a procession to the bench: Boykoff, Payak, and Boven followed, leaving all of Waterloo's five eligible-and-able players on the court. The Nationals took their first lead of the game at 84–82 midway through the fourth. Despite a game-leading 24 points from Leo Kubiak, Waterloo could not keep up with Syracuse, falling 102–98.

The loss left the Hawks at 12–37 for the season and 4–10 under Smiley.

●

The Indianapolis Olympians paced the NBA's Western Division by two and a half games when they visited the Hippodrome on February 15. It was the Olympians' first trip to the Cedar Valley since crumbling on Christmas night. With Indianapolis ahead by just a single point during the final seconds of the rematch, the Olympians' Bruce Hale attempted to steal the basketball. A foul against him yielded a game-tying free throw for Harry Boykoff, who had been on the court for the entire game. A jump ball automatically followed the converted foul shot in the closing minutes, and Waterloo's center won control of the toss. Receiving the basketball back from Dick Mehen, Boykoff boosted the Hawks past Indianapolis, 76–74, with a fifteen-foot field goal as time expired.

The loss sliced half a game from the Olympians' lead over the Anderson Packers. The Tri-Cities Blackhawks and Sheboygan Red Skins—both below .500—were well behind the leaders in the midst of their own race for third. The Denver Nuggets, the only NBA team without a double-digit win total, were last in the division. Waterloo was still firmly in fifth place, seven games short of a playoff position with only eleven left to play.

The Hawks had made their final roster changes earlier in the month. Elmer Gainer added his size to the lineup, returning to basketball while working at Rath Packing. The 6-foot-7-inch thirty-one-year-old had remained in Waterloo after playing for the Hawks in 1948–49. St. Louis Bombers castoff Johnny Orr was also signed for the remainder of the season. Supplanted as a University of Illinois starter by the return of the Whiz Kids from World War II plus his own later service in the U.S. Navy, Orr had completed his amateur career at Beloit College. He joined the Bombers at the outset of 1949–50. Despite a fair shooting percentage, Orr had received only scant minutes with the struggling St. Louis club.[16]

The additions were made, in part, because Ken Menke's regular job had left him with only limited opportunities to take to the court for Waterloo. Hoot Gibson was also shelved in early February for violating team rules. The eccentric center, who had a penchant for nightlife, was caught out far beyond curfew, as late as 2:00 a.m. His contract prevented Waterloo from trading or cutting him, so he was placed on indefinite suspension ahead of the league's February 10 trade deadline.

As postseason play looked unlikely, maintaining discipline and keeping morale up sometimes proved challenging during the late stages of the season. Ahead of a long trip east, Boykoff missed the team's train out of Waterloo. He had to fly to Chicago to catch up with the rest of the Hawks there for the second leg of the trip. Later, Boykoff and Mehen were both involved in the most disruptive incident of Jack Smiley's tenure as coach.

The Syracuse Nationals were a tired and shorthanded team completing a strenuous road sequence at the Hippodrome on March 1, yet it was the Hawks who lagged as the evening commenced. The sloppy game was poorly attended in the midst of a winter storm. Despite their own troubles, the Nationals dashed off a 20–0 run in the fourth quarter, and Smiley took Boykoff and Mehen off the court with just over four minutes remaining. As the clock melted down under a minute and with the eventual 93–72 result all but settled, Waterloo's two stars left the bench early for the locker room.

The seeming show of indifference aggravated the already disappointed fans. Waterloo's board of directors suggested that Smiley should punish both players. In a letter to the coach—published two days after the incident, presumably for the public relations effect—the executive committee called the situation "a disgrace that we cannot explain to the fans," continuing:

> . . . Wednesday night's exhibition during the last quarter was inexcusable from our viewpoint and also that of many fans who have contacted us today. Some of your ball players very apparently were not interested in winning the ball game, and we feel that you know they were not giving you and us their best efforts. When Boykoff and Mehen leave the bench before the game is over, in our opinion they deserve a stiff fine at least, if not a suspension.
>
> . . . We can't sell that kind of an exhibition to the public that has so loyally supported major league professional basketball here. . . .
>
> It is not our intention to try and run your ball club. That's your job. But when our employees, who are getting good salaries, don't feel like working, you have the authority to suspend them or fine them or do anything else necessary to get the proper cooperation to produce interesting basketball.
>
> We don't expect you to win every game, but we do expect you to look good losing.[17]

Smiley diffused the situation, saying that he had addressed the incident immediately, adding, "Because these men have consistently played fine ball for us in the past and because of my uncertain status here as an interim coach, I did not assess fines on the spot."[18] Team officials reaffirmed Smiley's authority to use any discipline he saw fit. They also provided him with a contract to remain Waterloo's player-coach for the 1950–51 season.

Unfortunately, the incident against Syracuse overshadowed several good results. The Hawks celebrated a runaway 21-point win against Tri-Cities, a game that included Don Boven decking an opposing Blackhawk with a right-handed swing during a shoving match. Waterloo also claimed a rare road win in Sheboygan as Leo Kubiak led four visitors in double figures. Victories against Denver by 24 and 19 points had been earned at the Hippodrome after Waterloo bought one of the home games from the Nuggets. By saving money on traveling expenses, the investment proved worthwhile, even though the game was attended by a smaller than average crowd. Fans on hand for the first of the two Denver matchups found themselves also attending a wedding as the guests of Letha Baumgartner and Ken Hutchinson when the couple was married on court at halftime.

Johnny Payak made increasingly significant contributions as a reserve during Waterloo's late-season improvement. By the final few games, Payak had earned the opportunity to start as a guard. The wiry twenty-three-year-old with a straight, narrow nose and slightly cleft chin was from the same Polish and Ukrainian area of Toledo, Ohio, as Kubiak. The two Toledoans, who both attended nearby Bowling Green State University, established a friendship that later included Payak serving as best man at Kubiak's wedding.

The Philadelphia Warriors had intended to use Payak as a reserve center at the outset of the 1949–50 schedule. However, the rookie was released and signed by Waterloo after scoring just 37 points in seventeen Warriors appearances. Initially playing in a more comfortable role as a forward for the Hawks, Payak averaged nearly 8 points per game. He could also create plays and was credited with six assists in a March 15 win against the Red Skins during the second-to-last game of the season. After Waterloo's final contest, *Waterloo Courier* writer Al Ney would suggest, "The best $500 the Hawks spent all season probably was for Payak, claimed from Philadelphia for the waiver price."[19]

The last game on the schedule was at home against the Blackhawks. The rivalry affair brought 4,456 to the Hippodrome, and

Payak began the afternoon well, contributing 8 first-quarter points. With a gap-closing 7-2 run to finish the period, the Hawks were within 1 point, 20–19, at the end of twelve minutes. By halftime Waterloo led, 40–36.

Perhaps inspired by being named Waterloo's Most Popular Player at halftime, Boykoff hit six shots in the third quarter, accounting for half of the Hawks' 24 points during the frame. The center would finish the game with a team-high 22. However, Waterloo had fallen behind by 5 when Smiley brought Boykoff and Mehen to the bench with 2:36 remaining in regulation. In their place, he sent out a small lineup with an unorthodox strategy.

Under NBA rules, the late-game jump ball after a free throw conversion had to be taken by the two players involved in the foul. Smiley wanted his team to foul Murray Wier. Although percentages suggested that Wier would hit the single foul shot, the 5-foot-9-inch Blackhawk was unlikely to win the jump against bigger players like Payak and Orr. The plan worked, and repeatedly trading 1 point for 2, Waterloo eventually tied the game at 77–77. A Payak layup provided the tie and boosted his point total to 18 with 1:26 to go.

The teams exchanged unsuccessful possessions and were still tied with thirty-three seconds remaining. Waterloo controlled the ball and stayed on the edge of the front court, dribbling away the seconds in order to try the last shot of regulation. Momentarily, it appeared that the Hawks might have taken too long: the ball landed in Payak's palms at the baseline as he faced away from the basket with two seconds to go. An awkward, whirling, leaping shot left Payak's right hand over a defender, and the ball fell through the cylinder as the expiring clock triggered the Hippodrome horn.

79–77.

The Hawks won the last game on the last shot in the last second of their 1949–50 NBA schedule.

●

By winning six of their final nine games, Waterloo completed the season with a 19–43 record. Only the Denver Nuggets ended the year with fewer wins. Playing Jack Smiley's running, up-tempo style, the Hawks were 11–16 during the two months after Charlie Shipp's dismissal. However, neither coach found success away from the Hippodrome; Waterloo won just twice outside the Cedar Valley. Yet at home the Hawks were formidable, earning a respectable 17–15 mark.

Fans who had voted Harry Boykoff the team's Most Popular Player also honored Leo Kubiak as its Most Valuable Player. Kubiak appeared in every game and led the squad with 202 assists, a statistic that had not been officially measured in the National Basketball League. Averaging 11.5 points per night, he was one of three players in double figures on a season-long basis. Dick Mehen paced the Hawks with an average of 14.3 points; he also connected on a team-best 41.9 percent of his shots from the field.

While Waterloo players — stars and substitutes alike — moved into summer jobs selling insurance or studied for advanced degrees, the NBA playoffs opened for the twelve qualifying teams. By percentage, the Syracuse Nationals finished with the league's best record and shortest path to the finals. The Nationals dispatched the Philadelphia Warriors and New York Knicks in successive best-of-three series. Syracuse's championship round opponents, the Minneapolis Lakers, had also won two divisional series, as well as defeating the Anderson Packers in an intermediate playoff round. Playing for their third title in three years — first in the NBL during 1947–48, then in the BAA during 1948–49 — the Lakers became the first NBA champions, winning the best-of-seven finals in six games.

The World Professional Basketball Tournament had been discontinued after 1948. Minneapolis had won the final event, yet the Lakers' 1950 NBA title could be considered far more prestigious. The NBL-BAA merger had put the country's top professionals (setting aside the issue of segregation) together on the same courts under the same rules for an entire season, rather than just one week in March. However, the marriage of the two leagues had not brought prosperity. Many clubs that struggled financially in either league during 1948–49 continued to face losses as members of the NBA during 1949–50.

Waterloo's 2,973 per game average attendance at the Hippodrome fell well shy of preseason estimates for the mark needed to break even. Budget-saving decisions, made from the middle stages of the season onward, limited the shortfall, and the Hawks generated more than $93,000 in revenue. Operating expenses—not counting the purchase of the team from Andy George and Charlie Shipp—totaled more than $113,000. Taking into account the working capital raised during the stock drive, the final deficit at season's end was $1,500.

The Waterloo Basketball Inc. board of directors planned to sell new shares to cover that relatively mild loss and continue operations into a new season. Almost half the original stock offering had covered acquisition of the franchise. Additionally, the purchase of the Hammond Calumet Buccaneers' roster had been among the substantial expenses on the 1949–50 balance sheet. Hawks leaders were optimistic that a similar line item would be unnecessary in 1950–51. Thus, the board hoped that selling the same quantity of shares in 1950 would allow the team to open a new season with a balance considerably more robust than had been available the previous summer. After the strong on-court finish, Waterloo's roster was a valuable asset, since standard professional basketball contracts allowed teams the exclusive right to negotiate with their own players the following season or to monetize residual contracts by selling them to another club.

A league meeting and college draft were scheduled for Chicago on April 24 and 25. Just two weeks before the gathering, the Hawks learned all teams would be required to make a $50,000 performance guarantee to the NBA, underwritten by a bank or insurance company that would be liable for that amount if Waterloo failed to complete the 1950–51 schedule. Although it was not necessary to deposit $50,000 with the league office, some teams—especially in smaller communities—would be stretched just to find that degree of fiduciary confidence among their backers. The promissory notes were due by the start of the league meeting.

This additional requirement was more than the Anderson club could manage. Within hours, Packers representatives announced that they would not be in the NBA during 1950–51. Other small-market teams were defiant. According to the *Milwaukee Sentinel*, Sheboygan Red Skins president Magnus Brinkman demanded concessions in return for providing the surety bonds, specifically, "'better business methods' including a monthly accounting of all league operating expenses; equalization of schedules and the certainty that if the bond is posted, Sheboygan will be assured of NBA membership."[20]

Comments by NBA president Maurice Podoloff four days before the Chicago meeting convinced the Hawks, Red Skins, and Nuggets that there was an ulterior motive for the new performance guarantee. "Something will have to be done to make the league more workable," he told reporters. "Sheboygan and Waterloo are not as attractive at the gate as some other cities. . . . Denver extends the league too far and makes it a major travel problem."[21]

On a Monday morning in Chicago's Morrison Hotel—less than a year after the NBA's foundation had been laid there during initial merger discussions—the league's size and shape changed dramatically. "Only once was there any mention of Waterloo and Sheboygan staying in the NBA," wrote a disgusted *Waterloo Courier* sports editor Al Ney. "That was in a preliminary confab when the question was asked whether or not Waterloo had a $50,000 bond to post if it was decided the Hawks could remain in the NBA. The Waterloo representatives said they were prepared to guarantee posting the $50,000 bond. That was the end of bond talk."[22]

The league's endangered small-city teams had interpreted the $50,000 guarantee as a mechanism designed to dislodge them from the NBA. This suspicion was strengthened by the special dispensation for the Chicago Stags. The bond was waived for Chicago, while the Stags were also provided with a $40,000 financial aid package. Keeping the club afloat in the 18,000-seat Chicago Stadium was worthwhile to the NBA, league owners reasoned, even if the Stags needed to be given nearly the same amount of backing that other teams in smaller markets were being asked to pledge.

During the formal afternoon session, the NBA's other members

voted not to include Waterloo, Sheboygan, and Denver when building the following season's schedule. Magnus Brinkman described
the Indianapolis Olympians' attempt to abstain, saying, "Mr. Podoloff's eyes snapped and he said he would entertain a motion to include Indianapolis in the original ouster motion. Indianapolis fell in
line immediately and voted with the other teams."[23]

Speaking to the press later in the day, Podoloff portrayed the
changes as voluntary. Sheboygan's Brinkman would have none of it,
responding firmly, "Anyway you look at it, we were kicked out. We
did not resign. They simply wouldn't have us in and they told us so
in the morning meetings."[24]

7

COLD-BLOODED, CUT-THROAT BUSINESS

Waterloo Hawks officials refused to passively accept their removal from the National Basketball Association. Within minutes of their dismissal from league meetings, representatives from Waterloo, Sheboygan, and Denver were structuring a new, Midwest-centric professional basketball league. In the same Chicago hotel—and on the same afternoon as the NBA purge—the three uprooted teams pledged to continue together into the 1950–51 season. Anticipating the addition of five to seven other franchises from regional cities, the Hawks' Chris Marsau, Sheboygan's Magnus Brinkman, and Denver's Gerry L'Estrange arranged to meet again with other prospective owners during mid-May. They also hired Doxie Moore to be the new league's commissioner.

Moore, the former commissioner of the National Basketball League, remained active during the NBA's first year, initially as the business manager for the Anderson Packers. Near midseason, following a brief stint in which Packers owner Ike Duffey had appointed himself as coach, Moore took over the team's coaching duties to conclude the 1949–50 schedule. The Packers ended the winter just two games behind the Western Division–winning Indianapolis Olympians. Anderson claimed two playoff series before being stopped shy of the championship round by the Minneapolis Lakers.

Besides Moore, the newly formed league also expected to rely on the leadership and experience of Lon Darling. The former Oshkosh All-Stars owner and coach was provisionally awarded a franchise to be operated in Oshkosh, Milwaukee, or possibly a combination of

Wisconsin cities. Darling had been instrumental in 1937 when the Midwest Conference had evolved into the NBL. Like Moore, he was on hand in Chicago for the new league's creation.

In a sense, during the previous autumn, Darling's All-Stars had been the first club cut adrift by the NBA when it missed a preseason deadline to deposit its league dues. Nearly a year later, Darling expressed the sentiments of those representing the abandoned cities. As their initial meeting adjourned, he remarked, "Well, now maybe we can deal with men we like and can understand. We can trust each other and we're not going to have anybody in the league we can't trust."[1]

The circuit was eventually christened the National Professional Basketball League (NPBL), and Omaha was anticipated to be a nearly vital site for a club. As the transportation hub of the Great Plains — home to the headquarters of the Union Pacific Railroad — the eastern Nebraska city was located at a convenient stopping distance on the route to and from Denver. After a halting start, Omaha's basketball team appeared to be coalescing by early July with the announcement that former Waterloo Hawk Paul Cloyd would serve as the team's player-coach for games in the city's Municipal Auditorium. However, in the closing weeks of summer, the plan disintegrated, and Cloyd was relocated south to a hastily arranged NPBL outpost in Kansas City.

St. Louis was another targeted market where the league's ambition to field a team failed. The NBA's Bombers had dissolved when club owners accepted a $50,000 offer to sell their entire roster to the league. With such a large and regionally appropriate city left vacant, the NBPL courted a group of local businessmen, who raised $3,000 to meet the league's franchise fee. By the first days of June, NPBL officials sent the money back when the St. Louis outfit could not secure a venue.

The new league looked to the fan-fertile industrial cities of Ohio, where teams had flourished during the NBL's early seasons in the late 1930s. Toledo and Dayton were announced as NPBL members on the same day that St. Louis was scratched from consideration.

Doxie Moore, who traveled more than 5,000 miles throughout the summer to meet with potential owners and inspect possible playing sites, was hopeful about both additions. "We are having another meeting," he reported from Dayton in early June, "to set up a stock drive following a similar pattern to the one we went through in Waterloo last year."[2]

However, neither Dayton nor Toledo ultimately fielded a team in the NPBL. Representatives from Des Moines, Sioux City, and Rockford attended summer organizational sessions. Rumors suggested that Duluth, Muncie, and Colorado Springs could host franchises. None of these cities was home to a professional basketball club when the 1950–51 NPBL schedule eventually tipped off. The primary limitations involved finding appropriate auditoriums and securing financial backers.

Even Darling's new project failed to ripen. His seminomadic All-Stars always had difficulty finding gyms in Oshkosh that were large enough to attract profitable crowds. As had been the case during the previous off-season, arena space in Milwaukee could not be secured. The loss of Wisconsin Badgers star Don Rehfeldt to the NBA was another crippling disappointment for the embryonic organization. Darling had been optimistic that the All-American could be tempted to remain in the state, but instead Rehfeldt, the second player selected during the 1950 NBA draft, accepted a contract from the Baltimore Bullets. By July, Darling abandoned the plan. By 1951, he was dead from a heart attack after suffering a breakdown that his family attributed to the demise of the All-Stars.

Another location with an NBL heritage proved more hospitable for the NPBL. Basketball fans in Anderson, Indiana, had convinced Ike Duffey not to sell the Packers in the midst of the 1949–50 season. Given the team's impressive performance during the NBA playoffs — and just one year removed from winning the final NBL Championship in 1949 — local leaders were optimistic about the future, despite being positioned in the corridor between the NBA cities of Indianapolis and Fort Wayne. As Duffey moved to other pursuits,

Anderson turned to a community ownership model. The organization even expected to enter 1950–51 with a strong core of players from the previous season.

The other four cities that finally joined the NPBL had each fielded a team in Maurice White's failed Professional Basketball League of America three years earlier. The Kansas City club relocated from Omaha, settling in at the Pla-Mor Amusement Center and calling itself the Hi-Spots. In western Michigan, a partnership between former Rochester Royals player George Glamack and former Indianapolis NBL owner Frank Kautsky brought the Hornets to Grand Rapids Stadium, coached by legendary pro star Bobby McDermott. In St. Paul, Minnesota, either due to or in spite of the Lakers' success in Minneapolis, a group of young business executives attracted healthy investor interest as they founded the Lights, then signed a crop of college stars to be led by former Anderson coach Howie Schultz. On the league's southern extreme, the Louisville Aluminites had access to a 12,000-seat arena. They were backed by William Reynolds, at one time a nationally renowned polo player whose family owned the aluminum-producing Reynolds Metals Company.

While NPBL membership solidified, Brinkman, L'Estrange, and Marsau took formal leadership positions within the league. Brinkman and L'Estrange were installed as president and vice president respectively; Marsau became secretary. William Johns of St. Paul was voted treasurer once the Lights' franchise became a certainty. The NPBL's official address became that of the Harris, Van Metre & Buckmaster law firm on Sycamore Street in Waterloo.

Many NBA rule modifications, like jump balls after made free throws late in the game and clock stoppages in the closing minutes, were abandoned. College standards prevailed, with two significant exceptions. After long discussions, the NPBL retained a forty-eight-minute game span. Both Brinkman and Moore preferred returning to forty-minute contests. Their stance was based in part on the belief that teams could maintain slightly smaller rosters and enjoy corresponding salary savings by playing shorter games. Marsau and a majority of Waterloo's stockholders took the opposing view, backing the argument that won out: with a forty-minute contest—eight minutes shorter than the NBA—average scores in the NPBL were likely to be lower, thus giving the impression of an inferior on-court product. With the longer games, the NPBL also continued to set the personal foul limit at six, one more than the NCAA.

To a greater degree, the league founders busied themselves with setting the parameters for the NPBL's business operations. Bylaws approved in early August set the maximum roster size at fourteen with a minimum of eight. Each team was required to put at least eight men in uniform on game night. College-age players were not permitted to sign league contracts unless they had been deemed permanently ineligible by their schools. In a departure from NBA policy, visiting teams were to receive a $375 payment from their opponents to allay travel expenses.

One organizational policy was to have far-reaching, unanticipated implications for the 1950–51 NPBL campaign: "In the event a team drops out of the league without completing its schedule, all league games played with this team shall be classified as exhibitions and will not count in the league standings."[3]

The sixty-game NPBL schedule was revealed in mid-September. All clubs were slated to play eight games against their seven counterparts. Four additional matchups would pit each team against a natural rival. By geographic coincidence, in each case these rivalries paired a former NBA city against a newly organized opponent: Waterloo with St. Paul, Denver with Kansas City, Sheboygan with Grand Rapids, and Anderson with Louisville. The two latter combinations comprised the league's Eastern Division with the prior pairings becoming the Western Division.

Of Waterloo's thirty home games, twenty were planned for either Saturdays or Sundays. Most of the other dates at the Hippodrome were assigned to Wednesday nights. The Hawks were to play in front of a friendly crowd during almost every weekend throughout the winter. The new league's first game on November 1 pitted St. Paul against Louisville; 239 other contests were parceled out between the opener and the fourth weekend of March 1951.

●

Robert Buckmaster might have preferred to be knee-deep in cold, running water. Instead, the attorney and fly-fishing enthusiast spent a pleasant July day defending the Waterloo Hawks from a legal action by the NBA's Tri-Cities Blackhawks at the federal courthouse in Moline. Two months earlier, Waterloo had hired former University of Iowa basketball coach Lawrence "Pops" Harrison as the club's general manager. He replaced Perk Purnhage, who left the organization to attend to his baseball team in Davenport. Tri-Cities claimed that Harrison had tried to coax several players to abandon their Blackhawks contracts and come to Waterloo.

The case focused on phone calls between the new general manager and his former Hawkeye player Noble Jorgensen. Both men were sworn in to give testimony about the conversations. Jorgensen — who had played in Waterloo during 1947 as a member of the Pro-Hawks in the failed Professional Basketball League of America — told Judge Henry Graven that Harrison had first offered an $8,000 contract, then an agreement worth $10,000. Harrison countered that the calls had been strictly personal. Tri-Cities lawyers could not substantiate Jorgensen's account with a formal document; their claims that other players had been asked to break contracts were not corroborated in testimony by Blackhawks forward Dike Eddleman when he was later called to the stand.[4]

Buckmaster further shredded the Tri-Cities' argument for an injunction against Waterloo by pointing out that the Blackhawks had engaged in the very activities from which they were seeking legal relief. The *Waterloo Courier* recounted the testimony of Tri-Cities general manager John Fitzgerald on the witness stand:

> He revealed . . . under questioning by Buckmaster that he contacted Jack Burmaster, Max Morris and Bob Brannum of

Sheboygan and Dick Mehen of Waterloo about switching to the NBA.

Fitzgerald admitted he knew Mehen was bound by a Waterloo option and told of warning Morris not to tell Sheboygan of his offer.[5]

The six-hour hearing ended in the late afternoon. Judge Graven denied Tri-Cities' request for a restraining order, indicating that "there is not sufficient showing of dire need or repeated conduct."[6]

In the summer of 1950, the threat of lawsuits became a prominent feature in any serious discussion about professional basketball. NBA leaders cited the reserve clause in standard player contracts as the basis for possible legal action against any star player who considered defecting to the NPBL. The tactic was intended to preserve the league's prestige and forestall any type of bidding war that might have developed with its new rival. Years later, former St. Louis Bomber Ed Macauley captured the atmosphere when describing his negotiations with Boston Celtics co-owner Walter Brown. The Celtics had acquired Macauley's contract when the Bombers disbanded; however, as Macauley recounted:

> I indicated to them I signed with the Bombers, that was my hometown where I lived all my life, where I was planning to live, and I really didn't have any desire to go to Boston and that I was seriously looking to go to the other league [to take an offer from the St. Paul Lights].
>
> . . . While we were having our discussion, Maurice Podoloff, the commissioner, called Walter, who told him we were talking about it just then. He said, "Put Macauley on the phone." He said to me, "If you so much as think of going to the other league you'll be sued and you'll be out of basketball, and your career will come to an end." Well, Walter and I were getting along fine and I was really aggravated that Podoloff came in with that kind of language. So, I said, "Mr. Podoloff, do me a favor. You sue me. Let's go to court. Let's find out whether such things as the reserve clause are legal," and I hung up.[7]

Macauley and Brown eventually came to amicable terms that brought the future Hall of Famer to Boston rather than St. Paul.

The Moline court appearance was the most notable of several instances in which Buckmaster provided legal counsel to the Hawks and the National Professional Basketball League. The energetic and able thirty-seven-year-old—described as a perfectionist by his peers—served as one of the executive directors on the Hawks' board, in addition to an array of other activities and commitments.[8] The dark-haired attorney with prominent ears wore a narrow mustache that did not reach the corners of his mouth. Intentionally or otherwise, his appearance at the time resembled that of movie star Clark Gable.

A lifelong Black Hawk County native, Buckmaster graduated from Iowa State Teachers College in Cedar Falls before studying law at the University of Iowa. He began his Waterloo legal career in 1938 but interrupted his practice to serve in World War II, first as a military flight instructor, then as a Marine Corps lieutenant. Back in Waterloo after the war, Buckmaster became city attorney in 1946. At a city council meeting in May of the following year, Mayor Knapp Matthews suffered a heart attack and died before he could be moved from the council chamber. A little more than a week later, Buckmaster received the appointment to finish Matthews' mayoral term. Although active in the Republican Party, he did not run to retain the office in 1948, and his interests led him away from government into broadcasting, real estate, education, and other pursuits like serving on the Hawks' board.

One of the matters on which Buckmaster had advised team officials earlier in the summer of 1950 was the departure of Dick Mehen and Harry Boykoff. On a national basis, the two former All-Americans were Waterloo's best-known players. Mehen and Boykoff had courted controversy in March when they left the Hawks' bench before the end of a home game against the Syracuse Nationals. Despite this and despite their cool relationship with Coach Jack Smiley, both had been offered renewals for 1950–51. The sports business customs of the era dictated that if the team offered them contracts, they could only deal with Waterloo.

However, in late May the NBA announced that—as a league—it had signed the pair. Mehen, Boykoff, and other selected NPBL players were to be assigned to teams in the NBA when they jumped from one loop to the other. Whatever their value in Smiley's on-court plans, *Waterloo Courier* sports editor Al Ney decried the action, suggesting that the Hawks might have been able to sell the two stars' contracts for up to $12,500 even if they never played another game for Waterloo. "In this cold-blooded, cut-throat business," he wrote, "the best thing a team can do apparently is to keep its mouth shut and go out and do a little knifing of its own."[9]

Buckmaster phoned Podoloff after the Hawks learned of the NBA's tactic. The Waterloo lawyer suggested that there were grounds for a lawsuit or, alternatively, that the Hawks might respond in kind. Ultimately the matter did not appear before a judge. Waterloo management believed it had already earned a separate victory against the NBA, one that made Mehen and Boykoff expendable, regardless of their contracts' value.

The Celtics had selected 6-foot-11-inch Bowling Green center Charlie Share with the first pick during the 1950 NBA draft. The All-American had led the Falcons in scoring during all four of his NCAA seasons, finishing with a program-best career total of 1,721 points and averaging 19.8 per game in his senior season. The dimpled twenty-two-year-old with a neatly trimmed flattop and size-15 shoes had a notable hook shot, could rebound, and was quicker than Boykoff. Share was slender coming out of college; as his professional career continued, he filled out his frame and became an imposing figure. A teammate in later years would remember colliding with him in practice, saying, "Man, it was like getting hit by a truck. He rocked my teeth, my jaw and everything. I vibrated and hurt for two months."[10]

Playing at 230 pounds during his final season with Bowling Green, Share served as captain. The Falcons climbed briefly into the Associated Press rankings. Yet their 19–11 record fell short of the two prior years when Bowling Green had participated in the National Invitation Tournament, including a third-place run during Share's junior season. Still, his individual performance during 1949–50 led Smiley to compare the prospects for Share's pro career favorably with George Mikan's ascent in the sport.[11] With former Falcons Leo Kubiak and Johnny Payak already in Waterloo, the Hawks made a strong bid for professional basketball's most coveted newcomer, offering a two-year contract and a signing bonus.

"I made a personal trip to Bowling Green," remembered Smiley. "We beat [the Celtics] to him. I laid out 2,500 bucks of my own money to sign him. . . . Then, to make sure he was ours, I went to Chicago to get him, met his father, a 6-foot-6-inch teamster organizer, and personally drove Charlie to Waterloo."[12]

As the summer continued, the Hawks also impressed local fans by acquiring former Iowa Hawkeye and Tri-Cities Blackhawks guard Murray Wier. Although he was small even by college and professional standards at the time, Wier's acrobatic offensive style and in-state college success made him a phenomenon far bigger than his stature. The presence of his former Hawkeye coach, Pops Harrison, working in Waterloo as general manager likely contributed to Wier's choice. However, his signing did not represent an instance of league jumping; before making the deal, Wier had already been released by the Blackhawks.

Kubiak, Payak, Don Boven, and Wayne See renewed their contracts over the summer. The Hawks added more speed with Stan Weber, a college track athlete as well as a basketball player at Bowling Green. Weber had spent the latter part of World War II cooped up in an army kitchen. Able to stretch out in college, Share's 6-foot-5-inch classmate became just the third Falcons player to cook up 1,000 career points. A Knicks draft pick, Weber chose the Hawks over New York. Meanwhile, another newcomer, Claude Overton of Southwest Oklahoma College, came to Waterloo instead of going to the NBA's Washington Capitols. Bob Vollers of the University of Iowa was an additional rookie signing.

In September, the Hawks received $1,995 from the NBA. The payment represented Waterloo's equity in the league at the time of the April meeting in Chicago. Similar checks also arrived in Sheboygan and Denver. During the off-season, five players from NPBL teams, including Mehen and Boykoff, switched allegiances. The NBA encountered seventeen defections. An October agreement between the two leagues established a value for those who had moved back and forth, obligating the NPBL office to pay the NBA $11,000 to compensate for the imbalance. The peace was strained, but basketball was about to begin on both fronts.

●

Two months before the Hawks' first game of the 1950–51 season, dozens of young women circulated through Cedar Valley homes and offices searching for basketball season ticket buyers. Coached by general manager Pops Harrison, the members of the Waterloo Junior League were equipped with auditorium maps and rate cards, and their sales script undoubtedly highlighted the value and affordability of ticket packages. Team management had altered the pricing of some plans, but seats in reserved, arena floor, and box areas still ranged between thirty and fifty dollars on a season-long basis, as they had the previous year. Adding to the pitch, the Junior Leaguers could also remind buyers that a portion of each season ticket they sold would be contributed to their organization's service projects.

Through late August, before the Junior League's sales campaign, the Hawks already had commitments from stockholders and renewal customers for approximately 225 season tickets. Those orders represented half the count from the previous season at an estimated value of $10,000. The team's sales target was far more optimistic. The unlikely goal to sell 2,000 season tickets was based on both the financial health of the club and a competitive rivalry. "We set that 2,000 goal because we want to top the 1,600 season tickets sold by Tri-Cities," admitted Pops Harrison.[13]

The third full season of professional basketball in northeast Iowa was greeted enthusiastically by many, seeming to vindicate Harrison's expectations. As practices began in Cedar Falls at Iowa State Teachers College, hundreds of fans watched the team work into shape. There was even enough excitement surrounding the sport for former Hawks Charlie Shipp and Dale Hamilton, both still living in the area, to form the Waterloo Rockets semipro squad. Unfortunately, many Hawks fans found themselves in no position to purchase basketball tickets during the fall of 1950.

A year earlier, in 1949, members of the United Automobile Workers at Iowa John Deere facilities had been close to calling a strike. Instead, they accepted a raise of five cents per hour. Their agreement with the company also included maternity leave provisions and an expanded statement pledging Deere not to discriminate on the basis of "race, color, creed, religious beliefs, nationality, or sex."[14] For its part, the union affirmed a commitment not to strike. That precedent had originated during World War II at a time when workers and management felt a patriotic necessity to maintain high production rates. "The membership voted to accept the proposal with tongue in cheek, because they knew they were having problems with [some Deere policies]," remembered Waterloo UAW Local 838 leader Carl Dahl, and "by 1950 there was a great deal of unrest in the plant."[15]

In the years after the war, strikes and labor disputes were common throughout the United States. Broadly, the country expected prosperity after the sacrifices made for the war effort. Consumers wanted new houses, cars, radios, previously rationed foods, and other products that had been scarce. Businesses tried to meet the high demand as quickly as possible, at times dangerously pushing the limits of productivity. Their unionized employees responded with campaigns for higher wages and better conditions as they worked faster and harder to fill orders and meet deadlines.

The U.S. government was forced to intercede in some strikes. Coal mines and steel mills were vital to the nation's economic expansion and security, and work in those places could not be halted for long without tempting dangerous consequences. Federal officials and the U.S. military temporarily operated many striking railroads to prevent transportation stoppages. The 1947 Taft-Hartley Act reinforced the principle of government intervention when necessary, and its authors admonished employers and workers "that neither party has any rights in its relations with any other to engage in acts or practices that jeopardize the public health, safety, or interest."

Waterloo's most traumatic strike of the era had happened at Rath Packing in 1948. The United Packinghouse Workers of America called for a nationwide work stoppage beginning in March, pulling approximately 6,000 local unionized and nonunionized employees off their jobs. Although Rath had a broad distribution network for the meat it processed, its operations were highly concentrated in Waterloo. The company became increasingly vulnerable as its primary facility remained idle. After the shutdown had lasted several weeks, management decided to reopen the plant. Picket lines became hostile territory as a limited number of workers entered and left the red brick complex for their shifts. In May, tension turned to tragedy.

On a Wednesday afternoon, Fred Roberts, an African American worker crossing union lines, attempted to navigate his car to the Rath entrance through a crowd of striking UPWA members. The picketers began to close in, rocking Roberts' vehicle, and even climbing onto the running boards. Fearing for his safety, Roberts pulled a gun, pointing first to the crowd on his right, then turning left. That's where a white striker named Chuck Farrell was standing when Roberts fired. Farrell fell to the ground, fatally shot through the head.

A riot began and continued for the remainder of the day as the crowd crashed through the plant gates. Dozens of cars were overturned, fires started in pools of spilled gasoline, and windows were smashed. The threat of more widespread violence on Waterloo's east side increased as nightfall approached. The arrival of 350 National Guard soldiers restored an uneasy calm. They patrolled the streets in machine-gun laden armored cars and half-track trucks well into the following week.

Fortunately, racial violence did not result from the incident. No business or fraternal organization in the community was better integrated than Waterloo's UPWA Local 46. Black employees had played a fundamental role in founding the union chapter years earlier. The

UPWA emblem even suggested racial unity, depicting white and black hands clasped in a handshake. "It was noteworthy that the riot was directed solely against the Rath Company and not Waterloo's black community," concluded labor historians Rick Halpern and Roger Horowitz in their account of the violence.[16]

The shooting and its aftermath helped precipitate an end to the strike less than two weeks later. Roberts was eventually acquitted of manslaughter. Several union leaders were charged with inciting the riot; a few were convicted and given brief prison sentences. Having recently completed his term as mayor and back in the role of city attorney, Robert Buckmaster served as the special prosecutor during these trials, resulting in pronounced union enmity against him. Union members also viewed the arrival of the National Guard as a strike-busting tactic and campaigned against incumbent local and state politicians in subsequent elections. Rath and the UPWA remained hostile until the plant closed in 1985.

The 1948 strike won Rath employees a raise worth nine cents per hour.

Across the river two years later, during the late summer of 1950 when the Waterloo Hawks were at work selling season tickets and securing the footing of the new NPBL, John Deere workers began their longest and most acrimonious strike up to that time. The first Waterloo tractors had been built during the closing years of the nineteenth century. Moline-based John Deere purchased the Waterloo Gasoline Engine Company in 1918, expanding it throughout the 1920s and surviving the Great Depression. During World War II, the company forged parts for Allied tanks, submarines, and aircraft. Back to building farm machinery after the war was won, the Waterloo plant completed a new tractor every five minutes when operating at top efficiency and, by itself, generated $100 million in annual revenue, approximately a quarter of the company's total. However, the Deere brand still ranked second in tractor sales to International Harvester. New efficiency standards intended to increase capacity were a major point of contention during the Deere strike of 1950.

A simultaneous strike was taking place at International Harvester plants, where wages were already higher. UAW and IH representatives resolved their differences by early November, two and a half months after picketing began. Deere's strike would continue after International Harvester plants were back in production. The most challenging days were still ahead in Waterloo.

Early talks to settle the work stoppage in Deere facilities faltered in mid-September, with the two sides settling into a stalemate for the remainder of the month and all of October. For 5,000 Waterloo UAW members and others put out of work by the impasse, finding work in another factory or some other alternative profession was vital. Union financial support was limited largely to those with serious medical conditions or those who otherwise might have been destitute. "You could go out and get jobs, but you didn't make the money," remembered UAW member Bob Shelton, whose hourly wages were reduced more than 25 percent while he was working elsewhere in the midst of the strike.[17]

As Rath had done in 1948, Deere decided to reopen its Waterloo operation by mid-November, less than two weeks after the International Harvester strike ended. Workers willing to break with the union were invited to return to their jobs. Emotions rose as the small group became larger, eventually up to half of the workforce by the time the strike was resolved. There were some altercations and threats of violence but nothing near the magnitude of the Roberts-Farrell incident. With the holidays approaching, the UAW arranged to make temporary installment payments at local department stores so that families could purchase winter clothes for their children in time for Christmas. Other union chapters from across the country collected and shipped tons of food to their Waterloo brethren. Yet the hardship of the strike and rumors—in some cases true—that some union leaders were misappropriating relief funds hurt union solidarity.

The dispute burned itself out three weeks into December. UAW members—some grudgingly—voted to accept a new contract. The five-year term shielded Deere from most labor stoppages. Some employees still felt that they were not protected from what they believed to be unrealistic work standards. However, wages were boosted fifteen cents per hour with a provision for annual adjustments. More generous medical and pension plans were also a valuable legacy of the 111-day confrontation. It was more than a generation before another comparable strike idled John Deere's Waterloo operation.

Work resumed Christmas week. Holiday-scale wages helped begin mending management-worker relations and provided employees with a little extra money to cover the bills that had accumulated in August and September.

●

Charlie Share was the only rookie from the National Professional Basketball League selected for the *Chicago Herald-American*'s 1950 College All-Star Classic. The annual exhibition was staged in the final days of October between the defending NBA champion Minneapolis Lakers and the previous season's top college seniors selected by sports writers and college coaches. Share's ten All-Star teammates had all landed with NBA clubs. Waterloo coach Jack Smiley flew with his rookie center to the event only hours after the Hawks lost their first preseason game, 69–65, against the St. Paul Lights on a neutral floor.

Despite the contrast of playing in front of several hundred fans in Willmar, Minnesota, one night and then taking to the court the next evening in Chicago Stadium with more than 19,000 on hand, Share was undaunted. He started the game across the jump circle from George Mikan. Share played well in the early minutes, contributing 6 points, limiting Mikan to one converted free throw, and blocking at least one field goal attempt by the Lakers' star. A syndicated account of the game noted, "Mikan met a man-sized rival . . . and had his hands full."[18] However, Share aggravated a chronic ankle injury before halftime and watched from the bench as the Lakers prevailed, 61–54. In Share's absence, Bob Cousy led the All-Stars with 13 points and was named the college team's co-MVP with Paul Arizin. Days later, both Cousy and Arizin would play the first NBA games in their respective Hall of Fame careers. After the game, College All-Stars coach Nat Holman of City College of New York highlighted Share's injury as a major factor in the outcome, remarking, "We'd have beaten the Lakers if Share would have been able to finish the game."[19]

Other ailments and accidents hampered the Hawks as they prepared for their November 5 debut. Leo Kubiak dealt with a knee injury almost from the time practices began. Claude Overton lost three teeth when he was clobbered by Don Boven's elbow during a scrimmage. Johnny Payak spent the first month of the season playing in a mask designed to protect his broken nose. Amid the sequence of mishaps, Waterloo signed Mac Otten, who had followed his older brother, Don, first to Bowling Green and then into professional basketball. While Don Otten became a familiar presence for the Tri-Cities Blackhawks over several seasons, Mac had bounced from Moline to St. Louis in 1949–50 and was in Minneapolis before the new schedule began, only to be released by the Lakers.

The arrival of 6-foot-7-inch Mac Otten gave Waterloo a full lineup of former Bowling Green Falcons: Otten, Share, Kubiak, Payak, and Stan Weber had all been teammates at the western Ohio school. The group liked to run the floor and was well suited to Smiley's style. Wayne See and Murray Wier also brought speed and experience to the court, and Don Boven was capable of keeping pace with anyone he was assigned to play with. The deep roster left little playing time for rookies Claude Overton and Bob Vollers.

Kubiak, Share, and Payak all played in the season opener versus Kansas City even though they had not fully recovered from their injuries. Despite outshooting their opponent, the Hawks fell 84–82 as the Hi-Spots sank forty free throws and were more effective at controlling rebounds. One week later, however, the Hawks were sharper during their first home game. In that instance, Waterloo capitalized on a free throw advantage to help force overtime against the Louisville Aluminites. Then, with the score tied at 65–65 on the final possession of the extra period, Wier eluded tight defense in a corner of the front court and moved the ball back to Payak beyond the top of the key. Payak's long shot dropped as time expired, giving the Hawks a 67–65 victory.

In another close November home game, Waterloo's Bowling Green contingent led the way to an 84–82 win against the Anderson Packers. Beyond Share's high-scoring 19-point contribution, the Hawks recorded the winning basket on what *Courier* sports editor Al Ney described as an "old Bowling Green play," elaborating: "With just 23 seconds left, Otten got the tip on a jump ball at the Waterloo free throw circle. He tipped to Weber, who in turn fed to Payak cutting around and in for a layup that provided the winning margin."[20]

Although Share fouled out before that winning basket, the star rookie's strong night was cause for excitement at the Hippodrome. Previously, during the Hawks' home opener, the twenty-three-year-old had been limited to a single point. Early in the season, in spite of his ankle ailment and some rookie miscues, Share generally played well at a time when his life was changing off the court. He missed an early December game after rushing to Chicago to be with his father, who had suffered a heart attack. Just over a week later, Share married college classmate Rose Bender in Cedar Rapids. In the midst of those emotional experiences, he continued to average just over 11 points per game.

Share's play was not spectacular but showed growth. The Hawks aspired to similar business results after early matchups at the Cattle Congress grounds. Crowds of 2,200 were on hand for each of the first two 1950–51 home games. Despite the Deere strike, Waterloo's average was 2,386 by the end of November, but down 13 percent compared with the first five home games of the 1949–50 NBA schedule. With a 6–4 record as December began, general manager Pops Harrison hoped to see steadily increasing attendance; he pegged 2,800 as the average figure the team needed for the season to ensure financial sustainability.[21]

The NPBL, meanwhile, attracted scant media attention. In a November *Courier* column, Al Ney noted, "National publicity has been so bad that few persons outside the eight NPBL cities know that the loop is playing major league basketball."[22] For that matter, many people within the league's markets were unaware of the circuit or, at least, reluctant to attend a game. By December, Kansas City was reporting losses in the range of $30,000.[23] The Grand Rapids Hornets' struggles were exacerbated when a howling snowstorm blew away hopes for a big Thanksgiving audience. A fund drive to collect money to cover road expenses was required in Anderson. One sportswriter in Louisville suggested that the widening number of homes with televisions was responsible for low Aluminites attendance.[24] St. Paul's average crowd was slightly larger than those drawn to a typical Waterloo home game, but receipts still failed to cover the large sums that Lights owners had spent while establishing the club.

In Denver, the Nuggets had struggled through 1948–49 and 1949–50 as a player cooperative with a profit-sharing arrangement similar to the Indianapolis Olympians. Ahead of the 1950–51 season, the organization's assets were sold to local shareholders. The team also received backing from a chain of service stations in the Rocky Mountain region and was rechristened the Frontier Refiners in the months leading up to its first NPBL contest. On a competitive basis, their schedule included few early road games, helping to vault the Refiners to the top of the league standings. However, even an 8–0 home record could not stir more than tepid interest from local fans. As in other NPBL markets, ticket sales lagged behind expectations. Crowds of around a thousand were typical in the community of 415,000.

Denver's basketball credentials were among the best of any city in the western states. Just a few years after inventing the game in Massachusetts, James Naismith relocated to the Colorado capital, working in the YMCA while attending medical school there. During the early 1930s, several strong Amateur Athletic Union teams were formed, and basketball became a prominent attraction. Around the same time Henry Iba, who had gained renown as an innovative and successful coach, arrived in nearby Boulder for a short stint leading the University of Colorado program. Moreover, by 1935, the AAU National Tournament was moved to Denver from Kansas City, bringing top amateur teams to the mountains from across the country each spring.

Denver's own AAU entries, playing under different names for various sponsors, had won three AAU national championships by 1948. During March in that final season as an amateur outfit, the Nuggets had been one of eight clubs to take to the court at Madison Square Garden in a special tournament to place players on the 1948 U.S. Olympic team. Despite this prestige, the organization had absorbed an $18,000 loss in 1947–48.[25] As the club's deficit mounted, ticket sales for the week-long annual AAU tournament in the city reached a record $73,000.[26] Convinced that new tactics were required to capitalize on evident local interest in basketball, Nuggets backers abandoned the amateur game. They hoped that professional status might be self-sustaining, though this failed to happen during the seasons that followed.

The Hawks had made three trips to Denver for games against the Nuggets during the 1948–49 and 1949–50 seasons. Despite finishing ahead of their hosts in the final standings each year, Waterloo had won just two of the six games played at high altitude. In mid-December of 1950, the Refiners led Waterloo by half a game in the Western Division before Wednesday and Friday matchups in Colorado. The Hawks went west after winning seven of their previous nine games but with expectations for limited production from Share, who had injured his elbow the week before.

In the opening game, Denver converted a free throw for the first point, and then the Hawks raced away with the lead. Waterloo's largest advantage was 14 before the end of the first quarter. The visitors were led by Kubiak on his way to a team-high 18. A Refiners rally closed the gap to 48–42 at halftime, but the Hawks stayed out of reach until the fourth quarter. Denver finally seized control in the last four minutes of regulation, ending the game on an 8–0 run. Bob Brown, a veteran and former star at Miami University in Ohio, led all scorers with 22 points in the 83–76 Refiners win. Rookie Ed Dahler, a Duquesne product, had 19.

Dahler proved even more difficult to stop coming off the bench two nights later. Whether from the field or the free throw line, the 6-foot-5-inch forward missed only four shots all evening and led both teams with 25 points. In this rematch, the Hawks played from behind throughout the game. Although Waterloo eventually tied the score at 73–73 late in the fourth quarter, the Refiners retook the lead and pulled ahead to an 88–82 final by hitting their foul shots. Share paced the Hawks with 14 despite his elbow injury.

Waterloo was unable to stifle the Refiners' perfect home record, and the losses shuffled the Hawks to third place in the division at 9–7. However, within a week, Waterloo would shoot up in the standings while making the biggest of several roster alterations in a refashioned NPBL.

AN EVEN GREATER CHALLENGE

The Hawks faced a daunting nine-game sequence during the final fifteen days of December 1950. After returning from consecutive losses in Denver against the Frontier Refiners, Waterloo was scheduled to play in five of the National Professional Basketball League's other seven cities before the calendar turned to a new year. Thrashing the Grand Rapids Hornets by 44 points in Waterloo Auditorium was an ideal start. The win moved the Hawks into a second-place Western Division tie with their geographic rivals, the St. Paul Lights.

During four regular-season meetings, the Lights had won three times. Two November trips to St. Paul had resulted in 7- and 13-point Hawks losses. On December 19, fewer than a thousand fans greeted the two teams when Waterloo visited St. Paul again. More than half those attending were Boy Scouts who had received free tickets. Murray Wier set the pace early, spurring the Hawks to a 16–13 lead by the end of the first quarter. However, St. Paul swung to an advantage in the second and led by 10 at halftime. Neither team was particularly sharp, and veteran Stan Miasek's 17 made the difference for St. Paul in the 76–70 result. Wier ended with a team-high 12 points for Waterloo.

The loss temporarily dropped the Hawks back to third place. However, before Waterloo could take to the court the next night versus the Sheboygan Red Skins, the team was back in second. The Lights' smallest crowd of the season convinced St. Paul's owners that their investment could not be salvaged. With reported losses of $40,000, the Lights were disbanded after just twenty games.

St. Paul wasn't the only club ready to abandon the NPBL. The Kansas City Hi-Spots simultaneously declared their intent to end operations. The Hi-Spots had already quit playing home games, surviving instead on the $375 stipend received from each road contest. A bid to secure more sponsorship money from the team's namesake soda brand went unrequited. However, Kansas City players were determined to see the season through. Within days, they successfully lobbied to have the team reinstated. Meanwhile, clubs across the NPBL arranged to send representatives to Chicago for a meeting. The league schedule needed to be patched and the standings recalculated with St. Paul's games reclassified as exhibitions.

Games continued in the middle of these alterations, with police intervention required so the Hawks could complete their 6-point December 20 win against the Red Skins at the Hippodrome. Late in the contest, following several instances of rough play and short tempers, a fight erupted between the Hawks' Johnny Payak and Sheboygan's Max Morris; officers on hand had to separate the two belligerents, in addition to several of their teammates and even a number of fans who raced into the tussle. Aside from the altercation, Payak and Don Boven each had 17 points. The next night in Sheboygan, the Red Skins responded by drubbing Waterloo 122–79.

Charlie Share had 10 points in the first game against the Red Skins. He was held to 5, all free throws, during the rematch. Arriving in Waterloo early the next morning after the long overnight car trip, the star rookie learned that his contract had been sold. The Hawks had accepted a $20,000 offer to move him to the Fort Wayne Pistons of the rival National Basketball Association.

When the deal was made, Share was averaging 11 points per game and ranked as Waterloo's third-leading scorer. He had been productive for the Hawks, but his play did not resemble the George Mikan–like dominance that the organization had hoped for. Moreover, Share had not attracted fans to the auditorium or to opposing NPBL buildings, as had been anticipated. Negotiations between the Hawks and the Pistons had quietly opened several weeks earlier with Waterloo asking for as much as $28,000. While the final price was closer to Fort Wayne's initial offer of $18,000, the sale was still one of the largest in professional basketball at that time.

Bringing Share onto the court in Fort Wayne was another matter. The Boston Celtics argued that he could only join their organization, because they had selected him in the 1950 NBA draft. The dispute continued through the remainder of the season, and the big rookie did not play an NBA game in 1950–51. Instead, he visited former teammates and fans at Bowling Green and later joined some little-used Pistons reserves for an exhibition tour as the title attraction of the Charlie Share All-Stars. Eventually, the Pistons and the Celtics reached an agreement. When the Washington Capitols later disbanded, Fort Wayne acquired guard Bill Sharman and swapped his rights for those of Share.

Hawks general manager Pops Harrison watched the Pistons and the Celtics maneuver for Share with only distant interest, noting, "It's strictly an NBA problem."[1] "We are doing it to strengthen our ball club," he said the day after Waterloo and Fort Wayne had come to terms. "This gives us even more financial security, and gives us an opportunity to deal for a more experienced center."[2]

As a boy, Lawrence Harrison had liked candy—lollipops in particular—and was thus known as Pops from his youth. He had built a reputation for athletics in Iowa City long before becoming the head basketball coach at the University of Iowa. First attending the university's junior high and high school in the early 1920s, he was noted for strong performances on the prep baseball and track squads as well as the basketball team. During his sophomore year at the college level, he was a guard on an Iowa team that won a four-way share of the Big Ten basketball championship. Upon graduating in 1928, he was hired by the Hawkeyes' athletics department as an assistant baseball and basketball coach.

During the two decades that followed, Harrison was absent from the University of Iowa only briefly. In the winter of 1930–31, he became head coach at western Pennsylvania's Westminster College.

Despite having only one senior on his roster, he led the school to a sparkling record. Yet he returned to Iowa as an assistant the following summer. Rollie Williams, who had coached the Hawkeyes' freshman team on which Harrison played, became Iowa's varsity coach in 1929. When Williams left to serve in the U.S. Navy in 1942, Harrison inherited the position and led the program to a 98–42 record over the next eight seasons. His greatest success came during the war years. In 1943–44, the Hawkeyes won their first twelve games and tied for second in the conference. The following winter, only a 1-point January road loss to Illinois blemished a 17–1 record as the Hawkeyes produced the school's first outright conference championship. The addition of a black transfer student, Dick Culberson, made Iowa the Big Ten's first integrated team.

The Hawkeyes' roster also included freshman Murray Wier. "Outside of my dad, Pops was the most important man in my life," Wier later remembered. "He made me go to class when I might have slacked off otherwise. All I really wanted to do was play basketball. I sometimes wonder where I'd be if it wasn't for him."[3]

Just before the 1949–50 college season tipped off, Harrison underwent emergency kidney surgery—the first of five operations—and was in the hospital for two weeks. He resumed his coaching responsibilities in late December, but complications forced him to step aside again in mid-January. His intent to return the following season was denied when the school fired him in April. The decision was attributed to "failure to attend staff meetings, improper teaching of classes and heated remarks to referees," according to the *Chicago Tribune*, rather than to the forty-three-year-old's medical problems.[4] At the time, Harrison's salary of nearly $7,000 was one of the highest in the Big Ten.

The balding, dimpled, round-nosed Harrison accepted an offer to be Waterloo's general manager less than a month later, pledging not to interfere with Jack Smiley's coaching decisions. "Frankly, I think this business end of the game will offer me an even greater challenge than coaching," he said, adding later in the summer, "I've had all the basketball coaching I want or ever want. I'm not going to be sticking my neck into Jack's business."[5]

While the lineup and game decisions were left to Smiley, the new Waterloo general manager occasionally found himself wandering to the bench on nights when games were close and his nerves took over. During the final days of December, both Harrison and the Hawks were almost constantly active. The team lost at home to Denver two nights before Christmas, suffered another setback on the road against the Louisville Aluminites on Christmas Eve, then made its way to Grand Rapids for a Christmas Day win versus the Hornets. Waterloo's weary club played two additional home games, splitting with Sheboygan and Louisville, before New Year's Eve. The Hawks lost four of their final six games of 1950, and their record, modified by changes in league membership, was 11–8.

Harrison, meanwhile, represented the team as the NPBL decided to reformat its standings without divisions following St. Paul's departure. In the dispersal of Lights players, Waterloo's general manager acquired a pair of former All-American forwards: Hamline product Hal Haskins and Brigham Young star Joe Nelson. Days later, the league shrank from seven to six teams as Grand Rapids, a club that had repeatedly failed to make payroll, left. Four wins and a loss against the Hornets evaporated from Waterloo's record, shuffling the Hawks to fourth place. However, during Grand Rapids' final days, Harrison acquired center Elmore Morgenthaler to replace Share. In return, the Hawks canceled the Hornets' $750 debt after the latter club had failed to pay the league-mandated $375 appearance fees when Waterloo visited twice earlier in the season.

The roster shuffling led to one departure in particular that surprised Hawks fans. Leo Kubiak's knee had never completely healed from a preseason injury. He did not miss a regular-season matchup and was averaging 9 points per game two months into the schedule, but the former team MVP felt his play was faltering. Fearing he might be cut, in early January Kubiak asked to be released. He later signed with Denver and played his final professional games with the

Frontier Refiners. Kubiak was the last link with the Hawks team that had taken to the court during 1948–49, prior to the National Basketball League–Basketball Association of America merger.

●

At 7 feet 1 inch, Elmore Morgenthaler was easy to spot in a crowd but still occasionally hard to find. From his time in college onward, Morgenthaler rarely stayed in one place very long. Born in Amarillo, Texas, "Big Mo" first gained notoriety in 1945–46 while playing at the New Mexico School of Mines. When the school dropped athletics, the "Texas Tower" went to Boston College for part of the following season. Morgenthaler was averaging more than 21 points per game for the Eagles before leaving school "upon losing a decision to the textbooks," as the student newspaper described it.[6]

Morgenthaler finished the 1946–47 campaign with the Providence Steamrollers during the Basketball Association of America's debut season. Later he played in the league for the Philadelphia Warriors. Morgenthaler found his way onto the court with the Birmingham Skyhawks of the short-lived Professional Basketball League of America. He attracted attention playing for eastern clubs in the American Basketball League as well as semiprofessional and touring teams.

During World War II, Morgenthaler had been too tall to serve in the armed forces. Married to a 5-foot-6-inch beauty queen whom he dwarfed, he had a personality as outsized as his frame. Upon his arrival in the Cedar Valley, the center described himself as "tall and tan and terrific."[7] *Waterloo Courier* sports editor Al Ney dubbed him the "Dizzy Dean of Basketball," expanding on that thought by noting, "Elmore is talkative and ready to play the role of a character at all times. Being seven feet tall 'is somewhat unusual,' Elmore says, 'but, heck, it has brought me more fun than grief.'"[8]

Waterloo's offensive pace pressed the new center, who had initially expressed concern that he might not be in shape to run with the Hawks' offense. Asked by player-coach Jack Smiley how he was feeling in the midst of one long spell on the court, Morgenthaler responded, "Push my tongue back in and I'll tell you."[9] However, he was capable of being an effective scorer. During early January in his third appearance for the Hawks, he recorded a team-high 22 points in a 116–69 road loss to the Anderson Packers.

Home games were decidedly more fruitful for the Hawks in January 1951. The biggest home win at the Hippodrome came on January 14 by a 55-point margin. In fairness, the Kansas City Hi-Spots team that visited Waterloo that afternoon was badly outmatched. Kansas City's roster had dwindled to four regular players; the team had found two replacements deemed suitable before making the trip. On arriving, the Hi-Spots added Clay Bristow, a former Morningside College player who had been cut from the Hawks' roster in the preseason, and former Waterloo East High School athlete Dick Gates to meet the NPBL's minimum roster standard.

Nonetheless, the game was close early on. Shooting poorly at the outset, the Hawks claimed their first lead only past the midpoint of the opening quarter. Ralph "Buckshot" O'Brien, who had moved into Leo Kubiak's spot on the Waterloo roster, recorded the basket that put the Hawks in front. O'Brien's backcourt running mate, Murray Wier, also helped Waterloo overcome its drab start. With four first-quarter field goals from Wier, the Hawks pulled ahead to a 25–13 lead through one period.

The rout was on in the second and third quarters. The lead was 18 points at halftime and up to 46 after thirty-six minutes. The Hawks wore down the Hi-Spots and attempted nearly twice as many shots (121 versus 65) in the 128–73 affair. In addition to Wier, Johnny Payak, Stan Weber, Buddy Cate (another January addition), Wayne See, and Joe Nelson all finished the game in double figures.

Waterloo was 7–0 at home during the month. All but one of the victories was by 19 points or more. Fans were willing to ignore the often hapless competition as well as the Hawks' 1–6 January road record, which kept the team hovering in or near fourth place. Despite occasionally frigid temperatures, more than 20,000 fans attended games during the first month of 1951, making Waterloo the NPBL's most financially stable franchise. The club was even secure enough to organize a benefit game pitting former Waterloo and Cedar Falls high school players against each other, which attracted a crowd of 2,000 and raised almost $1,300 for polio patients.

Fans of the struggling NPBL could take some solace in reports that most NBA teams were faring no better. The Tri-Cities Black-hawks' attendance was down more than 23 percent, and rumors suggested that the club might be sold, relocated, or moved to the NPBL. An early January report in the *Waterloo Courier* captured an array of other difficulties troubling the NBA:

> The National Basketball Association was rocked by three explosions Tuesday when one team quit, another threatened to quit and a third filed a circuit court suit to get back into the professional league.
>
> The Washington Capitols, uncapitalized by two years of financial losses, announced they would disband after Tuesday night's game with Philadelphia. The New York Knickerbockers threatened to leave because of the "disgraceful conduct" of the Syracuse Nationals, while the Chicago Stags, who were in the NBA last season, filed a suit asking for the return of their franchise and $150,000 in damages.
>
> Washington, which has been losing $3,000 to $4,000 a week this season, quit because Owner Mike Uline "didn't feel like taking it any longer," General Manager Rob Foster said.
>
> Ned Irish, vice president of Madison Square Garden, made far more noise than Uline as he threatened to pull the Knickerbockers out of the league because of the tactics used by Player-Coach Al Cervi of the Nationals. Irish said Cervi deliberately sent mediocre players into the game to pick fights with taller stars of the opposing team so both would be thrown out to the advantage of the Nationals.
>
> The Chicago club filed its suit against [President Maurice] Podoloff and officials of the league's member teams. It alleged the defendants conspired to oust the Stags and turn the franchise over to Abe Saperstein, owner of the Harlem

Globetrotters. The Stags were kicked out of the league last summer after failing to repay a loan received from the league.[10]

Still, the NPBL was far closer to unraveling than the NBA. In Anderson, almost half the team quit, including Coach Frank Gates. The players had accepted reduced salaries earlier in the winter; they regretted the decision when their original contracts were not reinstated as business conditions seemed to be improving. Even those who remained with the Packers were not fully committed to basketball. Star forward Milo Komenich skipped a trip to Waterloo when the restaurant he owned did not have enough staff to stay open without him.[11]

Despite the turmoil in Anderson, the Packers were still atop the league standings at the end of the month. Kansas City and Denver had fallen to the bottom. Both western teams were playing only road games and receiving regular thrashings. In one matchup against the Sheboygan Red Skins, Denver was trounced 157–72. Nearly half the Refiners' members had decided they would wait at home for the club's future to be settled before suiting up again. As Denver and Kansas City limped along, barely having the required minimum number of players on their benches, the NPBL considered combining their rosters into one team.

By the end of January, members of the Hi-Spots and the Refiners who wanted to continue playing were exploring drastic alternatives. Some hoped their clubs could be relocated. Commissioner Doxie Moore tried to shuffle the two teams to Indiana: Kansas City to Marion (between Anderson and Fort Wayne) and Denver to Terre Haute. A 6,600-seat high school gym in Marion offered a plausible home, but terms could not be reached, due in part to the building's already heavy schedule. A potential owner in Terre Haute expressed reservations about finalizing the move. Ultimately, both destinations proved unworkable, and the NPBL was down to just four active teams when February began.

Before leaving the league for a barnstorming tour of Wyoming and Montana, the Frontier Refiners provided the Hawks with the last player added to the 1950–51 Waterloo roster. Early in the season, center Ed Dahler had made a strong impression when the teams met. On Denver's final trip to the Hippodrome, he scored 15 points in a 96–74 loss, then traded in his Refiners jersey when his contract was sold on the spot after the game. The next morning, he was traveling with the Hawks to Anderson.

Waterloo created space for Dahler by releasing Morgenthaler in the days that followed. The entertaining pivot man had started well, but during his final two weeks in Waterloo, he was held to 6 points or less in seven of eight games. All totaled, Morgenthaler made sixteen appearances for the Hawks and averaged 8 points per game. Packing his size-15 shoes, the vagabond center moved on to the next stop in a career that, like the NPBL, was approaching its end.

●

Although Terre Haute and Marion had not proved viable as landing pads for relocating NPBL teams, another Indiana city did join the league early in February. The Evansville Agogans were affiliated with a nearby Baptist ministry and financed by Bill Butterfield, a successful business supplies merchant whose son had NCAA experience as a center with the Purdue Boilermakers. The club had played an independent schedule before entering the NPBL. Its unusual name, derived from the word "agog," reportedly described "those with intense interest and excitement."[12] League officials bequeathed their newest members with the Denver Frontier Refiners' record, which was near .500 (14–15), a decision that would contribute to confusion about which games should be counted toward NPBL standings and which games should be considered exhibitions.

Starting the Agogans with fourteen wins put all five teams in contention for first place with fewer than six weeks remaining in the season. The *Waterloo Courier* reported these standings as of February 8:

Anderson Packers: 17–11
Sheboygan Red Skins: 17–12

Waterloo Hawks: 18–14

Louisville Aluminites: 16–14

Evansville Agogans: 14–15[13]

Less than a week later, the NPBL suffered its final franchise departure. The Reynolds Metals Company lost an estimated $120,000 on basketball during the 1950–51 season. In addition to offering high-priced contracts to lure several veteran players away from NBA teams, the Louisville Aluminites also chartered an airplane and flew to nearly all their road games, boosting travel expenses substantially. Still, Louisville's decision to leave the league was publicly attributed more to an on-court incident than to the club's extravagant spending.

Beginning in mid-January, the league began relying on home teams to schedule referees. With just six active clubs at that time, NPBL leadership determined that there were not enough games to keep a regular officiating staff active. The cost of paying referee travel expenses may have also factored into the decision. Suspicions of hometown favoritism arose quickly. Louisville's displeasure about referees roiled toward Sheboygan after a 108–97 loss, during which the Aluminites were charged with seven technical and fifty-three personal fouls.

"You just can't win on the road with the officiating," complained Louisville coach Alex Downing. "There's no sense in playing. We shot 47 percent against Sheboygan there and still got beat."[14] The Red Skins countered that the foul differential was the result of stylistic differences. Sheboygan coach Ken Suesens suggested that the Aluminites were a perimeter team, while his squad forced more fouls thanks to aggressive offensive tactics. "It is common knowledge," he claimed, "that the Red Skins, combining a fast-breaking style of offense with a liberal use of driving attacks at the basket from our set pattern, will usually draw more fouls, especially when the game is a close one."[15]

Waterloo players and fans soon empathized with Louisville. Three days after the Aluminites' aggravating defeat, the Hawks lost a 117–

102 contest at Sheboygan's Municipal Auditorium and Armory. Four Waterloo players were marooned on the bench after reaching the foul limit, and the Red Skins converted seven more free throws than the Hawks even attempted.

Notwithstanding their choice of referees, the Red Skins were the model for community-owned professional basketball teams and had operated on that basis since joining the NBL in 1938. The club's directors worked at a variety of Sheboygan businesses and institutions. Shares of Red Skins stock were available to purchase in the community for a dollar. Ahead of late-season home games during lean years, the team could appeal directly to the community to "help balance the budget" by attending late-season games or fund-raisers.[16] Generally, Sheboygan was competitive as a member of the NBL, finishing above .500 in eight of eleven seasons between 1938–39 and 1948–49. Although its only championship came in 1943, the organization reached the league finals on four other occasions, finishing as runners-up.

Suesens and Magnus Brinkman led Sheboygan from the NBL through the NBA merger and into the NPBL. Except for his service in World War II, Suesens had been a Red Skin since playing for the club as a rookie in 1938–39. The University of Iowa graduate had been on the court for the Hawkeyes when Pops Harrison was an assistant coach in Iowa City. A quick guard who excelled in match-ups against high-scoring opponents, Suesens was twice named to the NBL's All-League Second Team as a player. In 1948, he was entrusted with the position of head coach in Sheboygan, succeeding Doxie Moore.

Brinkman, meanwhile, was president of both the Red Skins and the NPBL. He took the first of those roles in 1944 and had served as a member of Sheboygan's board of directors since the club's third season. Like Hawks president Chris Marsau, Brinkman was also involved with local baseball during the summertime. Professionally, he was president of the DeLand Cheese Company, which by the mid-twentieth century had been producing dairy products for more than eighty years.

Sheboygan may have been known for making fine cheese and manufacturing furniture, but its industrial reputation was built around the plumbing components and other goods assembled by the Kohler Company. Known for bathroom fixtures and other durable home products, Kohler's factory was located just west of Sheboygan. The company thrived during the postwar years, churning out faucets, sinks, bathtubs, and more as builders across the country scurried to keep up with the demand for new houses. Because Kohler was the major employer in the community of just over 40,000, many Red Skins fans clocked in and out of the plant each day.

"Sheboygan was very interesting," remembered Wally Osterkorn, who joined the Red Skins at midseason from St. Paul. "The only thing you could do there was watch the snow come down during the winter and watch whatever sport was around. So we used to pack them into the old armory."[17] During Osterkorn's stay with the team, the two story Municipal Auditorium and Armory was actually only a few years old. Opened downtown just in time for Sheboygan's 1942–43 championship season, the gray concrete venue faced east toward Lake Michigan near where the Sheboygan River spilled into the lake. As many as 3,161 Red Skins supporters could pack tightly around the court, which had almost no out-of-bounds space between players and fans. The atmosphere in the building was often raucous and intimidating.

Beginning with Waterloo's 1948 entry into the NBL, the Hawks' first six regular-season trips to the armory resulted in losses. Through the end of 1950–51, Waterloo won only twice in Sheboygan during fourteen games there. However, the banks of the Cedar River proved kinder than the Lake Michigan shore during the series. The Hawks' very first NBL game was a home win against the Red Skins. In three seasons of matchups at the Hippodrome, Waterloo finished 10–5 when hosting Sheboygan.

In both 1948–49 and 1949–50, the Red Skins had slipped into the last playoff spot just ahead of the frustrated Hawks. As the teams became the two strongest organizations in the NPBL, their rivalry flourished. Their games included the December matchup in Waterloo that required police to restore order and a bruising January rematch at the armory. After absorbing an elbow from Bobby Cook, Johnny Payak returned from that game with black eyes and a broken nose. "That one was an accident," conceded Hawks coach Jack Smiley, "but the one in that game that wasn't an accident was one Don Boven caught. Bob Brannum of Sheboygan poked Boven and sent Boven down to one knee, and the officials didn't see it. We told Brannum that we didn't miss it even if the officials did."[18]

One of the best games ever played between the teams took place on a neutral court in mid-February 1951, far from either the Hippodrome or the armory. With both clubs seeking to generate additional revenue, they made a seven-day, in-season exhibition tour, playing nonleague games in Mitchell and Aberdeen, South Dakota, as well as Sioux City and Muscatine, Iowa. The novelty of professional basketball matchups in those cities yielded several thousand dollars for each team and provided the NPBL with insight about prospective host cities for new teams in 1951–52. The only game that counted toward the league standings during this wandering week was held in Fargo at the North Dakota Agricultural College (later North Dakota State) Fieldhouse.

For twenty-four minutes, 2,500 Fargo fans watched a complete performance by the Hawks. Waterloo scored from inside and out, relying on Boven in the pivot as counterpoint to Buckshot O'Brien, who displayed his range, showering down shots from a considerable distance. By intermission, both players had 19 points; O'Brien would finish with 31. The Hawks extended a 10-point first-quarter lead to a 58–44 advantage at halftime.

The game changed early in the third quarter when Boven was dismissed following his sixth foul. The Red Skins rallied, erasing the 14-point deficit, even going ahead briefly before the period ended in a 75–75 tie. With Waterloo's veteran interior defender on the bench, Sheboygan's big-small combination of Osterkorn and Johnny Givens mirrored what Boven and O'Brien had earlier done for the Hawks. Givens would complete the night with 24 points and Osterkorn with 21.

The Red Skins surged to a 7-point lead early in the fourth quarter, but the Hawks reeled themselves back into the game. Free throws from Murray Wier and a field goal by Joe Nelson capped a 13-4 run, returning the Hawks to a 97-95 lead with about three minutes to play. Max Morris tied the score on Sheboygan's next possession.

At this point, Smiley unexpectedly changed tactics. The Hawks' player-coach—with a reputation for an aggressive, running approach—was on the floor and called for the basketball. For more than two minutes, Smiley maintained his dribble, eluding all Red Skins efforts to force a turnover as the clock clicked into the closing seconds. Calling time-out to run a set play, Smiley waved for the inbounds pass. From just inside midcourt, he arced a shot that glanced off the backboard as it fell through the cylinder. Without enough time remaining for Sheboygan to attempt a response, Smiley's surprise stall and sensational shot won the 99-97 decision.

●

By Waterloo's reckoning, the win in Fargo against the Sheboygan Red Skins put the Hawks one and a half games ahead of the Anderson Packers and an additional half game clear of Sheboygan. The Packers visited Waterloo three times during the latter half of February. The Hawks won each of those matchups, helping flip Sheboygan to second place and Anderson to third. Waterloo's lead on Sheboygan was two and a half games by the time the Red Skins came to Waterloo Auditorium on the final day of the month.

This entertaining meeting teetered between the teams with regular lead changes through the midstages of the third quarter. From there, the Hawks stayed just out of reach until deep into the final period. Waterloo tried to stall with a 3-point lead and four minutes to go in regulation. More aggressive than they had been in Fargo, the Red Skins fouled, in addition to forcing at least one turnover. Eventually, Johnny Givens landed at the foul line, one free throw away from tying the score with just over a minute to play.

Givens missed.

The Hawks controlled the rebound and ended the game with a 7-0 run. Buckshot O'Brien was responsible for 3 of the final 7 points in the 84–76 win. For the game, his 18 points led five Waterloo players in double figures. The Red Skins could not slow the Hawks' guards: O'Brien and Murray Wier combined to record 27 of Waterloo's 45 second-half points.

At just 5 feet 9 inches, O'Brien was right at eye level with Wier. Both became popular with fans across the Midwest due, in part, to college success that had been achieved despite their small statures. O'Brien came to national prominence at Butler University after starring nearby for Washington High School in Indianapolis. In college, he played on the varsity basketball team all four years while splitting his athletic time as an infielder on the Bulldogs baseball squad, both coached by Tony Hinkle.

With Hinkle's guidance, O'Brien was able to improve his defense and diversify his offensive skills at Butler. Always highly accurate at long distances with a two-handed set shot, the guard found the touch for transition layups and running, airborne shots cutting out from the Bulldogs' set offense. From his sophomore season in 1947–48 through his senior year, O'Brien was Butler's leading scorer. Named an All-American by *Look Magazine* in 1949–50, he averaged more than 18 points per game that winter.

The NBA's Indianapolis Olympians acquired him ahead of the 1950–51 season. "They didn't really want me," O'Brien explained regarding his decision to leave his hometown. "They had Ralph Beard. . . . Beard and I play a bit alike, and Beard doesn't want any competition. Indianapolis didn't even come to me about signing, but told the newspapers I refused to sign because of money."[19]

The advent of the NPBL provided O'Brien with an alternative, and he joined the Grand Rapids Hornets. During five appearances for Grand Rapids against Waterloo, the Hawks could not hold O'Brien to fewer than 12 points. In an early December matchup, he was the key figure in a 16–0 run that helped the Hornets overcome a 14-point deficit to Waterloo. When Grand Rapids disintegrated midway through the schedule, the Hawks remembered O'Brien's exploits and made sure to acquire him. O'Brien lived up to Waterloo's expectations and more; in early March, after two months with the team, he was averaging more than 14 points per game.

Entering the final month of the schedule, the Hawks' roster still included six of the ten players who had appeared on opening night. Besides Murray Wier, veterans Jack Smiley, Don Boven, Wayne See, and Johnny Payak had all seen the season through. Stan Weber was the only original remaining rookie. In addition to O'Brien, Buddy Cate had been salvaged from Grand Rapids. Meanwhile, Joe Nelson and Ed Dahler had floated to Waterloo from the sinking St. Paul Lights and Denver Frontier Refiners, respectively.

This group of Hawks had solidified in early February to represent Waterloo during the closing games of the 1950–51 season as well as the forthcoming NPBL Tournament. Scheduled to be played in Waterloo during late March, the event was to include the league's three other remaining teams: Sheboygan, Anderson, and the Evansville Agogans. It was planned with a single elimination format to be completed entirely in one weekend. However, on March 12, one day after the Red Skins had edged the Hawks at the Hippodrome, Sheboygan players decided not to attend, "owing to the lack of a [monetary] guarantee and the necessity of staying . . . for three days."[20]

Although the Red Skins had played many heated games in Waterloo, little about their final visit suggested they would not want to return. Sheboygan led from the outset and enjoyed a 16-point margin at halftime. The Hawks cut the deficit to 8 by the end of the third quarter. The rally continued into the final minutes, and with two seconds remaining Buddy Cate was fouled with Waterloo down 102–100. Cate made his first shot, but the second free throw rimmed away; the loss ended a seventeen-game home winning streak and was the Hawks' first defeat at the Hippodrome since December 27, when they had also fallen to Sheboygan.

Pops Harrison quickly scheduled a pair of exhibition home games to replace the canceled NPBL tournament. One was against a team of African American college players; the other pitted Waterloo against a group of touring semiprofessionals. A previously slated contest versus a squad of top Big Ten seniors had already been arranged as an additional ticket sales opportunity. Although attendance had lagged during the schedule's closing weeks, the Hawks were still in a position to show a profit or, at least, break even from day-to-day operations. Adding the money received from selling Charlie Share's contract to the Fort Wayne Pistons, Waterloo was ensured of a financially positive season.

On a competitive basis, two final NPBL road games in Indiana would conclude the Hawks' league schedule. The two matchups were actually part of a four-game swing against Anderson and Evansville, with the first and last games of the trip planned as exhibitions. Waterloo started with losses in both the friendly and then the formal meeting with the Packers. That left the Hawks with one meaningful contest against the Agogans. Waterloo was ahead of Sheboygan by one game in the standings. Two Red Skins home games remained against Anderson later in the week. A Hawks win would result in a lead of one and a half games, clinching the NPBL title.

Payak and See, two of the four remaining players who had been with Waterloo the previous year, ensured a Hawks win. Payak's first eight field goal attempts all found their way through the net. He helped Waterloo spring to a 6-point lead in the first twelve minutes. Despite a disastrous second quarter, in which the Agogans outscored the Hawks 26–13, the visitors tied it up again early in the final period. From there, Waterloo pulled away to an 88–80 victory, with 31 total points from Payak and 17 from See, who had been voted the team's Most Popular Player by Waterloo fans. The two long-tenured Hawks combined to record twenty-two of the club's thirty-seven converted shots in the game.

Waterloo residents believed their team had clinched the NPBL championship with a 25–17 record, insurmountable for the 21–16 Red Skins. However, the story in Sheboygan was different. Three days after the Hawks' win in Evansville, a *Sheboygan Press* article proclaimed the Red Skins to be "proud possessors of the championship of the National Professional Basketball League."[21] Team organizers there put Sheboygan's results at 29–16, including 17–10 in games they counted toward the standings. By contrast, they believed the Hawks were actually 17–14.

The muddled situation was the result of many factors. Anderson skipped its final two games against the Red Skins—perhaps considered forfeits by the Wisconsin club and its fans—in retaliation for Sheboygan forcing the cancellation of the NPBL tournament (the Red Skins' response was to schedule an intriguing exhibition on one of those dates against a different team of Packers: the National Football League's Green Bay Packers). To a greater degree, the withdrawal of five original teams had led to repeated recalculation of the standings. While league bylaws indicated that games against those departed opponents were to be treated as exhibitions, in at least Denver's situation, the Frontier Refiners' results were reassigned to the Agogans. The policy may also have been modified as it related to games involving the Louisville Aluminites. Finally, the in-season exhibitions between member clubs were likely understood to count toward the standings by one team but not the other, especially after the original schedule began to be altered by December defections.

Considering all nights on which the Hawks took to the court believing the game would be counted in the league standings, their record was 32–24. Tallied by opponent, those results are as follows:

> Anderson Packers: 6–4
> Denver Frontier Refiners: 4–3
> Evansville Agogans: 2–0
> Grand Rapids Hornets: 4–1
> Kansas City Hi-Spots: 2–1
> Louisville Aluminites: 6–3
> Sheboygan Red Skins: 7–8
> St. Paul Lights: 1–4

In the week after the season ended, many newspaper readers across the country scanned a variation of this Associated Press story, whose headline "No Champion! Just Confusion" summarized the state of the NPBL:

There will be no playoff in the National Professional Basketball League, Commissioner Doxie Moore announced Thursday night.

The NPBL finished with three teams—Sheboygan, Waterloo, and Anderson—and a new member, Evansville. A playoff among the four had been scheduled at Waterloo, but Sheboygan had announced previously it would not take part. Moore said no league champion has been determined; the changing membership caused some confusion.[22]

9

I DON'T WANT TO GO OUT
WITH A BAD SHOWING

"I do know we're going to have professional basketball here next year. Who we're going to play or where, I don't know. Basketball has sold itself in Waterloo, and we're not going to let it drop."[1]

Waterloo Hawks president Chris Marsau made that confident statement to players, media, and the team's board members during a late March gathering to celebrate and reflect on the season. Team attorney Robert Buckmaster echoed the message, while Coach Jack Smiley and General Manager Pops Harrison each noted appreciation for the players on the 1950–51 roster. Members of the team dutifully expressed optimism about returning in the autumn and competing for spots on the squad.

However, the disintegration of the National Professional Basketball League illustrated the challenges of raising a new league. Only a limited number of viable markets with the proper venue, geography, and local interest existed. The failure of more than half the NPBL's teams in 1950–51 would give pause to investors considering whether to work with Waterloo and the remnant of the shriveled circuit. At a minimum, the fate of teams in Kansas City, Grand Rapids, and Louisville suggested that professional basketball needed considerable time to become established and a requisite willingness by team owners to absorb financial losses until then.

Other challenges also diminished the likelihood of creating a successful new basketball league. Although Waterloo was more than two years from having its own television station, TV sets were becoming more common in midwestern communities, especially in areas within close proximity to a broadcaster. The Federal Communications Commission had temporarily stopped issuing television licenses to new stations in 1948 in order to settle several technical questions. Yet the medium's potential to attract an increasing share of Americans' leisure time was ensured everywhere that new broadcasters went on the air. This was evident in any market with a station launched prior to the FCC freeze.

Elite basketball was also being closely scrutinized by fans and the press early in 1951. The sport still had a much broader following among college fans, and January's news of a New York–based college basketball point-shaving scandal captured regular headlines. For months, near daily newspaper dispatches indicated that many of the sport's star players from top NCAA programs were implicated. While the racketeering did not involve professional games, the effects reverberated into the NBA: Alex Groza and Ralph Beard of the Indianapolis Olympians lost promising careers when they were convicted of participating in illegal activities while playing at the University of Kentucky. At a minimum, pro teams were put on the defensive, explaining why gamblers would not be interested in attempting to fix professional contests.

Beyond these difficulties, the greatest uncertainty for professional basketball—and every other organized sport in America—was the Korean War. "Of several hundred experts who answered an Associated Press year-end questionnaire," explained a widely circulated wire story early in 1951, "fewer than a dozen are ready to predict that sports will do 'business as usual' in the face of the draft and possible all-out mobilization."[2]

The Hawks, along with other clubs, had already been affected during 1950–51. After Hal Haskins was signed from the defunct St. Paul Lights, a prior commitment to the Naval Reserve forced his almost immediate departure from Waterloo. By March 1951, many college and professional athletes had been called into service. The war—which looked at first as though it might be lost, then won, within just a matter of months—was nearly a year old. The addition of Chinese forces suggested that the conflict had the potential to escalate dramatically, including the dreaded scenario of all-out, multifront hostilities between the worldwide alliances of capitalist and communist powers. Less than six years after World War II, another conflict on that scale seemed possible.

Yet Marsau and Hawks leaders were determined to make good on the promise to keep professional basketball active in northeast Iowa. By early June, a group of prospective owners from throughout the region congregated at Sunnyside Country Club in Waterloo. In circumstances similar to the previous summer, numerous cities were rumored to be interested. Waterloo and Sheboygan led the effort and were the only certain clubs. Anderson was another strong early possibility. Community sponsors of the Packers may also have been approached by Doxie Moore, who was separately organizing a professional league in several Indiana cities. The Hoosier league was aborted when Moore accepted an offer to coach Milwaukee's new NBA team, the relocated Tri-Cities Blackhawks.

In July, the Waterloo-Sheboygan project looked certain enough to be formally announced. The Hawks and the Red Skins would play a sixty-game schedule in the new Western Basketball Association (WBA) with teams from Sioux City, Iowa, and Sioux Falls, South Dakota. The Hawks–Red Skins February exhibition tour had seemingly been vindicated by the interest in professional basketball that it had stirred in the Siouxland. Pops Harrison—who had helped coordinate that series of games—was named commissioner by WBA team representatives. Despite the evident conflict of interest, he was to work in that capacity while retaining his role as the Hawks' general manager.

At least two, but preferably four, additional cities were to join the new WBA, making it either a six- or an eight-club circuit. Cedar Rapids was consistently mentioned as a destination, and Harrison visited Coe College there to see if school leaders would be amenable to opening the campus gym for games. Detroit, Mason City (Iowa), Austin (Minnesota), Huron (South Dakota), and Peoria (Illinois) were reported to have an interest. By autumn, Moline also became a candidate after more than $27,000 in debts spurred the Tri-Cities Blackhawks to move to Milwaukee.

The new WBA was introduced in Syracuse under circumstances that would have been unthinkable the prior summer. Initially, Robert Buckmaster and, later, league president-elect Magnus Brinkman negotiated an affiliation arrangement with the NBA. Completing the particulars by the second week of August, the new association was to be a minor league, an outcome Waterloo and Sheboygan had refused to accept in 1950. The NBA-WBA pact depended on the WBA fielding at least six teams. "We agreed to that," indicated Buckmaster, "because we don't want to operate anyway with less than six clubs."[3]

Even with the promise of players supplied by the NBA and the potential to see stars from Minneapolis, Indianapolis, and other top clubs during NBA-WBA exhibition games, the final two franchise commitments were not easily secured. In early October, the new league still had only four members, and leaders of the Sioux City team were beginning to have misgivings. A final gathering was convened in early October at the Montrose Hotel in Cedar Rapids. Prospective owners who had flirted with the WBA were called upon to make a tangible commitment of $1,000 in order to open the season.

The league's formation rested partly on Otto Kohl of Cedar Rapids, and the meeting was delayed as his flight from Pennsylvania was stalled by weather. In business, Kohl owned a successful industrial gas company with operations across the U.S. Athletically, he had the distinction of coaching two of the state's greatest sports stars in central Iowa more than a decade earlier while they were in high school: Iowa Hawkeyes Heisman Trophy winner Nile Kinnick and Cleveland Indians ace pitcher Bob Feller. However, so close to the typical start of the professional basketball season, Kohl and the other owners could not finalize a plan for the embryonic league, even if the first games were delayed until early December.

Hopes for the WBA—and a 1951–52 basketball schedule in Waterloo—ended that day. "It is impossible to operate this year without a league," Marsau reported to the directors of Waterloo Basketball

Inc. when the organization convened ten days later and voted to disband.[4]

Some hope was expressed for professional basketball to return after a short hiatus. Some board members suggested that the remaining assets from the 1950–51 season could be used to fund a future team. However, major league basketball would not return to Waterloo or to the other small communities that had fielded clubs in the National Basketball League prior to the formation of the National Basketball Association. The Tri-Cities' move was a harbinger of what would follow in other former NBL markets. Even the larger cities with NBL roots would see their franchises depart. After the 1952–53 season, the Olympians disbanded, albeit in large part due to the absence of former player-owners Groza and Beard. The Pistons entered the 1957–58 season representing Detroit rather than Fort Wayne, while the Rochester Royals moved to Cincinnati the same summer. After George Mikan's retirement, the Lakers slipped toward the bottom of the standings, then moved from Minneapolis to Los Angeles in 1960. The Syracuse Nationals were the last vestige of the NBL through 1962–63, eventually relocating to Philadelphia and rebranding themselves as the 76ers.

●

Don Boven gave the Western Basketball Association—or any arrangement that would have kept professional basketball in Waterloo—every opportunity to develop. The Hawks' Most Valuable Player of 1950–51 finally signed with Milwaukee on October 18, days after Waterloo Basketball Inc. admitted the inevitability of not taking to the court in 1951–52 and just weeks before the NBA season was to begin. Boven's new team was also the Hawks; upon moving from Moline—where the name "Blackhawks" carried regional significance—the club shortened its nickname. With Doxie Moore installed as head coach, the former NPBL commissioner's familiarity with Boven may have spurred the team to make the deal. Other Milwaukee staff had also seen him play as a rookie in 1949–50 when Waterloo and Tri-Cities had both been in the NBA.

Boven was a fixture in Milwaukee's lineup, appearing in every game during the season, averaging nearly 10 points and just over five rebounds per game. His biggest performance was a 28-point showing against the Boston Celtics in February 1952. That night, he made fourteen of seventeen free throws before fouling out. Yet from the bench he was able to watch Milwaukee complete a fourth-quarter comeback to win, 97–95.

Also celebrating Milwaukee's victory that night was Dick Mehen, who had 13 points. After leaving Waterloo ahead of the 1950–51 season, Mehen played for the Baltimore Bullets, the Boston Celtics, and the Fort Wayne Pistons before being reunited with Boven on a different iteration of the Hawks. Mehen mirrored Boven in 1951–52, contributing similar scoring and rebounding statistics and sitting out just one game during what would be his final season. Milwaukee finished last that winter and was one of only two clubs in the ten-team NBA to miss the playoffs.

After his simultaneous departure from Waterloo with Mehen, Harry Boykoff had been nearly as wayward in the months that followed. Boykoff initially joined the Celtics, spending part of the 1950–51 season there with Mehen. Near the end of January, he was dealt to Tri-Cities, arriving not quite two months after Noble Jorgensen—another former Waterloo center—had been shipped to Syracuse. However, Boykoff was limited to just forty-eight total games in 1950–51 and scored fewer than 7 points per night. He retired at the end of the season.

Although Boykoff did not relocate with the Tri-Cities' franchise, two additional former Waterloo Hawks did play in Milwaukee. Johnny Payak arrived there via an unlikely route. Stepping away from league basketball temporarily, Payak joined up with a promoter from his hometown in charge of the Toledo Mercurys—the opposing team that toured with, played against, and lost to the Harlem Globetrotters throughout 1951–52. Waterloo and Bowling Green teammate Stan Weber was on the Mercurys, too. Later, Ed Dahler joined the squad after spending the first month of the season with the Philadelphia Warriors. It was a strenuous but financially rewarding season; the teams played almost every night for six months, and the players earned as much money as they had in the top professional leagues.

Payak joined Milwaukee in 1952–53, periodically having notable showings. He recorded 21-point performances in December and January, but during the sixteen games in between he reached double figures only twice. His season included sixty-eight appearances at 6.4 points per game. As the Hawks finished ninth and missed the playoffs again, Payak retired. "It was something you wanted to do your whole life, you know, play pro ball, and then it kind of wore thin," he remembered.[5]

No former Waterloo player went on to greater NBA success than Charlie Share, who spent two seasons in Fort Wayne before landing in Milwaukee during December 1953. The Hawks brought Share along when they relocated again—this time to St. Louis—in 1955. There, the organization's fortunes changed. Through Share's final season in 1959–60, St. Louis earned the best record in the NBA's Western Division four times. The Hawks fell in a seven-game NBA Finals series to the Celtics in 1957 but won a six-game championship rematch in 1958. Share contributed 8 points in the series-clinching 110–109 win.

By the time Share retired at age thirty-three, the former Bowling Green All-American had played in 596 regular-season games. In 1955–56, he grabbed a career-high 774 rebounds, ranking sixth in the league. Share also enjoyed his highest scoring average that winter: 13.6 points per game, well above the 8.3 cumulative mark of his nine NBA seasons. The onetime Celtics draft pick also earned a unique distinction on December 22, 1956. At Boston Garden, Share had 18 points in a 95–93 loss while matching up against a rookie making his NBA debut: future Hall of Famer Bill Russell.[6]

Buckshot O'Brien was one of the rare players who remained in pro basketball after Waterloo without eventually playing for the Tri-Cities–Milwaukee–St. Louis franchise. O'Brien initially returned to Indiana to take a high school coaching job for the 1951–52 school year. The Indianapolis Olympians still held his NBA rights, and O'Brien became a valuable addition to the team following the October arrests of Ralph Beard and Alex Groza related to the point-shaving scandal. The hometown guard played in every game that season and contributed 9 points per contest, helping the Olympians to the playoffs, where the team made a quick exit against the eventual champions, the Minneapolis Lakers. O'Brien started the next year with Indianapolis but moved on to Fort Wayne and eventually Baltimore as the campaign progressed.

After 1952–53, O'Brien, Payak, Jorgensen, and Boven all left the NBA. Boven returned to his hometown to teach at his alma mater — Western Michigan University in Kalamazoo — where he served as an assistant coach for the Broncos' basketball, football, and baseball teams as well as a physical education instructor. In 1958, he began an eight-year tenure as the school's head basketball coach. Boven's best season was in 1961–62, when the Broncos finished 13–11; overall, Western Michigan's record was 75–112 during his time leading the squad.

Johnny Payak doubtlessly encountered Boven in Kalamazoo and other midwestern university towns. They had first been college opponents, then professional teammates, and their circumstances changed again with Boven coaching and Payak working as a referee for the Mid-American Conference and other regional leagues. Payak's nearly two decades carrying a whistle were augmented by thirteen years spent as the conference's supervisor of officials.

Charlie Shipp also found a place in college basketball. Although he had never played in the NCAA, Shipp spent much of the 1950s and early 1960s working as a part-time coach for Purdue's freshman team.

Other former Waterloo players stayed in the game on the sidelines. Buckshot O'Brien served as a television analyst for Butler University games. Stan Weber led basketball and track squads while teaching high school math for thirty years in western Ohio. Prep coaching opportunities brought 1947 Pro-Hawk Price Brookfield to Indiana. Wayne See led the Camp Verde High School team — his alma mater — to runner-up results during consecutive appearances at the

Arizona Class 1A State Championship in 1967 and 1968. Stan Patrick was the long-standing basketball coach and athletics director at the high school in his wife's hometown of Belvidere, Illinois.

Jack Smiley briefly played with Patrick for a semiprofessional team sponsored by a Rockford, Illinois, jewelry store. However, Smiley's return to his home state was for business rather than basketball. He worked for several companies supplying agricultural products to farmers. Later relocating to the Des Moines area, Smiley opened his own seed treatment and water purification business in the early 1970s.

Leo Kubiak turned his competitive focus first to entrepreneurship and then toward a new sport. Thanks in part to a recommendation from his college coach, Harold Anderson, Kubiak became a successful executive for Autolite. He sold wiring and electrical components for the company before starting his own sporting goods business. Moving across the country from Toledo to Milwaukee to San Diego, Kubiak was a member of several country clubs and developed into an exceptional golfer. He qualified to play in ten U.S. Golf Association championships, including three U.S. Senior Opens. During the 1983 U.S. Senior Men's Amateur Golf Championship, he defeated two-time winner and USGA president William Campbell in a first-round match. "I have no complaints, but I would have liked a shot at the pro tour," Kubiak remarked while playing in his first Senior Open in 1981. "But it just never got to that point."[7]

Like Kubiak, both Boykoff and Patrick had notable pursuits outside their principal postbasketball careers. Living in Los Angeles after retiring as an accountant, Boykoff had several small acting roles while in his seventies. He appeared in commercials, a few television shows, and had a pair of credited roles in two feature-length films: *The Crew* and *Town and Country*. Patrick taught high school government classes in addition to coaching. The curriculum may have inspired his own political career, which included eight years of service on the Boone County (Illinois) Board of Commissioners as well as a prominent role within the county's Republican Party.

Regardless of their skills or renown, none of Waterloo's stars of the 1940s and '50s retired to live on a basketball fortune. Charlie Share founded a successful company in St. Louis that produced cardboard boxes. Dick Mehen served as a union executive for retail workers in Toledo and Cleveland. Dale Hamilton found his way back to his hometown, Fort Wayne, and returned to the Zollner Corporation as a permanent employee after playing basketball for the Zollner Pistons at the beginning of his pro career. Rollie Seltz became an insurance salesman. Johnny Payak opened an insurance agency in addition to officiating. Swede Roos sold parts from salvaged warships for Zidell Explorations in Portland, Oregon. Bennie Schadler worked as a pharmacist in northern California, eventually owning his own stores.

●

The Waterloo Hawks' final game at the Hippodrome was a lopsided exhibition win in front of fewer than a thousand spectators on March 24, 1951. Many of Waterloo's players spent the remainder of that month and much of April touring Iowa and playing a variety of opponents. These remaining Hawks won all eleven of their games. The group included Don Boven, Johnny Payak, Stan Weber, Buddy Cate, and Ed Dahler, but the star attraction for the Hawkeye-minded spectators was Murray Wier.

"We took the first $50 in the gate, and 60 percent after that," Wier said after the mostly in-state odyssey ended. "We didn't get rich, but we made money and had fun."[8] The participating Hawks split the proceeds, with attendance counts numbering mostly in the hundreds. Occasionally, they met local amateur teams. Other games were against top seniors collected from Iowa's small colleges to form an all-star squad.

The tour took Wier back to Iowa cities and towns where he had first become famous in high school. His modest origins—as well as his limited size—had helped endear him to fans from the time he transferred from the small high school in the town of Grandview to nearby Muscatine, a move that gave him an opportunity to play against some of southeast Iowa's best prep teams in 1943–44.

Although Muscatine was stopped short of the state tournament, Wier led the squad with 14 points per game and led the voting when writers from thirty-two Iowa daily newspapers selected their All-State team.

Wier gained national acclaim for his wavy red hair, impish features, and willingness to shoot from anywhere on the court while at the University of Iowa. As a 145-pound, 5-foot-8-inch freshman, he played forward and proved to be a timely reserve. With 7.8 points per game from the "Mighty Mite," the Hawkeyes flew to a 17–1 overall record and a Big Ten championship. As a junior, Wier averaged more than 15 points per contest, winning the first of two team MVP awards. In 1947–48, the conference's leading scorer was recognized as an All-American and the Big Ten's Most Valuable Player. He left college as Iowa's career scoring leader.

Wier spent two seasons with the National Basketball League's Tri-Cities Blackhawks but never consistently produced the sparkling scoring figures or dazzling play for which he had been known in college. However, he signed with the Waterloo Hawks in the summer of 1950, attracted by Jack Smiley's running, hustling style and the presence of Pops Harrison as general manager. Arriving in the city, Wier went to work on the night shift at Rath Packing while conditioning for the coming season. East side residents up late or rising early might have seen him running the fifteen blocks to and from the Rath plant, preparing for the three to six miles he would run during an average game for the Hawks.

Overcoming an early-season ankle injury, Wier established himself within the Hawks' rotation, playing in the manner to which he was accustomed, as described by *Waterloo Courier* sports editor Al Ney:

> Wier dribbles down the floor like a new born colt, with legs and arms wobbling in all directions.
> He starts to stumble when he drives in and you never know where his legs might be when he finally gets off a twister or an underhand shot. The next time he'll hook one over his head.

Even when he gets a clear shot, Wier can't just stand still and shoot. He kicks up his legs, waggles his shoulders and fires for two points.

Murray's answer to his own comeback is simple: "Gee, this is the first time I've had fun playing pro basketball."[9]

Perhaps Wier's best performance as a professional came on February 3, 1951, against the Sheboygan Red Skins. Playing in the backcourt with Buckshot O'Brien, he accumulated 19 first-half points as the Hawks swaggered to a 62–35 halftime lead in front of 3,573 Hippodrome fans. Sheboygan whittled its way to within 5 midway through the fourth quarter, but O'Brien—who finished the game with 21—and Wier quashed the comeback and extended the margin. A Wier layup just before time expired delighted the crowd and pushed the Hawks over 100. The basket closed Waterloo's 21–7 finishing run and gave Wier 28 points in the 101–82 win.

Wier ended the 1950–51 season with 9.6 points per game. Unlike Boven, he did not wait to see if the National Professional Basketball League or some other league might be refashioned in Waterloo for 1951–52. In early May, he announced his retirement as a player. "I've seen too many guys play too long. I don't want to go out with a bad showing," he said.[10]

Wier spent the summer in Waterloo working as a playground supervisor while preparing for a new job at Waterloo East High School. During the first of his thirty-eight years teaching at the school, he served as the sophomore basketball coach, but just before the 1952–53 school year he was promoted to varsity. His Trojans were not showy. The team typically employed a straightforward man-to-man defense. The backcourt pressure and opportunistic fast-breaking that Wier had enjoyed while playing for Jack Smiley and Pops Harrison were naturally part of his tactics at Waterloo East. Especially early in his coaching career, some of Wier's players were amused at the irony when he yelled "knock off that Globetrotter crap" if the team's fundamentals became too fancy.

The Trojans earned berths to the state tournament in 1953, 1954,

1960, 1961, 1965, 1968, and 1970 but fell short of a title each time. Wier built his last state tournament team in the 1973–74 season. By February that winter, the Trojans were on a double-digit winning streak. Students, local media, and all the city's east side began to speculate on how long the run might last.

Waterloo East reached the state championship game and claimed a complete victory versus Dubuque Wahlert, 71–54. Wier's wife, Marge, provided the *Waterloo Courier* headline for the Sunday morning paper that followed the title game: "This Is Murray's Year."[11]

Wier coached for two additional seasons, finishing with 372 victories, and remained at the school as an administrator until 1989. Memories of the corduroy-suited, sideline-stalking coach linger longer in Waterloo than the fleeting image of a wild-shooting, redheaded Mighty Mite. Many who smile while reflecting on their humorous teacher and coach might struggle to imagine the All-American forward in Iowa City or the star guard at the Hippodrome. Yet his students, players, and East High School forever own the legacy of Wier's 1950–51 season playing professional basketball for the Waterloo Hawks.

EPILOGUE

D anny Steiber was a basketball player at Waterloo West High School when winter arrived in 1949. As the season approached, he wandered into the city's downtown YMCA for some extra practice. Once courtside, he discovered a kindred soul: John Pritchard, a young Waterloo Hawks player just weeks into the NBA's first season. Although the 6-foot-9-inch center had the height for professional basketball and experience from playing four years at Drake, he would appear in just seven Waterloo games.

With one shoulder toward the Y's backboard, Pritchard lifted shot after shot up over his head and to the rim. Steiber watched. The ball dropped through the cylinder and slapped the net as it fell. After a few minutes and several baskets, Steiber asked Pritchard to show him the technique.

Not long after, Steiber was sinking his own hook shots at West High. Wahawks coach Glenn Strobridge—near the midpoint of a thirty-five-year Iowa High School Athletic Association Hall of Fame career—asked about the new development in Steiber's game. With the secret told, Steiber came to practice days later and found Pritchard working with the whole West High team.

Steiber, meanwhile, was close to the Hawks in another way, working courtside during games at the Hippodrome assisting with the local radio broadcasts. Arriving on game nights, the teenager always had a parking spot because he could wedge his secondhand Model A Ford between a tree and a utility pole just across from the auditorium's entrance. When Red Auerbach and the Tri-Cities Blackhawks visited, it was Steiber's job to trail the temperamental coach from one side of the Hippodrome to the other until Auerbach provided his starting lineup for radio announcer Gene Osborn.

Nearly seventy years after Waterloo's season in the NBA, few people in northeast Iowa remember professional basketball at the Hippodrome as vividly as Steiber. "Waterloo could have been the Green Bay of basketball if they'd have been able to play a second and third year in the NBA," he says.[1]

●

It would be more than half a century before any form of professional basketball returned to Waterloo. In the summers of 2005 and 2006, the Waterloo Kings (renamed the Cedar Valley Jaguars for their second season) attempted to revive Waterloo's dormant NBA heritage while taking to the court at the minor league level in the International Basketball League. Former Olympian and NBA All-Star Tim Hardaway made a cameo appearance the first year. Basketball Hall of Famer Dennis Rodman was a Jaguar for one night the next summer. Despite these well-publicized stints by former NBA notables, the team never developed a following and disappeared before 2007.

Another attempt to attract community support for a pro basketball club began in 2016. The Cedar Valley CourtKings started operations with the modest goal of helping players prepare themselves for professional opportunities overseas in international leagues or—the best case—a tryout with an NBA Development League team. Although the CourtKings claimed immediate on-court success and celebrated Midwest Basketball League championships in their first two seasons, average attendance has been limited to several hundred fans per game.

Waterloo itself is much different from the factory city of the postwar years. Although its celebrated population swell of the early twentieth century ended long ago, many changes suggest other types of growth. The community is rebuilding the business district at the city's core and revitalizing its riverfront. In spite of lingering racial issues, Quentin Hart was elected Waterloo's first African American mayor in 2015.

John Deere still makes tractors, although its campus between the

Cattle Congress grounds and downtown looks far different. Some of the operations are now housed in satellite locations around the community. The imposing red brick production buildings, which attracted shifts of workers each day for decades, have been torn down or repurposed; one has even been renovated as a hotel. Despite occasional strikes and periodic layoffs, Deere still represents the foundation of the city's industry.

The Hippodrome also remains. Renamed McElroy Auditorium and renovated in the early 1960s, the building was home to hockey in the community for a time. Today the auditorium hosts concerts and the cattle shows for which it was originally opened. The basketball floor purchased from the bankrupt Professional Basketball League of America was put into storage long ago. Even the echoes of the ball bouncing during a high school game have long been silent.

The same silence has settled on Rath Packing. A long, slow decline led to bankruptcy and dissolution in the 1980s while the community and much of the Midwest suffered through a farm crisis. Many of Waterloo's other factories and plants that were active in the 1940s and '50s have also disappeared.

A decade after Rath shut down, professional baseball was also extinguished in Waterloo. As minor league teams do, the White Hawks changed names and affiliations through the years. However, by the early 1990s, the ballpark, built just after World War II and expanded with a loan from the Chicago White Sox, was worn and lagging behind the facilities in other regional communities. Nine decades as a pro baseball city ended for Waterloo after the summer of 1993.

Like affiliated baseball and Rath Packing, NBA basketball is something Waterloo lost. More so than the others, basketball was taken away. "Waterloo pro basketball fans always have insisted that the city would be in the NBA today if the big city members had not forced out smaller cities," wrote the *Waterloo Courier* in its 1954 centennial edition.[2]

EPILOGUE

182

Seven decades removed, a curious basketball fan would be hard-pressed to find many reminders that Waterloo once had an NBA team. In fact, none of the various incarnations of the Hawks left behind any trophies from the little more than three years they spent on the court. There are no championship banners hanging from the Hippodrome rafters. There is no video archive offering evidence of games against the Knicks or Celtics or George Mikan's Minneapolis Lakers. When Murray Wier moved to Texas after retiring from Waterloo East, the community lost its last direct link to the men who played for the Hawks. Danny Steiber, now in his mid-eighties, is among a shrinking group of firsthand witnesses.

Meanwhile, the NBA has evolved into a worldwide phenomenon. Though the Waterloo Hawks, Anderson Packers, and Sheboygan Red Skins were left behind, other teams like the Tri Cities Blackhawks and Syracuse Nationals still have an active lineage in the current league. They endure, respectively reincarnated as the Atlanta Hawks and Philadelphia 76ers.

From warmer, sunnier retirement spots, Leo Kubiak and Wayne See are the only remaining former Hawks who can share the team's story.

"Nowhere did anybody anticipate how big the game would get. It's unbelievable how big it is," says Kubiak, reflecting on the current state of pro basketball compared to what he experienced. "Nobody thought it would be that way. . . . Kids nowadays who I meet who have talent, I say, 'Hey, you want to make the money? You want to make a living? Work your butt off and don't cause any trouble, and you'll make a lot of money as an athlete.'"[3]

Over time, the dream of kids on playground courts, aspiring to one day play professional basketball, hasn't changed. Like those kids today, See recalls the thrill of living out his childhood dream of playing in Madison Square Garden. Though his professional career was short-lived, his memories remain clear. He looks back in wonder at

EPILOGUE

183

the dream that brought him to America's most famous arena by way of Waterloo, Iowa.

"That was the center of all college and pro basketball, Madison Square Garden," says See, who played there with the Hawks in December 1949, scoring 8 points against the Philadelphia Warriors. "I went out in the middle of the floor and looked up at all of the seats to the rafters, like a little kid enjoying himself."[4]

APPENDIX A. INDIVIDUAL STATISTICS

These figures are gathered from contemporaneous numbers recorded by the *Waterloo Courier*, except in the case of the 1949–50 season, when official National Basketball Association statistics are provided. Marks from the 1950–51 National Professional Basketball League season are based on the fifty-six times the Hawks played believing the game would be counted toward the NPBL standings. Players were often asked to fill varying roles in the lineup at different stages of their careers by different teams and coaches. The positions noted in this appendix attempt to recognize how they were described upon arriving and during their tenure with the Hawks.

ANDERSON, CLARENCE "ANDY"   Guard   St. Mary's College

Season & league	Games	FG	FT	FTA	Pts	Avg	Assists
1947–48 PBLA	5	3	4	4	10	2.0	NA
Waterloo totals	5	3	4	4	10	2.0	NA

BOVEN, DON   Forward   Western Michigan University

Season & league	Games	FG	FT	FTA	Pts	Avg	Assists
1949–50 NBA	62	208	240	349	656	10.6	137
1950–51 NPBL	56	269	245	345	783	14.0	NA
Waterloo totals	118	477	485	694	1439	12.2	NA

BOYKOFF, HARRY   Center   St. John's University

Season & league	Games	FG	FT	FTA	Pts	Avg	Assists
1948–49 NBL	61	292	191	259	775	12.7	NA
1949–50 NBA	61	288	203	262	779	12.8	149
Waterloo totals	122	580	394	521	1554	12.7	NA

BROOKFIELD, PRICE   Forward   West Texas State/Iowa State Universities

Season & league	Games	FG	FT	FTA	Pts	Avg	Assists
1947–48 PBLA	6	28	10	17	66	11.0	NA
Waterloo totals	6	28	10	17	66	11.0	NA

BROWN, BILL   Guard   University of Maryland

Season & league	Games	FG	FT	FTA	Pts	Avg	Assists
1948–49 NBL	44	41	31	50	113	2.6	NA
Waterloo totals	44	41	31	50	113	2.6	NA

BRUCH, CARL   Iowa State University

Season & league	Games	FG	FT	FTA	Pts	Avg	Assists
1947–48 PBLA	1	0	0	0	0	0.0	NA
Waterloo totals	1	0	0	0	0	0.0	NA

CATE, BUDDY   Forward   Western Kentucky University

Season & league	Games	FG	FT	FTA	Pts	Avg	Assists
1950–51 NPBL	26	58	49	90	165	6.3	NA
Waterloo totals	26	58	49	90	165	6.3	NA

CLOYD, PAUL   Forward   University of Wisconsin

Season & league	Games	FG	FT	FTA	Pts	Avg	Assists
1949–50 NBA	4	6	2	5	14	3.5	1
Waterloo totals	4	6	2	5	14	3.5	1

DAHLER, ED   Forward/Center   Duquesne University

Season & league	Games	FG	FT	FTA	Pts	Avg	Assists
1949–50 NBA	12	18	28	43	64	5.3	NA
Waterloo totals	12	18	28	43	64	5.3	NA

DEATON, LES   Guard   Simpson College

Season & league	Games	FG	FT	FTA	Pts	Avg	Assists
1948–49 NBL	27	18	19	33	55	2.0	NA
Waterloo totals	27	18	19	33	55	2.0	NA

ELLEFSON, RAY   Center   Oklahoma A&M University

Season & league	Games	FG	FT	FTA	Pts	Avg	Assists
1948–49 NBL	7	4	8	12	16	2.2	NA
Waterloo totals	7	4	8	12	16	2.2	NA

FLICK, GORDON   Drake University

Season & league	Games	FG	FT	FTA	Pts	Avg	Assists
1948–49 NBL	2	2	0	0	4	2.0	NA
Waterloo totals	2	2	0	0	4	2.0	NA

GAINER, ELMER "AL"   Center/Forward   DePaul University

Season & league	Games	FG	FT	FTA	Pts	Avg	Assists
1948–49 NBL	35	33	30	41	96	2.9	NA
1949–50 NBA	15	9	6	8	24	1.6	7
Waterloo totals	50	42	36	49	120	2.4	NA

GIBSON, WARD "HOOT"   Center   Creighton University

Season & league	Games	FG	FT	FTA	Pts	Avg	Assists
1949–50 NBA	30	64	41	60	169	5.6	36
Waterloo totals	30	64	41	60	169	5.6	36

HAMILTON, DALE   Guard

Season & league	Games	FG	FT	FTA	Pts	Avg	Assists
1948–49 NBL	61	78	94	176	250	4.1	NA
1949–50 NBA	14	8	9	19	25	1.8	17
Waterloo totals	75	86	103	195	275	3.7	NA

HASKINS, HAL   Forward   Hamline University

Season & league	Games	FG	FT	FTA	Pts	Avg	Assists
1950–51 NPBL	3	0	2	4	2	0.7	NA
Waterloo totals	3	0	2	4	2	0.7	NA

JORGENSEN, NOBLE   Center   University of Iowa

Season & league	Games	FG	FT	FTA	Pts	Avg	Assists
1947–48 PBLA	6	27	17	26	71	11.8	NA
Waterloo totals	6	27	17	26	71	11.8	NA

KERBER, OTTO   Guard/Forward   DePaul University

Season & league	Games	FG	FT	FTA	Pts	Avg	Assists
1947–48 PBLA	6	16	3	8	35	5.8	NA
Waterloo totals	6	16	3	8	35	5.8	NA

KUBIAK, LEO   Guard   Bowling Green State University

Season & league	Games	FG	FT	FTA	Pts	Avg	Assists
1948–49 NBL	62	177	108	146	462	7.4	NA
1949–50 NBA	62	259	192	236	710	11.5	201
1950–51 NPBL	26	85	63	84	233	8.9	NA
Waterloo totals	150	521	363	466	1405	9.4	NA

LOWTHER, BOB Forward Louisiana State University

Season & league	Games	FG	FT	FTA	Pts	Avg	Assists
1948–49 NBL	9	11	5	7	27	3.0	NA
Waterloo totals	9	11	5	7	27	3.0	NA

LUSSOW, EMIL Forward University of Dubuque

Season & league	Games	FG	FT	FTA	Pts	Avg	Assists
1947–48 PBLA	5	3	0	0	6	1.2	NA
Waterloo totals	5	3	0	0	6	1.2	NA

LYNCH, DICK "LOOPER" Guard Loras College

Season & league	Games	FG	FT	FTA	Pts	Avg	Assists
1947–48 PBLA	6	13	2	7	28	4.7	NA
Waterloo totals	6	13	2	7	28	4.7	NA

MEHEN, DICK Forward University of Tennessee

Season & league	Games	FG	FT	FTA	Pts	Avg	Assists
1948–49 NBL	62	318	212	305	848	13.6	NA
1949–50 NBA	62	347	198	281	892	14.4	191
Waterloo totals	124	665	410	586	1740	14.0	NA

MENKE, KEN Guard University of Illinois

Season & league	Games	FG	FT	FTA	Pts	Avg	Assists
1949–50 NBA	6	6	3	8	15	2.5	7
Waterloo totals	6	6	3	8	15	2.5	7

MIKSIS, AL Center Western Illinois University

Season & league	Games	FG	FT	FTA	Pts	Avg	Assists
1949–50 NBA	8	5	17	21	27	3.4	4
Waterloo totals	8	5	17	21	27	3.4	4

MORGENTHALER, ELMORE Center New Mexico School of Mines/Boston College

Season & league	Games	FG	FT	FTA	Pts	Avg	Assists
1950–51 NPBL	16	47	35	56	129	8.1	NA
Waterloo totals	16	47	35	56	129	8.1	NA

NELSON, JOE Forward Brigham Young University

Season & league	Games	FG	FT	FTA	Pts	Avg	Assists
1950–51 NPBL	32	48	43	52	139	4.3	NA
Waterloo totals	32	48	43	52	139	4.3	NA

O'BRIEN, RALPH "BUCKSHOT" Guard Butler University

Season & league	Games	FG	FT	FTA	Pts	Avg	Assists
1950–51 NPBL	30	183	56	73	422	14.1	NA
Waterloo totals	30	183	56	73	422	14.1	NA

OLLRICH, GENE Guard Drake University

Season & league	Games	FG	FT	FTA	Pts	Avg	Assists
1949–50 NBA	14	17	10	14	44	3.1	24
Waterloo totals	14	17	10	14	44	3.1	24

ORR, JOHNNY Forward University of Illinois/Beloit College

Season & league	Games	FG	FT	FTA	Pts	Avg	Assists
1949–50 NBA	13	23	6	7	52	4.0	14
Waterloo totals	13	23	6	7	52	4.0	14

OTTEN, MAC Center Bowling Green State University

Season & league	Games	FG	FT	FTA	Pts	Avg	Assists
1950–51 NPBL	24	47	39	67	133	5.5	NA
Waterloo totals	24	47	39	67	133	5.5	NA

OVERTON, CLAUDE Southwest Oklahoma College

Season & league	Games	FG	FT	FTA	Pts	Avg	Assists
1950–51 NPBL	9	3	8	12	14	1.5	NA
Waterloo totals	9	3	8	12	14	1.5	NA

PATRICK, STAN Forward Santa Clara University/University of Illinois

Season & league	Games	FG	FT	FTA	Pts	Avg	Assists
1949–50 NBA	34	79	70	108	228	6.7	41
Waterloo totals	34	79	70	108	228	6.7	41

PAYAK, JOHNNY Forward/Guard Bowling Green State University

Season & league	Games	FG	FT	FTA	Pts	Avg	Assists
1949–50 NBA	35	86	108	152	280	8.0	78
1950–51 NPBL	56	234	251	326	719	12.8	NA
Waterloo totals	91	320	359	478	999	11.0	NA

PHELAN, JACK Forward DePaul University

Season & league	Games	FG	FT	FTA	Pts	Avg	Assists
1949–50 NBA	15	24	13	24	61	4.1	16
Waterloo totals	15	24	13	24	61	4.1	16

PRITCHARD, JOHN Center Drake University

Season & league	Games	FG	FT	FTA	Pts	Avg	Assists
1949–50 NBA	7	9	4	11	22	3.1	8
Waterloo totals	7	9	4	11	22	3.1	8

ROOS, HARRY "SWEDE" Forward

Season & league	Games	FG	FT	FTA	Pts	Avg	Assists
1947–48 PBLA	3	4	1	4	9	3.0	NA
Waterloo totals	3	4	1	4	9	3.0	NA

SCHADLER, BENNIE Forward Northwestern University

Season & league	Games	FG	FT	FTA	Pts	Avg	Assists
1948–49 NBL	42	92	39	58	223	5.3	NA
Waterloo totals	42	92	39	58	223	5.3	NA

SEE, WAYNE Guard Arizona State Teachers College

Season & league	Games	FG	FT	FTA	Pts	Avg	Assists
1949–50 NBA	61	113	94	135	320	5.2	143
1950–51 NPBL	56	252	82	133	586	10.4	NA
Waterloo totals	117	365	176	268	906	7.7	NA

SELTZ, ROLLIE Guard Hamline University

Season & league	Games	FG	FT	FTA	Pts	Avg	Assists
1948–49 NBL	62	186	127	173	499	8.0	NA
Waterloo totals	62	186	127	173	499	8.0	NA

SHARE, CHARLIE Center Bowling Green State University

Season & league	Games	FG	FT	FTA	Pts	Avg	Assists
1950–51 NPBL	19	62	86	128	210	11.0	NA
Waterloo totals	19	62	86	128	210	11.0	NA

SHIPP, CHARLIE Guard

Season & league	Games	FG	FT	FTA	Pts	Avg	Assists
1948–49 NBL	56	99	70	106	268	4.7	NA
1949–50 NBA	23	35	37	51	107	4.7	46
Waterloo totals	79	134	107	157	375	4.7	NA

SMILEY, JACK Guard University of Illinois

Season & league	Games	FG	FT	FTA	Pts	Avg	Assists
1949–50 NBA	47	92	124	177	308	6.6	147
1950–51 NPBL	56	99	100	141	298	5.3	NA
Waterloo totals	103	191	224	318	606	5.9	NA

SPEHN, JACK   Forward   University of Detroit

Season & league	Games	FG	FT	FTA	Pts	Avg	Assists
1947–48 PBLA	6	12	6	13	30	5.0	NA
Waterloo totals	6	12	6	13	30	5.0	NA

SPENCER, JACK   Guard   University of Iowa

Season & league	Games	FG	FT	FTA	Pts	Avg	Assists
1948–49 NBL	10	6	4	4	16	1.6	NA
Waterloo totals	10	6	4	4	16	1.6	NA

STUMP, GENE   Guard/Forward   DePaul University

Season & league	Games	FG	FT	FTA	Pts	Avg	Assists
1949–50 NBA	26	36	30	40	102	3.9	21
Waterloo totals	26	36	30	40	102	3.9	21

TOUGH, BOB "RED"   Guard   St. John's University

Season & league	Games	FG	FT	FTA	Pts	Avg	Assists
1949–50 NBA	21	32	32	34	96	4.6	36
Waterloo totals	21	32	32	34	96	4.6	36

VODICK, NICK   Forward   Northwestern University

Season & league	Games	FG	FT	FTA	Pts	Avg	Assists
1947–48 PBLA	6	12	3	9	27	4.5	NA
Waterloo totals	6	12	3	9	27	4.5	NA

VOLLERS, BOB   Forward   University of Iowa

Season & league	Games	FG	FT	FTA	Pts	Avg	Assists
1950–51 NPBL	18	18	7	11	43	2.3	NA
Waterloo totals	18	18	7	11	43	2.3	NA

WAREHAM, DAVE   Guard/Forward   Loras College

Season & league	Games	FG	FT	FTA	Pts	Avg	Assists
1948–49 NBL	3	1	1	1	3	1.0	NA
Waterloo totals	3	1	1	1	3	1.0	NA

WEBER, STAN   Forward/Center   Bowling Green State University

Season & league	Games	FG	FT	FTA	Pts	Avg	Assists
1950–51 NPBL	54	190	102	185	482	8.9	NA
Waterloo totals	54	190	102	185	482	8.9	NA

WHITE, OLLIE   Guard   Michigan State University

Season & league	Games	FG	FT	FTA	Pts	Avg	Assists
1947–48 PBLA	6	8	9	13	25	4.2	NA
Waterloo totals	6	8	9	13	25	4.2	NA

WIER, MURRAY   Guard   University of Iowa

Season & league	Games	FG	FT	FTA	Pts	Avg	Assists
1950–51 NPBL	51	186	117	194	489	9.6	NA
Waterloo totals	51	186	117	194	489	9.6	NA

FG: field goals made, FT: free throws made, FTA: free throws attempted, Pts: points, Avg: scoring average. Assists were not formally tracked in the PBLA, NBL, or NPBL.

APPENDIX B. LEAGUE STANDINGS

The final standings from each season and league in which Waterloo played professionally appear below. These records are taken from the *Waterloo Courier*.

PROFESSIONAL BASKETBALL LEAGUE OF AMERICA: 1947–48

Northern Division

Chicago American Gears	8–0	1.000
St. Paul Saints	6–3	.666
Grand Rapids Rangers	3–3	.500
Louisville Colonels	2–4	.333
Omaha Omahawks	2–4	.333
Kansas City Blues	1–5	.167
Waterloo Pro-Hawks	1–5	.167
St. Joseph Outlaws	1–6	.143

Southern Division

Houston Mavericks	2–0	1.000
Atlanta Crackers	7–1	.875
Birmingham Skyhawks	5–2	.714
Tulsa Ranchers	7–3	.700
Chattanooga Majors	3–3	.500
Oklahoma City Drillers	2–3	.400
New Orleans Hurricanes	3–5	.375
Springfield Squires	1–7	.125

Note: The PBLA announced it had disbanded on November 13, 1947.

NATIONAL BASKETBALL LEAGUE: 1948–49

Western Division

Oshkosh All-Stars	37–27	.578
Tri-Cities Blackhawks	36–28	.563
Sheboygan Red Skins	35–29	.547
Waterloo Hawks	30–32	.484
Denver Nuggets	18–44	.290

Eastern Division

Anderson Packers	49–15	.766
Syracuse Nationals	40–23	.635
Hammond Calumet Buccaneers	21–41	.339
Dayton Rens	16–43	.271

Note: The Anderson Packers won the NBL Championship. The Dayton Rens' standings include a 2–17 record inherited from the Detroit Vagabond Kings. The Rens themselves were 14–26 in league play.

NATIONAL BASKETBALL ASSOCIATION: 1949–50

Eastern Division

Syracuse Nationals	51–13	.797
New York Knicks	40–28	.588
Washington Capitols	32–36	.471
Philadelphia Warriors	26–42	.382
Baltimore Bullets	25–43	.368
Boston Celtics	22–46	.324

Central Division

Rochester Royals	51–17	.750
Minneapolis Lakers	51–17	.750
Chicago Stags	40–28	.588
Fort Wayne Zollner Pistons	40–28	.588
St. Louis Bombers	26–42	.382

Western Division

Indianapolis Olympians	39–25	.609
Anderson Packers	37–27	.578
Tri-Cities Blackhawks	29–35	.453
Sheboygan Red Skins	22–40	.355
Waterloo Hawks	19–43	.306
Denver Nuggets	11–51	.177

Note: The Minneapolis Lakers won the NBA Championship.

NATIONAL PROFESSIONAL BASKETBALL LEAGUE: 1950–51

Waterloo Hawks	25–17	.595	17–14	.549
Sheboygan Red Skins	21–16	.567	17–10	.629
Anderson Packers	16–18	.471	12–12	.500
Evansville Agogans	9–21	.300	6–16	.271
St. Paul Lights	12–8	.600		
Denver Nuggets	14–15	.483		
Louisville Aluminites	13–14	.481		
Grand Rapids Hornets	4–11	.367		
Kansas City Hi-Spots	1–18	.053		

Note: There was no playoff. The Waterloo Hawks and the Sheboygan Red Skins both claimed the championship. The second column of records and win percentages represents the final standings as reported by the *Sheboygan Press*. Evansville's record includes elements of the Denver Frontier Refiners' record; the Agogans themselves were 0–6 in league play. Records for Denver, Louisville, St. Paul, Grand Rapids, and Kansas City are as reported when the teams disbanded, including any adjustments for games that had been reclassified as exhibitions.

APPENDIX C. GAME-BY-GAME RESULTS

Exhibition games are indicated by an asterisk after the game date. Games played at neutral sites are noted in parentheses. The Hawks played their last three games of the 1950–51 season against touring teams.

Professional Basketball League of America: 1947–48

Oct. 27	vs. St. Paul		49–55 (OT)	L
Nov. 1	vs. Chicago		56–82	L
Nov. 3	vs. New Orleans		53–58	L
Nov. 5	at Tulsa		44–46 (OT)	L
Nov. 8	vs. St. Joseph	W	45–36	
Nov. 10	vs. Omaha		61–63	L

National Basketball League: 1948–49

Oct. 21*	Tri-Cities		38–47	L	(Tama, IA)
Oct. 24*	Famous Globe Trotters	W	57–35		(Marshalltown, IA)
Oct. 25*	Famous Globe Trotters	W	69–40		(Newton, IA)
Oct. 26*	Famous Globe Trotters	W	54–25		(Centerville, IA)
Oct. 27*	Famous Globe Trotters	W	63–40		(Humboldt, IA)
Oct. 28*	Famous Globe Trotters	W	55–33		(Denison, IA)
Oct. 30*	vs. Cedar Rapids Danceland	W	59–33		
Oct. 31*	vs. Famous Globe Trotters	W	57–37		
Nov. 1*	Tri-Cities		48–62	L	(Dubuque, IA)
Nov. 7	vs. Sheboygan	W	64–61		
Nov. 8*	Oshkosh		50–60	L	(Eau Claire, WI)
Nov. 9*	Oshkosh	W	65–69		(La Crosse, WI)
Nov. 10	vs. Denver	W	51–48 (OT)		
Nov. 14	vs. Detroit	W	72–53		
Nov. 16	at Tri-Cities		63–67	L	
Nov. 17	vs. Hammond	W	51–45		
Nov. 21	vs. Oshkosh	W	54–49		
Nov. 24	vs. Syracuse	W	68–59		
Nov. 25	at Hammond	W	58–57		

Nov. 28	vs. Tri-Cities	W	61–59	
Nov. 30	at Detroit	W	65–63	
Dec. 2	at Syracuse		59–68	L
Dec. 3	at Syracuse		71–72	L
Dec. 5	vs. Oshkosh	W	41–36	
Dec. 6	Oshkosh		56–58	L (Appleton, WI)
Dec. 7	Oshkosh		49–64	L (Elgin, IL)
Dec. 9	at Anderson		59–71	L
Dec. 12	vs. Denver		51–53	L
Dec. 14	at Denver		60–65	L
Dec. 16	at Denver		51–69	L
Dec. 19	vs. Oshkosh	W	47–46	
Dec. 22	vs. Anderson	W	50–45	
Dec. 23	at Sheboygan		56–77	L
Dec. 26	at Hammond		61–64	L
Dec. 28	at Oshkosh		65–71	L
Dec. 29	vs. Anderson		50–51	L
Dec. 30	at Anderson		68–80	L
Jan. 2*	vs. Cedar Rapids Raiders	W	62–45	
Jan. 3*	at Cedar Rapids Raiders	W	54–46	
Jan. 5	vs. Sheboygan	W	52–43	
Jan. 6	at Sheboygan		51–54	L
Jan. 9	vs. Oshkosh	W	62–39	
Jan. 12	vs. Anderson	W	46–40	
Jan. 13	at Tri-Cities		68–72	L
Jan. 16	vs. Dayton	W	59–45	
Jan. 19	vs. Tri-Cities		42–45	L
Jan. 26	vs. Denver	W	82–60	
Jan. 30	vs. Sheboygan	W	60–46	
Feb. 2	vs. Tri-Cities	W	79–50	
Feb. 3	at Tri-Cities	W	63–56	
Feb. 6	at Syracuse		75–79 (OT)	L
Feb. 7	at Anderson		63–74	L
Feb. 9	vs. Dayton	W	56–44	
Feb. 10	at Sheboygan		63–78	L
Feb. 12	at Oshkosh		50–51	L
Feb. 13	vs. Sheboygan		54–55	L
Feb. 15	Dayton		52–53	L (Springfield, OH)

Feb. 16	at Tri-Cities		58–63	L	
Feb. 20	vs. Anderson		54–58	L	
Feb. 21	Syracuse		65–76	L	(Rockford, IL)
Feb. 23	vs. Hammond	W	63–61		
Feb. 25	vs. Hammond	W	65–52		
Feb. 27	at Hammond	W	73–63		
Mar. 2	vs. Hammond	W	64–58		
Mar. 3	at Sheboygan		57–63	L	
Mar. 6	at Hammond		72–81	L	
Mar. 7	at Anderson		53–69	L	
Mar. 9	Syracuse		51–61	L	(Albany, NY)
Mar. 10	at Syracuse	W	65–61		
Mar. 13	vs. Tri-Cities		49–50	L	
Mar. 15	at Denver	W	60–58 (OT)		
Mar. 17	at Denver	W	68–64		
Mar. 20	vs. Dayton	W	52–50		
Mar. 26	Dayton		45–61	L	(Anderson, IN)
Mar. 31	vs. Syracuse	W	69–68		

National Basketball Association: 1949–50

Oct. 13*	Tri-Cities	W	83–82 (3OT)		(Muscatine, IA)
Oct. 22*	at Albert Lea Packers	W	70–47		
Oct. 25*	Sheboygan	W	70–63		(Cedar Falls, IA)
Oct. 29*	Sheboygan		67–82	L	(Mason City, IA)
Nov. 2	vs. New York		60–68	L	
Nov. 6	vs. Boston	W	80–66		
Nov. 9	vs. Denver	W	80–65		
Nov. 10	at Fort Wayne		59–89	L	
Nov. 12	at Tri-Cities		89–99	L	
Nov. 13	vs. Anderson		69–81	L	
Nov. 16	vs. Sheboygan		73–76	L	
Nov. 17	at Sheboygan		95–97	L	
Nov. 19	at Indianapolis		74–106	L	
Nov. 20	vs. Tri-Cities	W	75–62		
Nov. 22*	at Wartburg College	W	72–35		
Nov. 23	vs. Rochester		71–90	L	
Nov. 26	at Rochester		95–120	L	
Nov. 27	at Syracuse		62–80	L	

Nov. 28	at Anderson		87–101	L
Nov. 30	vs. Fort Wayne	W	95–71	
Dec. 2	at Denver		63–74	L
Dec. 4	at Denver		76–85	L
Dec. 7	vs. Sheboygan	W	77–67	
Dec. 10	vs. Anderson		83–87 (OT)	L
Dec. 14	vs. Philadelphia		70–73	L
Dec. 16	Baltimore	W	77–75	(Philadelphia, PA)
Dec. 17	Philadelphia		72–81	L (New York, NY)
Dec. 20	vs. Syracuse		70–95	L
Dec. 21	Chicago		70–78	L (St. Louis, MO)
Dec. 22	at Anderson		84–101	L
Dec. 25	vs. Indianapolis	W	97–93 (OT)	
Dec. 28	vs. Chicago		80–87	L
Dec. 29	at Sheboygan		92–94	L
Dec. 31	vs. Minneapolis		68–86	L
Jan. 1	at St. Louis		79–91	L
Jan. 3	vs. Sheboygan		69–73	L
Jan. 5	New York		70–82	L (Baltimore, MD)
Jan. 7	at Washington		83–101	L
Jan. 8	at Syracuse		68–84	L
Jan. 10	vs. Syracuse	W	86–84 (OT)	
Jan. 12	at Anderson		69–80	L
Jan. 13	at Indianapolis		64–80	L
Jan. 15	at Tri-Cities		80–84	L
Jan. 18	vs. St. Louis	W	80–69	
Jan. 19	Indianapolis		87–104	L (Chicago, IL)
Jan. 21	vs. Denver	W	88–84	
Jan. 24	at Indianapolis		69–107	L
Jan. 25	vs. Denver	W	104–83	
Jan. 29	vs. Tri-Cities		79–85	L
Feb. 1	vs. Anderson		73–86	L
Feb. 3	at Syracuse		79–103	L
Feb. 4	Boston		82–100	L (Providence, RI)
Feb. 8	vs. Washington	W	77–70	
Feb. 12	at Syracuse		98–102	L
Feb. 13	at Anderson		80–93	L
Feb. 15	vs. Indianapolis	W	76–74	

Feb. 17	at Minneapolis		74–80	L	
Feb. 18	at Tri-Cities		93–116	L	
Feb. 19	vs. Tri-Cities	W	84–63		
Feb. 22	vs. Baltimore		77–84	L	
Feb. 23	at Sheboygan	W	86–81		
Feb. 26	vs. Denver	W	100–76		
Mar. 1	vs. Syracuse		72–93	L	
Mar. 8	vs. Denver	W	97–68		
Mar. 12	vs. Indianapolis		89–90	L	
Mar. 15	vs. Sheboygan	W	87–69		
Mar. 19	vs. Tri-Cities	W	79–77		

National Professional Basketball League: 1950–51

Oct. 26*	St. Paul		65–69	L	(Willmar, MN)
Oct. 30*	Kansas City		68–75	L	(St. Joseph, MO)
Nov. 2*	Denver	W	69–67		(Somonauk, IL)
Nov. 5	at Kansas City		82–84	L	
Nov. 6*	Kansas City	W	73–71		(Postville, IA)
Nov. 8*	Sid's Steak House	W	102–68		(Decorah, IA)
Nov. 9*	Des Moines Trotters	W	93–51		(Muscatine, IA)
Nov. 12	vs. Louisville	W	67–65 (OT)		
Nov. 14	at St. Paul		72–79	L	
Nov. 15	vs. Anderson	W	84–82		
Nov. 16*	St. Paul		69–76	L	(Waverly, IA)
Nov. 19	vs. St. Paul		74–75	L	
Nov. 21	at Grand Rapids	W	86–83		
Nov. 23	at Sheboygan	W	96–86		
Nov. 24	at St. Paul		73–86	L	
Nov. 26	vs. Grand Rapids	W	84–69		
Nov. 29	vs. Anderson	W	103–69		
Nov. 30*	Des Moines Trotters	W	123–66		(Iowa City, IA)
Dec. 2	vs. St. Paul	W	99–71		
Dec. 3	vs. Kansas City	W	108–67		
Dec. 6	vs. Sheboygan	W	89–80		
Dec. 10	vs. Grand Rapids		77–82	L	
Dec. 13	at Denver		76–83	L	
Dec. 15	at Denver		82–88	L	
Dec. 17	vs. Grand Rapids	W	114–70		

Dec. 19	at St. Paul		70–76	L	
Dec. 20	vs. Sheboygan	W	90–84		
Dec. 21	at Sheboygan		79–122	L	
Dec. 23	vs. Denver		51–52	L	
Dec. 24	at Louisville		91–101	L	
Dec. 25	at Grand Rapids	W	76–58		
Dec. 27	vs. Sheboygan		74–77	L	
Dec. 30	vs. Louisville	W	88–75		
Jan. 3	vs. Denver	W	81–61		
Jan. 4	at Anderson		69–116	L	
Jan. 6	vs. Louisville	W	82–76		
Jan. 10	vs. Denver	W	89–66		
Jan. 11	at Sheboygan		88–102	L	
Jan. 14	vs. Kansas City	W	128–73		
Jan. 17	Louisville		82–98	L	(Owensboro, KY)
Jan. 18	at Louisville	W	85–69		
Jan. 19	at Anderson		82–92	L	
Jan. 21	at Sheboygan		73–87	L	
Jan. 24	vs. Denver	W	125–75		
Jan. 27	vs. Anderson	W	88–69		
Jan. 28	vs. Denver	W	96–74		
Jan. 30	at Anderson		88–97	L	
Feb. 1	at Louisville		66–76	L	
Feb. 3	vs. Sheboygan	W	101–82		
Feb. 7	vs. Louisville	W	108–91		
Feb. 10	vs. Louisville	W	93–69		
Feb. 11	at Sheboygan		102–117	L	
Feb. 14*	Sheboygan		85–95	L	(Aberdeen, SD)
Feb. 15	Sheboygan	W	99–97		(Fargo, ND)
Feb. 17	vs. Anderson	W	86–76		
Feb. 18*	Sheboygan	W	114–88		(Mitchell, SD)
Feb. 19*	Sheboygan	W	98–91		(Sioux City, IA)
Feb. 20*	Sheboygan		95–105	L	(Muscatine, IA)
Feb. 21	vs. Anderson	W	84–77		
Feb. 24	vs. Anderson	W	103–92		
Feb. 28	vs. Sheboygan	W	84–76		
Mar. 1	at Sheboygan		89–101	L	
Mar. 3	vs. Sheboygan	W	107–103		

Mar. 8	at Sheboygan		76–93	L	
Mar. 10	vs. Evansville	W	118–88		
Mar. 11	vs. Sheboygan		101–102	L	
Mar. 12*	Anderson		84–99	L	(Brazil, IN)
Mar. 13	at Anderson		67–83	L	
Mar. 14	at Evansville	W	88–80		
Mar. 15*	Evansville	W	65–56		(Mt. Carmel, IL)
Mar. 18*	vs. Chicago Colored Collegians	W	102–52		
Mar. 21*	vs. Big Ten All-Stars	W	87–77		
Mar. 24*	vs. Chicago Majors	W	104–69		

NOTES

INTRODUCTION

1   See espn.com/nba/attendance/_/year/2014. Retrieved on August 14, 2017.

2   See, for example, usatoday.com/story/sports/nba/2014/02/13/adam-silver -commissioner-china-india-nfl-growth-basketball-age-limit/5464811/. Retrieved on August 14, 2017.

3   Millie Saffold, quoted in Gwenne Culpepper, "Shattered Dreams," *Waterloo Courier*, February 4, 1990.

4   See the National Basketball League's *PRO Magazine*, 1949 edition.

5   William Gates, quoted in Robert W. Peterson, *Cages to Jump Shots: Pro Basketball's Early Years* (New York: Oxford University Press, 1990), 13.

6   Phone interview with Leo Kubiak, April 22, 2017.

7   Clause 6 of Wayne See's 1949–50 contract with the Hammond Calumet Buccaneers, dated May 16, 1949, prior to the NBL-BAA merger.

8   Al Ney, "The Sports Alley," *Waterloo Courier*, November 25, 1949.

9   Clause 6 of Wayne See's 1949–50 NBA contract with the Waterloo Hawks, dated October 15, 1949.

10 Phone interview with Leo Kubiak, April 22, 2017.

1. ORGANIZED PROFESSIONAL BASKETBALL

1   New York Knicks coach Joe Lapchick, quoted in Jack Cuddy, "Rival Coach Rates George Mikan Tops," *Eugene Register-Guard*, February 28, 1949.

2   Richard F. Triptow, *The Dynasty That Never Was: Chicago's First Professional Basketball Champions, the American Gears* (n.p.: R. F. Triptow, 1997), 119.

3   Ibid., 137–44.

4   "Pro Basketball Here—Waterloo, Des Moines in League with Gears," *Waterloo Courier*, August 14, 1947.

5   "Waterloo Stood on Threshold of Boom Back in 1900," *Waterloo Courier*, December 29, 1950.

6   "$25,000 for New Seats at Stadium," *Waterloo Courier*, September 17, 1947.

7   Charles Einstein, "Des Moines Out; Waterloo In: Chicago Banker Heads New Pro Cage League," *Waterloo Courier*, September 5, 1947.

8   Ibid.

9 "Lack of Skilled Labor Slows Building," *Waterloo Courier*, August 3, 1947.

10 The Three-I League acquired its name by having teams in Iowa, Illinois, and Indiana.

11 Interview with Danny Steiber, Waterloo, August 18, 2017.

12 "Chicago Gears Win," *Waterloo Courier*, April 10, 1947.

13 Al Ney, "The Sports Alley," *Waterloo Courier*, October 1, 1947.

14 "Coach Seeking Talent; Build $8,500 Court," *Waterloo Courier*, September 18, 1947.

15 "Add Forward, Guard; Cagers Ready to Open," *Waterloo Courier*, October 26, 1947.

16 Advertisement, *Waterloo Courier*, October 20, 1947.

17 Al Ney, "Pro-Hawks Slip in Overtime," *Waterloo Courier*, October 28, 1947.

18 Ros Jensen, "Gears Romp, 82–56," *Waterloo Courier*, November 2, 1947.

19 Al Ney, "Professional Basketball League of America Folds," *Waterloo Courier*, November 13, 1947.

20 "New Pro Cage Loop Disbands," *Schenectady Gazette*, November 14, 1947.

21 Al Ney, "The Sports Alley," *Waterloo Courier*, November 19, 1947, and Bob Herdien, "Abe Is Lucky: Remember White?" *Waterloo Courier*, January 2, 1963.

22 Al Ney, "The Sports Alley," *Waterloo Courier*, November 14, 1947.

23 "Junior Chamber to Buy Pro-Hawk Floor for $4,000," *Waterloo Courier*, January 30, 1948.

2. THE REAL MAJOR LEAGUE THING

1 Robert W. Peterson, *Cages to Jump Shots: Pro Basketball's Early Years* (New York: Oxford University Press, 1990), 164.

2 Al Ney, "The Sports Alley," *Waterloo Courier*, May 26, 1948.

3 "Major Pro Loop Okehs City Switch," *Waterloo Courier*, August 17, 1948.

4 Information about Andy George's war service is compiled from declassified OSS files held in the National Archives at College Park, Maryland.

5 "Major Pro Loop Okehs City Switch," *Waterloo Courier*, August 17, 1948.

6 W. Blaine Patton, "Local Pro Quintet Wins First League Tilt from Akron Goodyears," *Indianapolis Star*, November 29, 1938.

7 James Enright, "Shipp, Peck's Bad Boy of Cagedom, Keeps Rolling," *Waterloo Courier*, December 26, 1948. Originally from the *Chicago Herald-American*.

8 Al Ney, "The Sports Alley," *Waterloo Courier*, August 18, 1948.

9 Phone interview with Leo Kubiak, April 22, 2017.

10 "Pro Cage Loop Vice-President Gets in Plug for Hawks, but Questions Low Ticket Prices," *Waterloo Courier*, September 17, 1948.

11 Various advertisements and classified ads, *Waterloo Courier*, November 2 and 3, 1949.

12 "769 Cars from 56 Other Counties and 13 States," *Waterloo Courier*, November 29, 1948.

13 Al Ney, "The Sports Alley," *Waterloo Courier*, November 30, 1948.

14 Frank Litsky, "Harry Boykoff, 78, St. John's Star in the 1940's, Dies," *New York Times*, April 15, 2001.

15 "Mehen on First All-NBL Team with Most Points," *Waterloo Courier*, March 25, 1949.

16 "Roughest NBL Team Hawks' Foe Sunday," *Waterloo Courier*, November 19, 1948.

17 "Andy George, Charlie Shipp New Hawk Owners; Pinkie Out under Doctor's Orders," *Waterloo Courier*, December 14, 1948.

18 Al Ney, "The Sports Alley," *Waterloo Courier*, December 17, 1948.

3. FOR THE SAKE OF LEAGUE PRESTIGE

1 Al Ney, "The Sports Alley," *Waterloo Courier*, December 21, 1948.

2 Ibid.

3 "Railroad Man 'Luckiest in World,'" *Spartanburg Herald*, April 11, 1952.

4 "Packer Prexy Suspends One, Fines Another, Orders Club Home on Railroad Coaches," *Waterloo Courier*, December 23, 1948.

5 Al Ney, "The Sports Alley," *Waterloo Courier*, January 16, 1949.

6 "Goal with 5 Seconds Left Tips Hawks," *Waterloo Courier*, March 14, 1949.

7 Al Ney, "The Sports Alley," *Waterloo Courier*, April 4, 1949.

8 Ibid.

9 Al Ney, "The Sports Alley," *Waterloo Courier*, March 8, 1949.

10 Al Ney, "The Sports Alley," *Waterloo Courier*, March 1, 1949.

11 Al Ney, "The Sports Alley," *Waterloo Courier*, January 25, 1949.

4. EVERYBODY'S BALL CLUB

1 Advertisement, *Waterloo Courier*, May 12, 1949.

2 Al Ney, "The Sports Alley," *Waterloo Courier*, May 16, 1949.

3 Ibid.

4 Al Ney, "The Sports Alley," *Waterloo Courier*, May 30, 1949.

5 "Set 10 Day Limit on Raising $2,290 Balance for Hawks," *Waterloo Courier*, June 9, 1949.

6 Brian Gaynor, "Iowa's NBA Team," *Des Moines Register*, December 10, 2006.

7 Neil D. Isaacs, *Vintage NBA: The Pioneer Era, 1946–56* (Kindle edition, 2013), location 11137 of 11238.

8 "Revive Rumors Rival Basketball Loops to Merge," *Ellensburg Daily Record*, July 1, 1949.

9   "Pro Leagues Make Peace," *Milwaukee Journal*, August 4, 1949.

10 R. G. Lynch, "Maybe I'm Wrong," *Milwaukee Journal*, August 4, 1949.

11 Waterloo Hawks game program, November 2, 1949. From the collection of Vicki S. Sidey.

12 This perception of the two styles and the merger leading to a more open game is referenced tacitly in various ways by *Waterloo Courier* sports editor Al Ney in columns on November 2, 18, and 25, 1949. An article in the March 1950 edition of *Sport Magazine* written by an anonymous NBA referee and quoted in the *Courier* on February 24, 1950, refers to "the rock-'em and sock-'em style of the west as opposed to the fancy-pants style of the east."

13 Alex Stoddard, "Waterloo Tips Sheboygan, 98–91, in Pro Game Here," *Sioux City Journal*, February 20, 1951.

14 Isaacs, *Vintage NBA*, location 4830 of 11238.

15 Al Ney, "The Sports Alley," *Waterloo Courier*, September 16, 1949.

16 Al Ney, "The Sports Alley," *Waterloo Courier*, November 1, 1949.

17 Robert Mellace, "Tall Youngster Praised, Court Coach Hails Boykoff as Greatest," *Pittsburgh Press*, January 24, 1943.

18 Al Ney, "The Sports Alley," *Waterloo Courier*, November 3, 1949.

19 Al Ney, "The Sports Alley," *Waterloo Courier*, November 9, 1949.

20 "Tri-Cities Go Here Sunday a 'Natural' as Hawks Try to Avenge Only NBL Loss," *Waterloo Courier*, November 26, 1948.

21 "Patrick Racks 21 as Hawks Win, 75–62," *Waterloo Courier*, November 21, 1949.

5. I WANT TO PLAY BASKETBALL

1   Al Ney, "The Sports Alley," *Waterloo Courier*, December 10, 1946.

2   Al Ney, "The Sports Alley," *Waterloo Courier*, December 1, 1949.

3   "You'll See See—Outstanding Rookie Set to Report Here," *Waterloo Courier*, September 4, 1949.

4   Phone interview with Wayne See and Vicki Sidey, July 12, 2017.

5   Neil D. Isaacs, *Vintage NBA: The Pioneer Era, 1946–56* (Kindle edition, 2013), location 3150 of 11238.

6   Al Ney, "The Sports Alley," *New York World-Telegram*, November 29, 1949.

7   "NBA Prexy Cracks Down: Orders Refs to Stop Burlesque Work, Call Fouls and Shut Up," *Waterloo Courier*, December 2, 1949.

8   Al Ney, "The Sports Alley," *Waterloo Courier*, February 24, 1950. Originally from "Confessions of a Basketball Referee," *Sport Magazine*, March 1950.

9   Al Ney, "The Sports Alley," *Waterloo Courier*, January 18, 1949.

10 Ray Meyer with Ray Sons, *Coach* (Chicago: Contemporary Books, 1987), 35.

11 Al Ney, "The Sports Alley," *Waterloo Courier*, December 19, 1949. Originally from the Associated Press syndicated "Sports Roundup" by Hugh Fullerton, Jr.

12 Al Ney, "The Sports Alley," *Waterloo Courier*, December 28, 1949.

13 Hugh Fullerton, Jr., "Chapter 4," *Waterloo Courier*, January 6, 1950.

14 Arthur Daley, quoted in Al Ney, "The Sports Alley," *Waterloo Courier*, December 22, 1949.

15 Note Waterloo's opponents during the Hawks' only visits to the following large cities: Philadelphia (Baltimore Bullets), New York (Philadelphia Warriors), Baltimore (New York Knicks), and Chicago (Indianapolis Olympians). Waterloo's only road game against the Boston Celtics was played in Providence, Rhode Island.

16 Al Ney, "The Sports Alley," *Waterloo Courier*, December 23, 1949.

17 Al Ney, "Down 12 Points with 58 Seconds to Play, Hawks Win in Overtime, 97–93," *Waterloo Courier*, December 26, 1949.

18 "Charlie Shipp Non-Playing Coach Now," *Waterloo Courier*, January 1, 1950.

19 Al Ney, "The Sports Alley," *Waterloo Courier*, December 26, 1949.

20 "Hawks vs. Powerful Syracuse at 8:15," *Waterloo Courier*, January 10, 1950.

21 Al Ney, "The Sports Alley," *Waterloo Courier*, January 9, 1950.

22 "Name Smiley Coach after Firing Shipp," *Waterloo Courier*, January 11, 1950.

6. THE BAND DID NOT STOP PLAYING

1 "Name Smiley Coach after Firing Shipp," *Waterloo Courier*, January 11, 1950.

2 "Smiley at Helm as Hawks Go on Road," *Waterloo Courier*, January 12, 1950.

3 Phone interview with Jack Smiley's son, Mark Smiley, December 13, 2016.

4 Phone interview with Wayne See and Vicki Sidey, July 12, 2017.

5 "Hoot Gibson, Ex–Waterloo Pro Cager, Killed in Car Accident in Des Moines," *Waterloo Courier*, February 24, 1958.

6 Ray Meyer with Ray Sons, *Coach* (Chicago: Contemporary Books, 1987), 49.

7 Al Ney, "The Sports Alley," *Waterloo Courier*, January 17, 1950.

8 "Put Bombers on Block, Welcome Any Purchaser," *Waterloo Courier*, January 29, 1950.

9 "Pro Group May Split into Major, Minor," *Milwaukee Journal*, February 3, 1950.

10 "Hawk Prexy Rejects Minor League Idea; Board Starts 1950–1951 Plans," *Waterloo Courier*, February 5, 1950.

11 John Barrington, "Sees Two Compact Divisions as Answer to NBA Problems," *Waterloo Courier*, January 13, 1950.

12 Al Ney, "The Sports Alley," *Waterloo Courier*, January 23, 1950.

13 Al Ney, "Hawks Slip, 85–79, before 4,264 Fans," *Waterloo Courier*, January 30, 1950.

14 Charles Salzberg, *From Set Shot to Slam Dunk: The Glory Days of Basketball in the Words of Those Who Played It* (New York: E. P. Dutton, 1987), 111.

15 Ibid., 109–11.

16 Although his time as a professional player was ultimately brief, Johnny Orr would make a lifelong career in the sport. The beloved coach of the Iowa State Cyclones spent fourteen years in Ames beginning in 1980 after first leading teams at the University of Massachusetts and the University of Michigan.

17 "Board Suggests Smiley Fine Players," *Waterloo Courier*, March 3, 1950.

18 "No Fines — This Time: Jack Smiley Promises 'First Rate' Basketball under 'New Status,'" *Waterloo Courier*, March 5, 1950.

19 Al Ney, "The Sports Alley," *Waterloo Courier*, March 20, 1950.

20 "Skins Get Extension on Bond," *Milwaukee Sentinel*, April 18, 1950.

21 "Skins, Three Other Clubs May Be Forced Out of NBA, Podoloff Hints," *Milwaukee Sentinel*, April 21, 1950.

22 Al Ney, "The Sports Alley," *Waterloo Courier*, April 25, 1950.

23 Ibid.

24 Al Ney, "New Pro Cage Loop Hires Doxie Moore," *Waterloo Courier*, April 25, 1950.

7. COLD-BLOODED, CUT-THROAT BUSINESS

1 Al Ney, "The Sports Alley," *Waterloo Courier*, April 26, 1950.

2 Russ L. Smith, "Sports of Sorts Report: Hint New Iowa Club: Hale to Coach Dayton," *Waterloo Courier*, June 7, 1950.

3 Al Ney, "The Sports Alley," *Waterloo Courier*, August 7, 1950.

4 "Court Denies Ban on Talks with Cagers," *Waterloo Courier*, July 18, 1950.

5 Ibid.

6 Ibid.

7 Charles Salzberg, *From Set Shot to Slam Dunk: The Glory Days of Basketball in the Words of Those Who Played It* (New York: E. P. Dutton, 1987), 86.

8 Jackie Young, "Buckmaster Remembered for Intensity," *Waterloo Courier*, April 25, 1993.

9 Al Ney, "The Sports Alley," *Waterloo Courier*, May 29, 1950.

10 Neil D. Isaacs, *Vintage NBA: The Pioneer Era, 1946–56* (Kindle edition, 2013), location 8255 of 11238.

11 "Cage Hawks Sign Top NBA Draft Choice," *Waterloo Courier*, May 10, 1950.

12 Isaacs, *Vintage NBA*, location 2687 of 11238.

13 Al Ney, "The Sports Alley," *Waterloo Courier*, August 23, 1950.

14 *UAW Local 838: Our History*, on file at the Waterloo Public Library.

15 Ibid.

16 Rick Halpern and Roger Horowitz, *Meatpackers: An Oral History of Black Packinghouse Workers and Their Struggle for Racial and Economic Equality* (New York: Monthly Review Press, 1999), 120.

17 Eileen Ambrose, "'50 Deere Dispute Still Strikes Chord," *Waterloo Courier*, January 12, 1987.

18 "Laker 'F' Beats All-Stars 61–54," *Winona Republican-Herald*, October 28, 1950.

19 "Share Holds Mikan to One Free Throw, but Lakers Triumph," *Waterloo Courier*, October 29, 1950.

20 Al Ney, "The Sports Alley," *Waterloo Courier*, November 16, 1950.

21 Al Ney, "The Sports Alley," *Waterloo Courier*, December 1, 1950.

22 Al Ney, "The Sports Alley," *Waterloo Courier*, November 15, 1950.

23 Al Ney, "The Sports Alley," *Waterloo Courier*, December 19, 1950.

24 Al Ney, "The Sports Alley," *Waterloo Courier*, November 13, 1950.

25 Adolph H. Grundman, *The Golden Age of Amateur Basketball: The AAU Tournament, 1921–1968* (Lincoln: University of Nebraska Press, 2004), 123.

26 Ibid., 129.

8. AN EVEN GREATER CHALLENGE

1   "Hawks Watch NBA Battle over Share," *Waterloo Courier*, January 7, 1951.

2   "Hawks Sell Share for 'About $25,000,'" *Waterloo Courier*, December 22, 1950.

3   Buck Turnbull, *Hoop Tales: Iowa Hawkeyes Men's Basketball* (Guilford, Conn.: Globe Pequot Press, 2006), 22.

4   "Iowa Fires Pops Harrison, Basketball Coach since 1942," *Chicago Tribune*, April 11, 1950.

5   Russ L. Smith, "Sports of Sorts Report: Hint New Iowa Club: Hale to Coach Dayton," *Waterloo Courier*, June 7, 1950.

6   "Elmore Leaves B.C.; Signs with Pros," *The Heights*, February 21, 1947.

7   Al Ney, "The Sports Alley," *Waterloo Courier*, January 1, 1951.

8   Al Ney, "The Sports Alley," *Waterloo Courier*, November 23, 1950.

9   Al Ney, "The Sports Alley," *Waterloo Courier*, January 8, 1951.

10 "NBA in Uproar: Caps Quit, NY Threatens, Stags Sue," *Waterloo Courier*, January 9, 1951.

11 Al Ney, "The Sports Alley," *Waterloo Courier*, January 17 and 30, 1951.

12 "Louisville, Hawks Clash Here at 8:15," *Waterloo Courier*, February 7, 1951.

13 *Waterloo Courier*, February 8, 1951.

14 "Only One Change in Hawks' Home Card," *Waterloo Courier*, February 13, 1951.

15 Ken Suesens, quoted in the Sheboygan Red Skins 1950–51 game program, on file at the Sheboygan County Historical Research Center in Sheboygan Falls.

16 Sheboygan Red Skins 1948–49 game program, on file at the Sheboygan County Historical Research Center in Sheboygan Falls.

17 Neil D. Isaacs, *Vintage NBA: The Pioneer Era, 1946–56* (Kindle edition, 2013), location 9012 of 11238.

18 "Wier, O'Brien Start for Hawks Here Today," *Waterloo Courier*, January 14, 1951.

19 Al Ney, "The Sports Alley," *Waterloo Courier*, March 7, 1951.

20 "Red Skins Win in Exhibition, Battle Drifts," *Sheboygan Press*, March 13, 1951.

21 "Red Skins Boast Great Record for 1951; Suesens Lauds Club," *Sheboygan Press*, March 17, 1951.

22 "No Champion! Just Confusion," *Milwaukee Sentinel*, March 23, 1951.

9. I DON'T WANT TO GO OUT WITH A BAD SHOWING

1 Al Ney, "The Sports Alley," *Waterloo Courier*, March 23, 1951.

2 "Minor Leagues Face Crisis," *St. Cloud Times*, January 17, 1951.

3 "Two Pro Cage Leagues Draw Tentative Pact," *Waterloo Courier*, August 9, 1951.

4 "No Professional Basketball Here This Year," *Waterloo Courier*, October 16, 1951.

5 Neil D. Isaacs, *Vintage NBA: The Pioneer Era, 1946–56* (Kindle edition, 2013), location 4006 of 11238.

6 Terry Pluto, *Tall Tales: The Glory Years of the NBA* (Lincoln: University of Nebraska Press, 2000), 125–27.

7 "Kubiak Low Amateur in U.S. Senior," *Toledo Blade*, July 12, 1981.

8 Russ L. Smith, "Dahler, Cate with Bradley; Rest of Hawks Hang up Shoes after 11 for 11," *Waterloo Courier*, April 20, 1951.

9 Al Ney, "The Sports Alley," *Waterloo Courier*, December 8, 1950.

10 Al Ney, "The Sports Alley," *Waterloo Courier*, May 2, 1951.

11 Burke Evans, "Mrs. Wier: This Is Murray's Year," *Waterloo Courier*, March 24, 1974.

EPILOGUE

1 Interview with Danny Steiber, Waterloo, August 18, 2017.

2 "Waterloo in Big Leagues in One Sport—Basketball," *Waterloo Courier*, June 20, 1954.

3 Phone interview with Leo Kubiak, April 22, 2017.

4 Phone interview with Wayne See and Vicki Sidey, July 12, 2017.

INDEX